PEACEFUL AIR WARFARE

PEACEFUL AIR WARFARE

The United States, Britain, and the Politics of International Aviation

ALAN P. DOBSON

CLARENDON PRESS · OXFORD
1991

Oxford University Press, Walton Street, Oxford OX2 6DP
Oxford New York Toronto
Delhi Bombay Calcutta Madras Karachi
Petaling Jaya Singapore Hong Kong Tokyo
Nairobi Dar es Salaam Cape Town
Melbourne Auckland
and associated companies in
Berlin Ibadan

Oxford is a trade mark of Oxford University Press

Published in the United States
by Oxford University Press, New York

British Library Cataloguing in Publication Data
Data available

Library of Congress Cataloging in Publication Data
Dobson, Alan P.
Peaceful air warfare: the United States, Britain, and the politics of international aviation/Alan P. Dobson.
p. cm.
Includes bibliographical references (p.) and index.
1. Aeronautics, Commercial—Political aspects—History—20th century. 2. Aeronautics, Commercial—History—20th century. 3. Aeronautics, Commercial—Law and legislation—History—20th century. 4. United States—Foreign relations—Great Britain. 5. Great Britain—Foreign relations—United States. I. Title.
HE9775.D63 1991 387.7'1'0941—dc20 91-11793
ISBN 0–19–827531–5

Typeset by Best-set Typesetter Ltd.
Printed and bound in
Great Britain by Bookcraft (Bath) Ltd.
Midsomer Norton, Avon

This is for
Bev

Preface

It is important—perhaps more so than for other works—to explain what this book is and is not about. It is not an account of British and American civil aviation. There is much herein which speaks of those matters, but in themselves they are not the main focus of attention. Developments within civil aviation, and the context within which the industry has operated in Britain and the United States respectively, are both dealt with on the basis of secondary and high-level government primary sources: mainly Cabinet records on the British side, and published and unpublished White House papers on the American. I have not, for example, delved into Air Ministry records nor their equivalent on the US side; instead, I have taken up policy developments at a higher level, usually when they have begun to have significant implications for foreign aviation policy, and more particularly when they were clearly going to count in Anglo-American affairs. The rationale for this was twofold. Firstly, there was the practical problem of time and space—if I had started to research policy developments at Air Ministry level, then both would have run on out of control. Secondly, it would have involved a great deal of bureaucratic politics and technical information, neither of which are of main concern to my studies.

The book is about international civil-aviation policy in the US and Britain; the way their respective policies were moulded and how they interacted diplomatically; and the influence that the two countries had in determining the character of the international aviation system. Clearly, these matters cannot be dealt with without some mention of the development of aviation policies in general and the various political dispensations under which they took form, but they are, so to speak, simply the preliminaries which allow the study of international civil aviation as a subject of Anglo-American diplomacy to be conducted effectively.

My interest in aviation goes back to my childhood hero Biggles, in the novels of Captain W. E. Johns, but my academic interest began in the mid-1970s, during my doctoral studies in Durham. Charles Reynolds (Senior Lecturer, Department of Politics) drew my attention to the wartime correspondence between Churchill and Roosevelt concerning the 1944 Chicago Civil Aviation Conference. The letters involved were some of the most ill-tempered the two leaders exchanged throughout the course of the war, which caused me to think that there was scope for work to be done on the political and diplomatic aspects of civil aviation. Ever since then, I have nurtured the idea of this present manuscript.

I started specific plans for the book in 1986, and, as always, I was strongly supported by Charles Reynolds, Professor Peter Calvert (Department of Politics, Southampton University), and Professor Warren Kimball (History Department, Rutgers University). They helped me to get financial support from the British Academy, the Franklin D. Roosevelt Foundation (A Four Freedoms Award), and University College, Swansea. Without the backing from my referees and the generosity of the various bodies which awarded me grants, the research for this book would not have been possible and I am therefore most grateful to them all.

During the course of my researches, more people were helpful and kind to me than I can mention. So to all those librarians and archivists who played an important part in what follows: thank you. I must also thank those who were kind enough to grant me interviews: Lord Callaghan, Michael Colvin MP, the Right Honourable Edmund Dell, and a senior official at the Foreign Office.

Once the manuscript was completed, I received the benefit of comments on it from a number of people. In 1989 Professor Robert McCormack (Department of History, University of Winnipeg) published an article in which he expressed a slightly revisionist view of Churchill's role in the Air Ministry after the Great War and it was so strikingly similar to the view I had developed in Chapter 2 of this book that I immediately sent a copy of the relevant part of it to him. He was kind enough to reply with some detailed comments and with some interesting ideas and bibliographical references for which I am indebted to him.

Dr Dick Richardson (Teeside Polytechnic), who is an authority on inter-war disarmament, read Chapter 3 and gave me the benefit of his detailed knowledge and strong views about how it ought to be interpreted. I amended the chapter considerably after what he had to say, but I fear he will still disagree with what he views as my too charitable reading of the actions of Baldwin and Simon.

Mike Simpson, my friend and colleague (History Department, University College, Swansea), read large chunks of the manuscript, including Chapters 4, 5, and 6. He gave me useful comments based on his great knowledge of American history of the 1930s and 1940s and, more importantly, he gave me words of encouragement. Edmund Dell read part of Chapter 8, from the beginning down to the end of the section on Bermuda 2, and approved it, after minor factual corrections and words about two matters of interpretation which resulted both in the recasting of some of the comments I had made and in further clarification of his position. My thanks go to him for his courtesy and for the frank and clear way in which he spoke to me about the political and diplomatic affairs concerning Bermuda 2.

Finally, regarding the manuscript, I must thank Michael Colvin (Chairman of the Conservative Aviation Committee). Not only did he give me an interview, but he also supplied me with some much-needed material on the problem of Computer Reservation Systems (CRSs), and then read and commented on the final manuscript.

Oxford University Press have been considerately patient in awaiting the manuscript. For various reasons, some of which were out of my control (but not all, for example the arrival of our third child), my time was taken up by other things which forced me to put back the completion date to May 1990. I must also compliment OUP on their choice of Keith Hayward (North Staffordshire Polytechnic) as a reader for my original proposal. I hope that he finds that his initial enthusiasm, kind words, and strong support have been justified by the work I have produced.

Last of all, acknowledgements would not be complete without mentioning friends and family who have helped to revive me when my spirits have flagged. Thanks in particular to Adrian Knuszhka for good conversation—often aided by an odd pint or two—to Tony Lamb and the collective Bodycombe family for similar reasons, but also for the former's digging out of useful bibliographical references for me. Thanks also to Alison and Ian Jenkins, especially for salvaging some of the interviews I had arranged by lending me a tape-recorder at the eleventh hour, when the one I had borrowed from the University turned out to be a dud. I am also indebted to Dr Richard Jenkins of the Sociology Department, University College, Swansea, for the semi-permanent loan of a number of books on civil aviation. At times I felt that with his obvious enthusiasm for, and knowledge of, civil aviation it should have been he writing the book not I.

Finally, Bev, and my older two girls, Becky and Jessie, have borne my moods stoically, knowing only too well that the elation of having finished one chapter would soon give way to the gloom and conviction that 'I'll never be able to finish it' on starting the next. Naomi was too young to know, but she has helped me in her own way no less than the others—and she gradually came to understand what 'shut up' screamed at several decibels meant.

It is above all to them that my thanks—and many other feelings which are far too sentimental to mention here—must go.

Of course, all those mentioned only contributed to whatever is of value and interest herein: responsibility for whatever defects there are is mine alone.

A.P.D.

Swansea
May, 1990

Contents

Abbreviations

ACC	Air Co-ordinating Committee
ACCA	Advisory Committee on Civil Aviation
AMEX	American Export
AOA	American Overseas Airways
APEX	Advance Purchase Excursion
ATAC	Air Transport Advisory Council
ATLB	Air Traffic Licensing Board
BA	British Airways
B.CAL.	British Caledonian
BCPA	British Commonwealth Pacific Airline
BEA	British European Airways
BIS	Bank for International Settlements
BOAC	British Overseas Airways Corporation
BOB	Bureau of the Budget
BSAA	British South American Airways
CAA	Civil Aeronautics Authority (US), Civil Aviation Authority (British)
CAB	Civil Aeronautics Board
CAT	Committee on Postwar Civil Air Transport
CATC	Civil Aerial Transport Committee
CID	Committee of Imperial Defence
CRP	Committee on Reconstruction Problems
CRS	Computer Reservation System
DOT	Department of Transport
EAMS	Empire Airmail Scheme
ECAC	European Civil Aviation Conference
FAA	Federal Aviation Authority
GPO	General Post Office
HMSO	Her Majesty's Stationery Office
IA	Imperial Airways

IATA	International Air Transport Association
ICAO	International Civil Aviation Organization
ICC	Interstate Commerce Commission
ICIAC	Interdepartmental Committee on International Air Communications
IDCIA	Interdepartmental Committee on International Aviation
IMF	International Monetary Fund
JAL	Japan Airlines
MTCA	Ministry of Transport and Civil Aviation
NWA	Northwestern Airlines
OPEC	Organization of Petroleum Exporting Countries
PAA	Pan American Airways
PANAGRA	Pan American-Grace Airlines
PICAO	Provisional International Civil Aviation Organization
QANTAS	Queensland and Northern Territories Aerial Service
RAF	Royal Air Force
R. & D.	Research and Development
SCADTA	Sociedad Colombo-Alemán de Transportes
SST	Supersonic Transport
TWA	Transcontinental and Western Air, later became Trans World Airlines
UA	United Airlines

Note on Sources

The following abbreviations occur in relation to presidential libraries.

AW	Ann Whitman File
CF	Central File
CF CF	Central File, Confidential File
DDE	Dwight D. Eisenhower Library
FDR	Franklin D. Roosevelt Library
GEN CO	General Correspondence
HST	Harry S. Truman Library
JFK	John F. Kennedy Library
LBJ	Lyndon B. Johnson Library
MR	Map Room
NSF	National Security File
OF	Official File (after 'JFK' = Office File)
PSF	President's Secretary's File

The following abbreviations also occur in the bibliographical material.

CAB	Cabinet
CMD	Command Paper
CP	Cabinet Paper
FO	Foreign Office
FRUS	*Foreign Relations of the United States*

All Cabinet and Foreign Office papers are to be found in the Public Record Office.

All decimal references are to State Department files, National Archives, Washington DC. When no separate date is given, it is included in the decimal number.

1
Civil Aviation: Origins and Character

> And I said, O that I had wings like a dove: for then would I fly away, and be at rest.
>
> King David, Ps. 55, *c.*1000 BC

FOR three thousand years there has been written testimony to man's desire to take to the air and disappear into the blue in search of peace and pastures new. In the twentieth century, that desire became a reality for an ever-growing number of people, though there were few pastures left to discover by then, and the contribution to man's peace and tranquillity has been more than offset by flying's contribution to the frenetic life-style of the contemporary world and the dimension it has given to war. Nevertheless, man's interest abides. From 'flying by the seat of one's pants' to 'flying by wire', the world of aviation has fascinated people. This has been widely recognized and there is a growing number of books to meet the demands of an interested public. However, some aspects of aviation have attracted relatively little attention, in particular where aviation comes into contact with politics and diplomacy. The story which follows refers to many aspects of aviation, but it concentrates on the policies of Britain and the United States, which have been the two most important actors in international civil aviation, and on their respective international carriers. This involves diplomatic and political considerations which have led Britain and the United States to mould both their bilateral relationship and much of the international aviation-system in the way that they have.

Civil aviation has been tangled up with politics from its very beginning. There has always been more to it than just carrying mail, freight, or passengers for a profit from one point to another. Civil aviation, apart from commercial considerations, has also been deemed important for military and intelligence purposes, as a means of encouraging national and imperial cohesion, and as an important status-symbol. In all these aspects politics plays an important part.

Commercial aviation has had to rely upon political and diplomatic sponsorship in order to obtain routes and landing rights; furthermore, notwithstanding the move towards deregulation which took place in 1978 in the United States, airlines have often been subsidized and fares regulated to ensure profitability. The free market has repeatedly submitted to political interference.

The difference between civil and military aviation is more obvious now than in the days when bombs were dropped by hand from open cockpits, but in fact they remain closely related. There is a prolific cross-fertilization of ideas between military and civilian aviation on matters of design, with the latter often benefiting from the former's research and development (R. & D.). According to one historian, every large commercial engine designed in the United States began life under military specifications.[1] The commercial carriers of today would perform ill as bombers or fighters, but they can be commandeered as troop-carriers, which are valuable in contemporary warfare, where the premium is placed on speed and mobility. From the French wish for controls over civil aircraft in the early 1930s, in order to prevent conversions for military purposes, to Soviet paranoia about both secrecy and espionage, which resulted in the shooting-down of a South Korean airliner in August 1983, civil aviation has been unable to divorce itself from military matters.

During the 1920s and 1930s the political importance of cohesion in the continental United States and the British Empire respectively was highly valued. In the United States this resulted in political discretion being exercised in the award of mail contracts, in order to establish four large, viable commercial domestic carriers which would help unite the country. In Britain similar considerations resulted in the creation of Imperial Airways (IA), the Empire Airmail Scheme (EAMS), government concentration on Empire routes, and the mobilization of diplomatic pressure to try to get Empire and Commonwealth co-operation in negotiating commercial rights.

As a status symbol, civil aviation has had different effects in

[1] C. Solberg, *Conquest of the Skies: A History of Commercial Aviation in America* (Little, Brown, and Co., Boston, 1979), 52.

different countries. In Britain there was for many years a policy of 'buy British', even though repeated failures meant that the country had no competitive long-range airliner. Such a decision was very costly, but thought to be necessary, primarily because of political considerations. In the United States it was taken for granted by the 1940s that the country's rightful position in aviation should be one of leadership, if not supremacy, and the will of government was repeatedly exercised to achieve that.

Politics has thus been as ubiquitous in the history of civil aviation as modern airliners are in the skies of today. But was it inevitable that things would turn out like this? Given what we now known about the vulnerability of states to air and missile strikes the answer for the long term is probably yes, but that is not to say that states have not tried to take politics out of the skies. Internationalization has been seen as a possible means of doing this, as has maritime law, which was a model for dealing with aviation in its early days.

MARITIME LAW AND INTERNATIONALISM

The rules governing sea-borne commerce grew up in an age very different from the one in which aircraft developed. By the twentieth century, there was little evidence left in maritime affairs of the influence of mercantilist controls; instead, the dominant notion was freedom of the seas, derived from Grotius' *mare liberum* doctrine and from Britain's nineteenth-century espousal of *laissez-faire*. And although practice often conflicted with principle, even when free trade was at its height, the ideals associated with freedom of the sea continued to have great purchase on the minds of international statesmen. The right of innocent passage and unrestricted entry into ports, which in itself implied the right to conduct trade, was well established. When aviation began to come of age, maritime trade was not generally regulated directly by individual governments in peace-time, apart from cabotage—water-borne commerce between two points in the same country (one very notable exception was and is the US Jones Act, which reserves a high percentage of US trade for American bottoms). Providing a ship abided by international maritime law and the law of the country in whose territorial waters it was sailing, there were no restrictions on carriers and few either on entry into trade or on the amount conducted. As the twentieth century progressed, economic nationalism, made manifest in tariffs, quotas, and the like, began to change this, as did cold war trade embargoes. However, economic nationalism and strategic considerations affected the infant aviation industry long before the traditions of the maritime trade upon which it was initially modelled.

When governments began to think about regulating civil aviation, they turned to maritime law for help, although in a sense that model was rapidly becoming outdated. The air industry took much of its vocabulary from that of maritime trade: pilots, portholes, port and starboard, stewards, and cabotage were all used, and ports and liners were simply given the prefix 'air'; however, the overlap in language did not mean that the two kinds of commerce were wholly analogous. Those who took part in early air-conventions did see many similarities between air and sea commerce. But it was one thing to grant innocent passage through territorial waters and to accept free entry to ports for peacetime carriers (though even the days of these rights in their pristine form were numbered); it was quite another to grant innocent passage for aircraft and to allow foreign airlines to disembark and embark passengers at will from airports situated deep inside one's country. Consequently, another kind of legal analogy was soon invoked which was somewhat at odds with the prevailing ethos in maritime law. Property law, with its concept of private ownership of land to the centre of the earth, was invoked to give legal substance to the claim of national air-sovereignty *usque ad cœlum* (to a point in the sky). Thus, although many characteristics of maritime trade have been carried over into air transport, the waiving of sovereignty has not been one of them. In fact, states did just the opposite, by claiming exclusive control over their air space.[2]

The failure of maritime law to provide an acceptable paradigm for regulation was largely a consequence of the growing concerns of nation-states with the non-commercial potential of civil aviation, and this in turn resulted in jealously possessive and defensive political attitudes towards the airlines. National

[2] R. Y. Chuang, *The International Air Transport Association* (A. W. Sijthoff, Leiden, 1972), 14–16; C. Jonsson, *International Aviation and the Politics of Regime Change* (Frances Pinter, London, 1987), 78.

considerations have often damaged the economic health of the overall system of world aviation, caused strange route-configurations, and resulted either in cutthroat competition underwritten by government subsidies, or in excessively high fares. In addition, the existence of large civil fleets with the potential for conversion to military use have also posed persistent problems. From time to time, in trying to solve these, politicians have resorted to advocating various forms of internationalism. They have included: full internationalization, whereby all civil aviation, domestic and international, would be operated by an international company overseen by the United Nations or, in former times, the League of Nations; a system under which the airlines of the world would continue to fly under national flags but would be strictly regulated by a powerful international organization; a system which would establish an international model for states to follow in establishing aviation relations with another state; and finally, though this is seldom seen as internationalism, a system of deregulation under which market forces would determine the fares and the operation of civil aviation.

None of these have ever come into being. In fact, the more idealistic forms of internationalism have sometimes been used to further nationalist ends, either by being put forward as bargaining-ploys, or because it was believed that national interests could best be served through international controls. At other times internationalist proposals have been made by the politically naïve, with all sincerity; or by the politically worldly in a somewhat cynical way because it was in accordance with their party's publicly expressed doctrines. Nevertheless, to dismiss internationalism in the sphere of civil aviation as the instrument of the naïve idealist and the political scoundrel would be a mistake. For although it has not triumphed in any of its pristine forms, it has influenced world aviation and helped to mould it into a procession of forms.

THE EARLY CONVENTIONS

In mid-1910 an international conference on aerial navigation was convened by the French in order to attempt to come to terms with the new phenomenon of flying. The Germans and the French wanted freedom of the air, but the British opposed them and asserted the principle of national air-sovereignty. In the end, the conference was adjourned at the request of the British to allow proposals to be considered by the delegates' governments. It never reconvened. The conflict between freedom of the air and national air-sovereignty could not be resolved and the conference failed.[3] States soon began to declare sovereign control over their airspace. The British Air Navigation Act of 1911 (and further legislation in 1913) maintained that air above Britain, her Empire, and her Dominions was inviolable. Given the developments in military aircraft and aerial bombing during the First World War, the wisdom of doing this seemed to be confirmed. The first hopes of bestowing an international character on civil aviation and of minimizing the play of nationalist interests was thus defeated.

If there had been any doubts about the importance politics was to play in civil aviation, articles 1 and 15 of the Convention Relating to International Air Navigation, signed in Paris in 1919, ended them. This Convention originated from France, which suggested that a formal body should be created from the Inter-allied Aviation Committee, established in 1917, to take part in the Peace Conference. The French proposal was accepted and an Aeronautical Commission was formed, composed of the five Allied and Associated War Powers—Britain, France, the United States, Italy, and Japan—and seven minor powers—Cuba, Greece, Romania, Brazil, Serbia, Belgium, and Portugal.

The British, French, and American delegates were the most influential, particularly the former two, who, unlike the latter, came to the Commission well armed with ideas and proposals. The British position was virtually unchanged from that of 1910. The government's Civil Aerial Transport Committee (CATC), appointed in 1917, had concluded that the analogy of maritime law was not appropriate for aviation: 'The case of the upper air presents no true analogy to the case of the high seas outside the limits of territorial waters.' Decisively, security dictated that

[3] See R. Higham, *Britain's Imperial Air Routes 1918–39* (Shoe String Hamden, Conn., 1961), 19; and *Foreign Relations of the United States* (US Government Printing Office, Washington, DC, printed from time to time and hereafter referred to as *FRUS*), 1919, 1, 550–1, Acting Secretary of State, Polk, to Commission to Negotiate Peace, 2 Jan. 1919.

ultimately a state must have sovereignty over its airspace. And this was the basic position adopted by the British delegation.[4]

Ironically, however, it was no longer the main exponent of the most exclusive form of air sovereignty. Realizing that there was potential for commercial gain and, perhaps more importantly, that they needed good communications with the Empire, both of which would involve flying over European and Middle Eastern nations, the British wanted to combine air sovereignty with a liberal formula to facilitate international services. They proposed that regulations should be used only to protect the security of the State and to uphold its laws, otherwise they should permit 'the free navigation of foreign aircraft'. It was the turn of the French, in the light of wartime experience, to insist on a more exclusive form of air sovereignty.[5]

The Convention granted rights of innocent passage to the private planes of member states without discrimination (non-members needed special permission), but the Convention did not create a framework for commercial aviation. Innocent passage was not accorded to scheduled commercial flights. According to article 15, commercial carriers would have to fly in lanes allocated to them by national governments. In other words, routes, landing-rights, and all the other commercial aspects of air travel were open to negotiation. For the rest, the Convention was mainly concerned with safety and technical and navigational matters. The British government gave legal effect to the convention with the passage of the 1920 Air Navigation Bill.

This cautious and limited form of international collaboration was far from being of universal effect. The Americans, after some initial hesitancy, had taken an active part in the Aeronautical Commission's work, but in the end isolationism and President Wilson's arrogant treatment of the US Congress resulted in the Senate refusing to ratify any of the agreements which arose out of the negotiations in Paris. The United States was thus left the most significant of outsiders.[6] The Convention

[4] Cmd. 9218, 1918, 'Civil Aerial Transport Committee Report'; Jonsson, *Regime Change*, 84.

[5] Cmd. 266, 1919, 'Convention Relating To International Air Transport'; John C. Cooper, 'Some Historic Phases of British International Civil Aviation Policy', *International Affairs*, 23 (1947), 189–202.

[6] *FRUS*, 1919, 1, 551, Secretary of Commission, Grew, to Acting Secretary of State, 25 Jan. 1919.

tried to put pressure on states to join by prohibiting members from bilaterally extending the privileges of the Convention to non-members, but in the long term this inadvertently further prejudiced the chances of the United States joining. Still, this was all some time before transatlantic flights and it must have seemed redundant to most Americans to involve themselves in a European air-convention when there was no aviation contact between the two continents. Developments in the Americas were a different matter, however, and because of them the United States felt the need to become involved in international controls.

In 1928 the Sixth International Conference of American States met in Havana, from 16 January to 20 February. One outcome of the Conference was the Havana Convention on Commercial Aviation, which aimed to regulate civil aviation in the Western hemisphere. It was patterned on the Paris Convention, dealing with technical, safety, and navigational matters—once again the commercial aspects were left aside.[7] Thus, during the inter-war years, the two main centres of civil aviation, America and Europe, were regulated by two separate conventions. In 1929, attempts were made to bring the two sides together by revising the Paris Convention, but they failed. Ironically, this was partly because of the discriminatory requirements of the Paris Convention, which had been designed to encourage membership rather than provide obstacles to it. In 1934 President Roosevelt ended US Senate consideration of the matter for the time being by recalling the relevant papers from Congress.

Even if the United States could have been drawn in under the aegis of the Paris Convention, this would not have solved the burgeoning problems of commercial aviation. Safety standards, navigation and other technical matters had to be properly dealt with—as the Paris and Havana Conventions tried to do—as a prerequisite for a flourishing system of international air-travel; but the political economy of the industry needed tending to as well, and here the two conventions were silent. This deficiency resulted in a mess, best described by a British government paper of 1944 which reviewed the past and discussed the need which then existed for a new universal convention. Speaking of both the Paris and Havana systems, the paper said:

[7] *FRUS*, 1928, 1, 585.

> Neither of these Conventions made provision for international regulation in the economic, as opposed to the technical field. In the result the growth of air transport was conditioned by political rather than economic considerations and its development as an orderly system of world communications was impeded. Summed up, the major evils of the pre-war period were, first, that any country on an international air route could hold operators of other countries to ransom even if those operators only wished to fly over or refuel in its territory; secondly, that there was no means of controlling the heavy subsidisation of airlines which all too often were maintained at great cost for reasons mainly of national prestige or as a war potential; thirdly, that the bargaining for transit and commercial rights introduced extraneous considerations and gave rise to international jealousies and mistrust.[8]

By 1944, when this paper was published, the main technical problems which had stood in the way of intercontinental commercial aviation in the 1920s and 1930s had been solved: the obstacles which remained were political. The great post-war boom in civil aviation was only possible because countries found a way, not so much of solving, but of coping with those political problems, and the two main protagonists in this were the United States and Britain. Much of the character of the international civil-aviation system was determined by these two countries. However, to understand how they interacted with each other in moulding this system, it is necessary to trace the development of their respective industries and to see how the two sides made their first transatlantic connections in the air. That story will be told in Chapters 2 and 4; for the moment the focus of attention is the year 1919—an important departure-point in the development of civil aviation.

BRITAIN AND THE UNITED STATES IN 1919

British aviation developed rapidly, and by the end of the Great War Britain was the world's leading air-power, with 27,000 officers and 260,000 other ranks in the Royal Air Force (RAF), 23,000 aircraft, and 700 aerodromes. For a while it appeared that technical and manufacturing advances and the creation of a large pool of trained pilots would be complemented by appropriate governmental organization and planning for both the transition to peacetime and the development of civil aviation.

[8] Cmd. 6561, 1944, 'International Air Transport'.

In 1917 the British government created an Air Ministry and in May of that year set up the CATC, under the chairmanship of the newspaper baron Lord Northcliffe. After its first meetings, Northcliffe had to go to the United States and so the Committee was then chaired by Major J. L. Baird, Under-Secretary of State for Air. The Committee's brief was to consider:

(1) the steps which should be taken with a view to the development and regulation after the War of aviation for civil and commercial purposes from a domestic, an imperial and an international standpoint. (2) The extent to which it will be possible to utilise for the above purpose the trained personnel and aircraft which the conclusion of Peace may leave surplus to the requirements of the Naval Military Air Services of the United Kingdom and Overseas Dominions.[9]

It took exactly twelve months for the Committee to make its recommendations. In the main, they were to do with technical matters, but the following had political implications: the adoption of the doctrine of air sovereignty; uniformity of legislation for the Empire; a requirement that some routes and civilian aircraft should conform to military standards; advanced planning of routes and the provision of landing-grounds; the placing of civil aviation under the authority of the Air Ministry; and 'To keep the expanded aircraft industry alive after the war, it will be necessary for the State to assist aerial transport and/or to own and participate in undertakings.' Interestingly, the most celebrated visionary on the Committee, H. G. Wells, dissented from the report on the grounds that its recommendations were too timid.[10] In fact, things turned out to be more timid than even Wells had feared, for, while most of the recommendations were accepted and implemented, the idea that civil aviation should be subsidized by the government was rejected. This was a costly mistake.

The post-war Secretary of State for both War and Air, Winston Churchill, had some enthusiasm for aviation but unfortunately used his impressive energies to argue against subsidies, partly because of his attachment to the principles of the free market, partly because of the severe financial difficulties in which the

[9] Cmd. 9218, 1918; and P. and G. Ford, *A Breviate of Parliamentary Papers 1917–39* (Basil Blackwell, Oxford, 1951), 289–90.
[10] Ibid.

British government found itself because of war expenditures. This early stand against direct subsidies was in sharp contrast with affairs in France, Britain's main competitor, where the government had no hesitation in granting such aid to their infant industry. Commercial flights in Britain began officially on 1 May 1919 and in July Captain H. G. Shaw flew the maiden cross-Channel commercial flight from Hendon to Le Bourget.[11] Britain's aircarft and pilots were second to none in 1919, but they soon had difficulty in competing with French operators. In addition, the British government's attention was not so much on what promised to be the potentially lucrative routes between Britain and Europe as on imperial ones.

In May 1919 Churchill called upon his predecessor at the Air Ministry, Lord Weir, to chair the newly established Advisory Committee on Civil Aviation (ACCA): on 28 May Weir agreed. Lord Weir was an eminent industrialist who had been drawn into government service during the Great War. Over the next twenty years he was never far from aviation matters and was one of the main architects of British air-power, which managed to win the Battle of Britain in 1940. He was eminently capable.

The ACCA included such illustrious names from British aviation history as H. M. Trenchard, Chief of Air Staff, and J. A. H. Moore-Brabazon. The brief of the Committee was to consider the future of Britain's imperial air-routes and any other matters referred to it by the Secretary of State for Air. In July 1919 it got down to serious work and by the end of October its recommendations for imperial air-routes were ready. Once again caution was the order of the day. The Committee made it clear that, 'their investigation kept always in view the present financial position of the country'. And thus, 'it is not practicable at the moment to recommend any large appropriation of public funds by way of investment in what is now an entirely novel business'. Nevertheless, the Committee got things moving, suggesting that priority should be given to the setting-up of a demonstration route between Cairo—envisaged as the Clapham Junction of Britain's imperial air network—and Karachi. It should be run by private enterprise, with government help in the form of surplus RAF engines and an infrastructure consisting of airports

[11] Higham, *Imperial Routes*, 29.

and navigational and meteorological facilities. Finally, it was suggested that the Post Office (GPO), in consultation with the Air Ministry, should draw up a form of tender for an airmail contract for the proposed route. At this time, although Weir thought that indirect government subsidies would be essential if civil aviation were to succeed, this was all the help that the Committee was prepared to countenance. The report was unanimous, but it masked serious reservations, for example by Lord Inchcape, about the estimated £4.5 million outlay for the Cairo to Karachi infrastructure.[12]

From the strong base that had been established in the Great War, British aviation was losing its way because of faint-hearted government policy. Civil aviation needed financial help, but the British government, partly because of difficult economic conditions and partly because of the overwhelming antipathy of ministers and officials to government intervention in what was seen as being properly the preserve of commerce and free enterprise, refused to come forward with adequate funds. Distracted by the greater priority accorded to the future of Empire routes, the government left Britain's commercial operators to their inevitable and sorry fate at the hands of subsidized French operators. Even indirect subsidies for the important political, strategic, and commercial task of developing Empire routes were only granted with difficulty and with much soul-searching. And the proposal that the GPO might help the development of British civil aviation did not come to anything of any consequence until the EAMS of the 1930s. The time-honoured British practice of muddling through would not do for the new aviation industry; but the British took some time to realize that, and even longer to take effective remedial measures, by which time they had lost their world leadership and had accumulated handicaps which were to continue to hamper progress for a considerable time.

For a while there was some consolation for the British because the situation of commercial aviation in the United States

[12] *Public Record Office* (all Cabinet and Foreign Office papers are to be found in the PRO) CAB 24/93, CP(19)191, 'Advisory Committee on Civil Aviation: Report on Imperial Air Routes to W. S. Churchill, Secretary of State for Air'; Cmd. 449, 1919, 'Imperial Air Routes', from Ford, *Breviate*, 290; and W. J. Reader, *Architect of Air Power: The Life of the First Viscount Weir of Eastwood 1877–1959* (Collins, London, 1968), ch. 4.

appeared, if anything, to be much worse than theirs. Americans pioneered heavier-than-air flying-machines, and Orville and Wilbur Wright achieved the first controlled flight in 1903. Americans also established the first scheduled air-service, carrying passengers from St Petersburg to Tampa, Florida. The service ran from January to April 1914; however, US commercial airlines were slow to develop after the war.

Unlike Britain and France, which had the English Channel to contend with in linking two large population-centres with a potentially lucrative demand for swift travel, and unlike Germany, which was barred from making military aircraft and thus had to concentrate on civilian if she wanted to stay in the air at all, the US did not have great inducements to develop civil aviation.

> In the United States . . . the social and geographic conditions were unfavourable; there were few situations involving a water crossing, and the densest inter-city routes were already served by efficient railways, often providing excellent service under the stimulus of competition.[13]

While the railways did provide relatively good transport, and were undamaged by war (unlike in Europe), they had their failings and did not effectively link the country in a cohesive communications network. For a modern state this was an important deficiency and it was not sufficiently alleviated by the road system. In 1919 a young army officer named Eisenhower traversed the United States east to west in a War Department-sponsored convoy and was disturbed by the poor state of communications. Just over thirty years later, impressions President Eisenhower gained in 1919 helped to convince him to fund the US interstate highway-system federally. In the 1920s the railways were still operating much as they had done in the previous decade, but in 1925 it was deemed politically important to have more efficient and effective national communications and from then on the government began to help airlines to provide it.

More important factors than the railways in the slow development of post-war American civil aviation were the lack of

[13] R. E. G. Davies, *Airlines of the United States Since 1914* (Putnam, London, 1982), 4.

government subsidies, the absence of central direction, and the primitive state of the infrastructure—in particular that of airports. Until 1925 there was really only one successful commercial line in the United States—Aeromarine, operating from the east coast. Apart from that, it was left to the Post Office to keep the spirit of civil aviation alive: it ran its own mail planes, developing skills such as night flying and the discipline to keep to tight schedules. It also established the necessary infrastructure for successful commercial flying. The carriage of mail by the US Post Office was much more important than private passenger services in the early days of American aviation. One historian's judgement is that: 'The aggregate effect [of the US Post Office's airmail service] was to give the United States a flying start in the field of commercial aviation, enabling it to overhaul Europe, in spite of the latter's eight-year head start, within two years of spectacular growth.' But that growth did not come until the privatization of mail carriage by the 1925 Kelly Act, and so before then, although invaluable experience and a sound infrastructure were being established, the potential still had to be realised and, until it was, it was not very obvious that the United States was actually in a good position to exploit commercial aviation.

The United States was a laggard in the early post-war period, but she had planes, pilots, a continent to draw together, a large potential domestic market, and plenty of entrepreneurial skills and investment money. All that was really lacking was: government initiatives to get the ball rolling—they came in 1925 with the Kelly Act; and something to capture the public's imagination—and that came two years later, in May 1927, when Charles Lindbergh flew solo across the Atlantic in the Spirit of St Louis.[14]

[14] R. A. Lee, *Dwight D. Eisenhower: Soldier and Statesman* (Nelson Hall, Chicago, 1981), 46. For section on the United States, see Davies, *Airlines*, chs. 1 and 2.

2
From Versailles to Depression: 1919–1930

POLITICAL attitudes towards civil aviation changed substantially during the ten years between the signing of the Treaty of Versailles and the onset of the Depression. There were two main reasons for this. Firstly, both the British and the US government changed their minds about subsidies and began to see them as necessary for nurturing the infant aviation-industry until it had commercial viability. In America the change was dramatic in the aftermath of the passage of the Kelly Acts of 1925 and 1928, which provided indirect subsidies for American airlines through generous airmail-contracts. In Britain subsidies were squeezed from a succession of reluctant and impecunious governments, but the imperative need for them was gradually accepted and the pattern for future development established. Secondly, as airplanes became faster, increased their range, and became capable of carrying larger payloads, concern deepened about their military potential. By the time of the Geneva General Disarmament Conference of 1932–4, not only was the danger from military aircraft acutely perceived, but so also were the dangers of civilian aircraft being used for intelligence-gathering or carrying troops, or being converted into bombers.

Civil aviation was not seen only as an end in itself. It was in the national interest to develop air communications and an infrastructure which would be invaluable in times of war. The civil-aviation industry, with its profit potential, was also an economical way of helping in the development of military aircraft and technology in general: there was considerable interdependence and mutual benefit to be had, particularly in R. & D. In other words, civil and military aviation were linked, not least in the minds of politicians and the military. The political and strategic aspects of civil aviation helped it to gain government support (most obviously through subsidies), but they also brought with them complications, in the form of conflicting priorities. This was something which did not arise in such a complex form in other industries which were more purely commercial in character.

DEVELOPMENTS IN THE UNITED STATES 1919–1930

Juan Trippe was to international airlines what Henry Ford was to the motor car. Born in the summer of 1899 into a wealthy East Coast banking family, Trippe became the most influential individual in the history of international commercial aviation. Stocky and Latin-looking, he was a twentieth-century man with the buccaneering spirit of the seventeenth and the acumen of the commercial empire builders of the nineteenth. His vision, courage, and political skill enabled him to pioneer US civil aviation abroad and to establish Pan American Airways (PAA), which in its heyday was the world's leading airline. He was involved in commercial aviation from its start and did not retire until 1968.

During the Great War he interrupted his university education at Yale to train as a navy pilot, but after the armistice he returned to his studies and then went on to become a bond salesman with Lee, Higginson and Company. That job lasted for two years. In 1923 he moved back to aviation. He had little success with the first two airlines with which he was associated—Long Island Airways and Colonial. But he went on to prepare the ground for his next venture with some Yale friends from Pittsburgh, who helped him to persuade their local congressman, Clyde Kelly, Chairman of the House Post Office Committee, to introduce a bill to end the Post Office's monopoly and allow private companies to tender for airmail carriage. This sparked off a flurry of government activity which established the framework for US civil aviation until 1934. While that activity was going on, Trippe was busy, and with backing from two wealthy associates, Cornelius Vanderbilt (Sonny) Whitney and John T. Hambleton, he started what was to become PAA. Trippe was soon ready to take advantage of the changes the US government made to civil aviation by its introduction of a heavily subsidized airmail system.[1]

[1] The Smithsonian National Aeronautical and Space Museum Archives, Trippe Papers, box 8, folder: 1956, Newspapers and Magazines, draft ch. by Vern Haugland; *New York Times*, 12 May 1968, 'Last of Aviation Pioneers

If Trippe can be regarded as the key figure in the private realm in developing American civil aviation—at least in the field of foreign operations—Herbert Hoover could be seen as his government counterpart. Hoover, an engineer by training, was an able man. He greatly expanded the importance and influence of the Commerce Department from the time of his appointment as Secretary by President Harding in 1921 until his resignation because of his own presidential campaign in 1928. Much of his energy during those years was devoted to the task of helping America's civil aviation. In April 1921, when President Harding unsuccessfully tried to get Congress to enhance the status of aviation in government, Hoover was undeterred by the failure and proceeded to promote aviation more energetically than ever. He had faith in its potential and was convinced of its importance for national defence. While Congress remained inactive, he tried to get the various parts of the industry to come together to consider problems of safety and standards; but it was the Morrow Board which provided the platform for him to urge his views upon the public, and eventually on Congress as well.[2]

In response to the accelerating growth of civil aviation, Harding's successor, President Coolidge, appointed Charles Lindbergh's father-in-law, Dwight Morrow, to chair a committee to consider national policy. The Morrow Board heard testimony and received recommendations from a wide range of sources—probably none more influential, however, than Herbert Hoover, who had been instrumental in persuading Coolidge to appoint the Board in the first place. The overall gist of his memorandum of recommendation was based on what he described as 'a complete analogy' between water and airborne commerce. According to him, it was the government's duty to provide the same kind of infrastructure for aviation that it had for water-borne commerce, namely: navigational and communication assistance (which among other things were to facilitate night flying), the maintenance of set standards, the

Retires'; R. Daley, *An American Saga: Juan Trippe and His Pan American Empire* (Random House, New York, 1980), pt. 1; C. Solberg, *Conquest of the Skies: A History of Commercial Aviation* (Little, Brown, and Co., Boston, 1979), 34.

[2] R. K. Murray, *The Harding Era: Warren G. Harding and His Administration* (University of Minnesota Press, Minneapolis, 1969), 410–11; R. L. Wilbur and H. M. Hyde, *The Hoover Policies* (Scribner's, New York, 1937), 215–16.

establishment and allocation of routes, and the development and improvement of airports.

In particular, Hoover emphasized the importance of three things: first, the establishment of an Aviation Bureau, which would give the government powers to act in the field of civil aviation; secondly, the contracting-out of mail carriage to private operators; and thirdly, the establishment of a nation-wide system of municipal airports. The justification for such action and public expenditure was largely in terms of the long-term commercial gains to be had from a well-established aviation industry. Subsidies in any form were seen as a short-term, but necessary, expedient. However, there was another theme to Hoover's argument of justification. He told the Board:

> I need not emphasise the importance of commercial aviation as an arm of defence. While it is not probable that the actual commercial plane will be much used in actual battle, yet the building up of the manufacturing industry behind such aviation is of the most vital importance, and we must develop the airways across our own country . . . for purposes of defence.[3]

Hoover's recommendations were embodied in the Morrow Board's report. A division of aeronautics was set up in the Department of Commerce, and the Post Office had the authority to grant airmail contracts. In addition, various other measures, along with mail contracts, constituted a substantial form of subsidy to aviation, but they were indirect subsidies, not direct like the ones granted by many European states, which the Board self-righteously described as un-American. Legislative effect was given to the proposals in the 1926 Air Commerce Act. If the US government had stopped at that point with its subsidy programme, there would have been considerable force behind what the Morrow Board saw as a favourable contrast between European and American subsidy-policies. However, that was not the case, for the Board also recommended that help given to aviation should be increased through airmail contracts granted by the federal government. As a result, the Kelly Act was altered

[3] Wilbur and Hyde, *The Hoover Policies*, 216–18, quoting from Hoover's memo; Solberg, *Conquest*, 64, 117; *Report of the President's Aircraft Board, 30 Nov. 1925* (US Government Printing Office, Washington, DC, 1925).

in 1926 and 1927; on both occasions the rate of subsidy was increased. For an airline like PAA this development was vital. Two years after flying its first airmail from Florida to Cuba, PAA had rapidly expanded its operations into the Caribbean area and Central America. By 1929 it still carried only a few passengers, but its income from the carriage of airmail was approximately $4 million.[4] With much of this being in effect government subsidy, the distinction between direct and indirect subsidies became rather a nice one: a rose by any other name . . .

The Morrow Board's conclusions concerning the needs of the civil-aviation industry were very perceptive. As a result, the industry was given form and direction by the actions of the federal government (along with state and municipal authorities), and that also helped to reassure a suspicious and sceptical public about the viability and safety of civil aviation. But, more than anything else, government in the United States put money into aviation. The 1929 air-expenditure estimate of the US federal government was 125 per cent above the 1925 level, some $145 million (the official rate of exchange was $4.86 for £1). In addition there was also vast expenditure by state and municipal governments. For example, the Commerce Department estimated that when the 890 projected airports were completed in the United States and their capital expenditure added to that already expended on the 726 existing airports, the total would be around $200 million: most of this money came from local, not federal, sources.[5]

The Morrow Board's brief was not restricted to civil aviation, and, following Hoover's line, it observed that aviation in general was important to the national interest. Among other things, this demanded that airplanes and airplane technology be developed with an urgent sense of purpose. Consequently, Congress passed a five-year aircraft-procurement programme for the

[4] Ibid. 90.

[5] *Daily Telegraph*, 17 Apr. 1930, quoted in 841.796/288 (all decimal references are to State Department files, National Archives, Washington, DC. When no separate date is given it is included in the decimal number). Atherton to Secretary of State, 21 Mar. 1930; CAB 24/201. CP(29)4, 14 Jan. 1929. 'Air Estimates and the Course of Air Expenditure in this Country and Abroad'; *Public Papers of Herbert Hoover 1929* (US Government Printing Office, Washington, DC, 1974), State of the Union Message to Congress, 3 Dec. 1929, 419–20, where combined figure for actual and projected airports is 2,200.

army and the navy. At the end of that five-year period, using 1925 as the base-year, US expenditure had risen by 140 per cent. In contrast, Britain's had declined by 2 per cent; she had 780 frontline machines to America's 1,310; and she had 1,550 pilots (including those in training) compared to over 2,100 pilots in America.[6]

Government money and the policy of planned aircraft-procurement gave much encouragement and stability to the American civil-aviation industry. In particular, aircraft-manufacturing companies began to emerge which were later to dominate the world market. The infrastructure for a modern air-transport industry was also taking shape, and the famous Lindbergh solo flight across the Atlantic in 1927 gave a major boost to aviation's public image: something which was effectively capitalized on by Trippe, who employed Lindbergh in PAA. However, the US domestic airline-system was ill-co-ordinated, and the goal of achieving a national network of air-communication routes which would bind the country together remained elusive. The story of America's venture into international aviation was rather different, but that will be related shortly. First, it is important to see how the domestic system took shape, because that had a bearing both on reforms which were later instituted under the Roosevelt Administration and on the challenge mounted by American domestic carriers during the Second World War to PAA's monopoly of foreign routes.

By 1930 the US aviation industry was thriving as a result of government help and individual initiative. In 1926 there were 369 miles of private and 2,665 miles of government-operated air-transport. In his State of the Union Message to Congress in December 1929 Hoover was able to report that there were then over 25,000 miles of government-improved airways. He went on to say that, 'Over 6,400 planes are in commercial use, and 9,400 pilots are licensed by the Government. Our manufacturing capacity has risen to 7,500 planes per annum. The aviation companies have increased regular air transportation until it now totals 90,000 miles per day—one-fourth of which is flown by night.'[7] This was an overwhelming justification of the imaginative and purposeful policies adopted in the wake of the Morrow

[6] *Daily Telegraph*, 17 Apr. 1930.

[7] *Hoover Public Papers*, 419–20, State of the Union Message.

Board's report, but American civil aviation was not without problems. The main deficiency of the domestic system was lack of co-ordination, which also affected the industry's profitability. The problem has been described well in R. E. G. Davies' definitive history of American airlines.

> Theoretically, a passenger could travel from New York to El Paso by American Airways. But this involved, first a trip due north up the Hudson as far as Albany (formerly a Canadian Colonial route); then along the Mohawk Valley to Cleveland (Colonial Western); on to Fort Worth (Universal); and finally to El Paso (Southern Air Transport). The Southern Pacific Railroad did the honours for the last part of the route to Los Angeles.[8]

It was these chaotic and byzantine route-configurations that President Hoover's Administration, in particular his Postmaster-General, Walter F. Brown, determined to reorganize. Hoover gave notice of changes to come in a press conference on 15 October 1929. Replying to a question about possible price-reductions in the airmail service, Hoover said that the 'Post Office is working on a very difficult problem of trying to discover some form of a rate structure for the airmail service. Hitherto, as you know, the routes have been let by competitive bid, and a great many distortions have grown up as the art has made progress'.[9] Republican administrations of the 1920s had the reputation of being well disposed to big business, and this was certainly the case with Walter Brown's plans for ironing out the 'distortions' in America's domestic airline-system. Brown wanted to mould a national integrated air-communications network which would benefit the United States politically and strategically. To do this it was necessary to encourage the emergence of three or four national carriers by the selective award of airmail contracts. This would bring order out of chaos and would also result in companies of a size which would be more viable and profitable. But Brown could not do this without first changing the law, so in 1930 he set to and managed to get through Congress a third series of amendments to the Kelly Act of 1925; they were known as the Watres Act. The Act allowed

[8] R. E. G. Davies, *Airlines of the United States Since 1914* (Putnam, London, 1982), 114.

[9] *Hoover Public Papers*, 326, News Conference, 15 Oct. 1929.

the Postmaster-General to consolidate and extend routes if he thought that it was in the national interest to do so; it favoured the airlines which already had mail contracts, and there were various provisions which effectively discriminated against both small and new airlines; and finally the act sought to encourage an increase in passenger travel and a reduction in the rate paid per mile for mail carriage.

Under the new regime, Brown held a series of what have disparagingly been described as 'spoils conferences', in which, while paying lip-service to the requirement of competitive tenders, he actively encouraged larger enterprises. There emerged from this, four firmly established commercial companies (though subsidized through mail contracts); Eastern, United, American, and Transcontinental and Western Air (later this became Trans World Airlines, but the initials TWA remained the same), which dominated the domestic system until the 1970s.

The new system, masterminded jointly by Hoover and Brown and implemented and overseen by the latter, came under intense criticism from the Roosevelt Administration, but it had many achievements to its credit. Airmail miles flown increased from 10,200 in the year ending June 1929 to 35,900 in the year ending June 1933. At the same time, the net cost per airmail mile to the government came down from \$1.26 to \$0.26. The character of the industry was also changed with the emergence of large companies carrying many more passengers: numbers increased from 165,000 in 1929 to over 550,000 in 1933.[10]

Major changes were also taking place in the sphere of the United States's foreign airline carriage. While it was necessary for government agency, in the form of Walter Brown, to provide the catalyst for the emergence of four large domestic national carriers, no such direct agency was required in the foreign field. Juan Trippe was the moving force there in creating a large, viable, and profitable airline, which established a *de facto* monopoly over the foreign routes of the United States.

PAA was incorporated in 1927 and within three years it was the dominant US overseas carrier. Its success was due to Trippe, who had a flair for generating good publicity—he hired

[10] Davies, *Airlines*, ch. 5; W. S. Myers and W. H. Newton, *The Hoover Administration: A Documented Narrative* (Scribner's, New York, 1936), 430.

Lindbergh (by then an American national hero) to carry out route surveys in South America—and who was astute enough to realize the potential of air routes throughout the Americas and to understand that the key to exploiting that potential lay in obtaining mail contracts from the government. By 1928 the grand strategy for PAA's development was clear. It involved three tactics. Firstly, care was taken to develop good relations with the political establishment, and in particular with Congressmen who could help create a favourable disposition towards PAA within the federal government. This was helpful when the company came to bid for mail contracts or needed assistance for persuading foreign governments to grant PAA routes and landing-rights. Secondly, Trippe had the foresight and the courage to plan ahead, commissioning both route surveys and the design and construction of new planes. Thirdly, Trippe bought over twenty airline companies, mainly in South America, which then became PAA subsidiaries, and he also entered into partnership with the W. R. Grace Shipping Line to form Pan American-Grace Airways (Panagra). As a result of all this, Trippe swept the decks so far as overseas mail contracts were concerned. In 1928 the government, worried by the threat from foreign airlines operating near the Panama Canal, promoted what became the 1928 Foreign Airmail Act, modelled on the 1925 Kelly Act, which provided similarly generous subsidies in order to help the expansion of America's overseas operators. The only serious potential rival to PAA gaining these heavily subsidized contracts in this period was the New York, Rio and Buenos Aires Airline, but the Wall Street Crash and the company's initial failure to obtain mail contracts caused it financial difficulties, and in 1930 it was bought out by Trippe.

As the web of PAA's routes spread down through South America, so the company's, and in particular Trippe's network of political contacts expanded. Political power and influence were important facets of PAA. And this was true in the spheres both of its foreign and of its domestic dealings, although it is difficult to separate these two aspects of the company's activities.

At home Trippe's political influence was based on his family and business connections. In 1928 he married Betty Stettinius, whose brother became a senior member of the State Department during the war and for a short period was the Secretary of State. The board of PAA in 1929 included such illustrious public figures as Sonny Whitney, Robert Lehman, and David Bruce, who came from a distinguished Virginian diplomatic family and whose father-in-law was Andrew Mellon. Any political influence Trippe lacked through inheritance, marriage, or business he cultivated by his own charm: best-known among this category of acquaintances was Owen Brewster, 'the Senator from PAA'.[11] This network of political influence was, however, also the result of PAA becoming a vital cog in the foreign policy of the United States, and to understand how that came about it is necessary to look briefly at PAA's South American operations.

One of the main dilemmas facing international airline operators like PAA, which were private rather than state-owned enterprises, was the diplomatic job of negotiating with foreign countries for commercial rights. PAA was more than willing to take on such a task and had considerable success, but as the international situation deteriorated in the late 1920s, it became of mutual interest for the US government and PAA to co-operate in diplomatic efforts to promote American aviation expansion, i.e. the expansion of PAA, in Central and South America.

Many of the South American airlines were under the influence or control of foreign interests, particularly French and German. The US government had always been wary about foreign planes flying near the Panama Canal—the umbilical cord between the main American naval force in the Pacific and its offspring in the Atlantic—and those considerations, along with commercially protectionist policies, had led them to deny landing-rights in 1926 to the Colombian airline SCADTA (Sociedad Colombo-Alemán de Transportes). The concerns and fears which the US government had were compounded as the 1920s progressed and the political situation in Europe deteriorated. Until 1929 the State Department's policy concerning overseas operations by US airlines had been one of acting as a benevolent onlooker, but in 1929, prompted by the Post Office, it changed its policy to one of more active support.

[11] Solberg, *Conquest*, ch. 7; A. Sampson, *Empires of the Sky: The Politics, Contests and Cartels of World Airlines* (Hodder & Stoughton, London, 1984) 45; Trippe Papers, box 8, folder: Newspapers and Magazines, draft ch. by Vern Haugland.

On 6 July Assistant Secretary of State Francis White conveyed to the Secretary of State, Frank Kellog, a request from the Post Office that active diplomatic support be given to US airlines which had been granted mail contracts. In effect this was an attempt to get preferential treatment for PAA. White pointed out that in the past the policy of the State Department had been one of non-discrimination between competing US companies abroad, but he then went on to point out some of the advantages of a 'chosen instrument'.

French and German companies were expanding in South America, were heavily subsidized, and thus advantaged in their competition with US airlines, which were expected to cope with this as well as to compete among themselves. White was concerned that 'a hands-off policy' could result in a proliferation of competing US lines which would damage each other and then fall prey in turn to foreign competition. Such an eventuality would not only be damaging commercially to the United States, but would also have serious strategic and security implications. It was important that US mail be carried in US planes to South America. This was desirable both for the expansion of business and for security reasons—not the least important consideration being the need to keep foreign planes away from the Panama Canal. In fact, it was important to the United States to control aviation in the whole Caribbean area. White suggested that if a chosen-instrument policy were adopted, the government could deflect criticisms of discrimination by saying that the Post Office had put up mail contracts for competitive bids and that PAA had proved to be the only capable airline to come forward. He also commented that there was no reason why the government should not support other US airlines for the passenger market and the carriage of other countries' mail.

On 12 July the Cabinet agreed to the Post Office's request. Hoover was ambitious for US airlines: after his election in 1928 he had undertaken a tour of South America, helping to prepare things for the further development of air services throughout the Americas. However, regarding the matter of diplomatic support, he entered the caveat that the mail contract awarded to PAA for the west-coast run down South America should not be used by the Post Office as grounds for preventing diplomatic support for other companies wanting to service the east coast of

South America (an oblique reference to the New York, Rio and Buenos Aires Airline).[12]

The State Department was soon involved in helping smooth things along for route surveying by Lindbergh on behalf of PAA in Colombia, which was a country that posed a particularly awkward problem for PAA. Not only was it an obstacle to linking Panagra on the west coast of South America with PAA in Central America, but also its main airline, SCADTA, was under German influence and, resentful of the denial of landing-rights in the United States, was being obstructionist. In the end the Colombian problem was solved by a two-pronged assault: the US government negotiated the Kellog-Olaya Pact for reciprocal US–Colombian landing-rights, and Trippe overcame SCADTA's obstructionism through a secret deal with its owner, Von Bauer, involving PAA buying up over 80 per cent of the company's shares in the spring of 1931, but leaving Von Bauer in nominal control. The deal was kept secret in Colombia, and in the United States Trippe informed only senior members of the State Department.[13]

It was this kind of active involvement in high diplomacy which inevitably drew PAA and the US government into a close working-relationship: a relationship which became ever more important as the Western democracies drew ineluctably closer to engaging the European Fascists and National Socialists and the Japanese militarists in war.

While PAA rapidly expanded its operations, flying American planes over, and landing its citizens in, foreign countries, the US government itself remained formally uninvolved in the regulation of much of this until 1928, largely because of the unwillingness of Congress to enter international regulatory agreements. After the Great War there had been a reaction in the United States against international commitments and involvements, particularly with Europe and European diplomacy. The Congress refused to ratify the Peace Treaty and the League Covenant, and traditional American isolationism from the affairs of Europe, and a policy of 'no entangling alliances', seemed to be the order

[12] *FRUS*, 1929, 1, 542–4, White to Under-Secretary of State, 6 July 1929, and Secretary of State to White, 12 July 1929; Wilbur, *Hoover Policies*, 222.

[13] *FRUS*, 1929, 1, 546–652, and *re* Lindbergh 546–50, letters 18 Jan. to 9 Feb. 1929; Daley, *American Saga*, ch. 39; Solberg, *Conquest*, 85–6; Davies, *Airlines*, 228.

of the day once again. In fact, things did not turn out quite like that. Developments in armaments during the Great War meant that the United States was now vulnerable to attack by sea and from carrier-borne aircraft. Consequently, it took an active part in naval armaments negotiations during the inter-war period. The years of the Republican ascendancy also witnessed an increase in America's overseas commercial activities, actively promoted by Hoover and his Commerce Department. The United States remained unentangled from more purely political world affairs, and in particular refused to become associated with the League of Nations in any way which might draw her into Europe's power politics and security affairs. Civil aviation, however, came under the heading of commerce and thus the government—while wary—was prepared to engage in international discussions.

The United States had taken an active part in drafting the Paris Convention, but, as with the other agreements negotiated there in 1919, it was never ratified. On 20 February 1929 the State Department, on the advice of the Commerce Department, asked the Senate to suspend consideration of the convention in view of provisions in the 1926 US Air Commerce Act. Another factor which had a bearing on America's relationship to the Paris Convention was that in 1928 US representatives signed the Havana Convention on Commercial Aviation, which held jurisdiction over the Americas. It covered very similar ground, and indeed was partly modelled on the Paris Convention, but it also differed at several points. And these were to cause problems, for, ironically, no sooner had the Senate suspended consideration of the Paris Convention than the United State was invited to attend an extraordinary session of the International Commission for Air Navigation in Paris. The meeting was prompted by proposals put forward by Germany for revision of the Paris Convention, specifically with a view to facilitating the admission of herself and other non-members.

On 25 April 1929 Secretary of State Henry Stimson explained the US position to President Hoover. In 1926 the then President and Secretary of State had recommended acceptance of the Paris Convention to the Senate subject to five conditions being met. First, private US planes would be allowed to overfly areas prohibited to foreign planes; this was contrary to the existing provisions of article 3. Secondly, the United States disliked the discriminatory provisions of article 5, which prohibited aviation agreements with states which were not members of the Paris Convention. One of America's main concerns regarding this was a 1926 agreement with Panama, which, in effect, had given the United States control of the airspace near the Panama Canal. Article 30 of the Havana Convention recognized the legality of existing aviation arrangements and therefore posed no problem for the Panama–US agreement; but there might be a serious problem if the United States but not Panama were to join the Paris Convention. Understandably then, the United States wanted to retain her right to have agreements with non-member states. Thirdly, the United States wished to retain absolute control over its customs regulations. Fourthly, it wished to retain the right to appeal to the Permanent Court of International Justice regarding any dispute which arose out of the Convention. And finally, the United States did not wish it to be implied that membership of the Convention in any way associated her with the League of Nations.

After the United States signed the Havana Convention, the force of most of these reservations was increased. Although it had not been ratified by the Senate at the time the invitation to attend the extraordinary session in Paris was issued, clearly the United States would have to ensure compatibility before she could join the Paris Convention. Thus America's objections to certain matters in the Paris Convention on grounds of principle and beliefs concerning American national interests were now bolstered by the commitments she had made to the legal requirements of the Havana Convention.

Given American prospects in international civil aviation, it seemed absurd to have two controlling conventions with different regulations, especially if those differences were likely to prejudice the expansion of US airlines into Europe and the vast territories of the European empires. Stimson believed that the Paris meeting afforded an opportunity to make the two Conventions compatible and thus arrive at universally acceptable rules. He recommended US participation and named a delegation, to be led by William P. MacCracken, an Assistant Secretary in the Department of Commerce. On 27 April Hoover accepted Stimson's recommendations.

On 28 June MacCracken reported from the conference that some progress had been made towards the US position and that the result could be 'a substantial improvement in the Convention'. In particular both the matter of overflights by private aircraft and the problem of relations with non-members of the Convention had been discussed sensibly. In support of the principle of granting liberal access to foreign airlines, the United States found itself in a minority of four including Britain, Holland, and Sweden, but by the end of November the State Department wanted to recommend ratification of the revised Convention to the Senate. It was still necessary, however, to reserve the US position on flights by private aircraft, on relations with non-members, and on customs duties, and to insist that there would be no implication that the United State, by adhering to the Convention, associated with the League.

Unfortunately, the promise of these talks was not fulfilled. The Commerce Department requested a delay in US action until existing members of the Paris Convention ratified the revisions that had emerged from the extraordinary session. The delay proved fatal, as subsequent attempts to gain ratification in the Senate collided with the growing strength of isolationism. On 12 January 1934 President Roosevelt requested that the Senate return the Convention and accompanying documents to the executive branch of government, and three days later the Senate complied. So died the hope of a major multilateral convention which would have linked civil aviation in the Americas and Europe.[14]

In contrast with the importance of the talks in Paris, negotiations on private aeronautical law in Warsaw from 4 to 12 October, at the invitation of the Polish government, were of only minor significance, but they had more success in the sense that the United States felt able to adhere, with reservations, to the Warsaw Convention which emerged from the talks. Its substance was of little political importance—the most important

[14] *FRUS*, 1929, 1, 489–517, in particular see Secretary of State to Hoover, 25 Apr. 1929, and the President's reply of 27 Apr.; Secretary of State to McCracken, 20 May 1929; McCracken to Secretary of State, 28 June 1929; Secretary of State to Secretary of Commerce, 26 Nov. 1929; and editorial comment, 517; J. C. Cooper, 'Some Historic Phases of British International Civil Aviation Policy', *International Affairs*, 23 (1947) 194–6.

aspect concerned provisions to cover compensation to individuals involved in air accidents—but apart from the Havana Convention it was the only multilateral aviation-arrangement that the United States participated in prior to 1944, and it was the only one that linked the United States with Europe.[15] Other links with Europe were left to bilateral company or state agreements, and it was these, and not international multilateral treaties, that determined the character of international aviation in the 1930s.

DEVELOPMENTS IN BRITAIN 1919–1930

In February 1919 Winston Churchill became Secretary of State for Air. He was also in charge of the War Department, which undoubtedly distracted him from aviation matters and in particular from civil aviation. Much of his ministerial time was spent tidying things up after the Great War, coping with crises in the Middle East, and overseeing the British military intervention on behalf of the White Russians. However, not only did Churchill have time-consuming responsibility for this major department, but the Air Ministry was also a difficult portfolio, because of the conflicting priorities between the RAF and civil aviation and because the existence of an independent airforce was under attack from the Army and Royal Navy. Churchill's main aviation concern was to maintain a powerful independent airforce for the purposes of defence and to help to bind the Empire together through better and speedier communications. Consequently, civil aviation in its own right was rather neglected, but it could never be wholly divorced from military developments and political considerations, which thus helped to carry it along.[16]

Churchill presided over the Air Ministry at an important stage in its early life, but his handling of civil aviation has been

[15] Ibid. 540–1; R. Y. Chuang, *The International Air Transport Association* (A. W. Sitjhoff, Leiden, 1972), 89–91 and 95–6; R. Hurst (ed.) *Pilot Error: A Professional Study of Contributing Factors* (Granada, London, 1978), 250.

[16] For Churchill's main concerns in this period, see Martin Gilbert, *Winston S. Churchill*, iv: 1917–22, Companion (Heinemann, London, 1977), and in particular for his views about the RAF, 1287–9, quoting sources CAB 27/71, Cabinet Finance Committee mins., 4 Jan. 1921 and Lloyd George Papers, Churchill to Lloyd George, 4 Jan. 1921.

criticized by at least two leading air-historians, in particular because of his attitude towards subsidies. Such criticisms are not entirely justified. When one looks at the context in which Churchill worked, involving conflicting priorities, financial constraints imposed by the Treasury, an overall drive for economy by the government—most obviously manifest in Sir Eric Geddes' Committee on National Expenditure—and general opposition to subsidies, his policy on civil aviation appears more defensible than has been allowed.[17]

Churchill was assisted by Sir Frederick Sykes, Controller-General of Civil Aviation, and by Major-General Sir Hugh Trenchard, Chief of the Air Staff. Of the two, Trenchard was the more dominant, and a formidable character by all accounts. Nicknamed 'Boom' because of his resonant voice, he got his flying-certificate after ten days of training: he was an ardent air-enthusiast and a fanatic for an independent air-force, and he helped to reinforce Churchill's existing disposition to favour the RAF over civil aviation. On 11 December 1919 Churchill presented a White Paper to Parliament, authored by Trenchard, on the permanent organization of the RAF. This was part and parcel of their ongoing battle to help the RAF to survive intact. However, it was not so much politics at home which saved the most junior of the services, but rather troubles in Mesopotamia and with 'the Mad Mullah' in Somaliland which allowed the RAF to demonstrate its potential for imposing order over unruly and recalcitrant natives in the vast tracts of the Empire. Policing actions from the air were effective and, more important in some ways, they were cheap. This strategy of 'control without occupation' did much to save the RAF from reabsorbtion by the Army and Navy. The establishment of a permanent, independent RAF was an acknowledgement of the importance of air power, and in the 1930s this had significant consequences for civil aviation. First of all, 'control without occupation' was something that the British were unwilling to abandon at the Geneva Disarmament Conference, and this helped prejudice what little chance there was for air disarmament and international control of civil aviation. Secondly, in the 1930s civil

[17] R. Higham, *Britain's Imperial Air Routes 1918–39* (Shoe String, Hamden, Conn., 1961), 23 and 40; Sampson, *Empires*, 26–7.

aviation found itself fighting a losing battle with the RAF for resources in order to compete with the United States on the transatlantic route.[18] Things might not have been so bad if more imaginative policies and more generously funded ones had been adopted by the British government in the 1920s; sadly they were not.

In January 1920 Churchill asked the Weir Committee to consider measures that the British government could take within the existing air-estimates to develop civil aviation. Weir refused to be so tightly constrained, and his brief was altered so that instead of having to operate within a set framework he simply had to bear in mind the need for the utmost economy. Weir favoured a more generous policy than Churchill for civil aviation, but his Committee was still cautious. It decided against subsidies on the basis of miles flown, which the French granted to their operators, and instead proposed more limited subsidies on selected demonstration-routes such as the Cairo–Karachi one. At the same time as the Committee came to this conclusion, Churchill made a famous remark in the House of Commons on 11 March: 'Civil aviation must fly by itself; the Government cannot possibly hold it up in the air.' This apparently took Weir somewhat by surprise and has been seized on by some to prove that Churchill took a hard *laissez-faire* line on civil aviation, as well as neglecting it for other concerns. There is some truth to this, but on close scrutiny Churchill's position does not seem to have been all that far from Weir's. In defence of Churchill, one should bear in mind the pressures that he had to cope with, including the powerful influence of Trenchard, which resulted in the RAF being given priority over civil aviation regarding the meagre amounts of money allocated by the Treasury in the Air Estimates. Furthermore, Churchill's main aim was only to argue against 'floods of money' being poured into civil aviation. He was not against some government assistance in order to get civil aviation established. For, while thinking that the government should get out of the way, he also wanted it to 'smooth the way'

[18] Cmd. 467, 1919, 'Note by the Secretary of State for Air on a Scheme for the Permanent Organisation of the Royal Air Force, outlined by the Chief of the Air Staff'; Sir Samuel Hoare, Viscount Templewood, *Empire of the Air: The Advent of the Air Age 1922–29* (Collins, London, 1957), 36–8 and 46–8.

for civil aviation, and that conviction, as circumstances developed, led him to argue for moderate subsidies. Later on in his career, when Chancellor of the Exchequer, he opposed what many saw as necessary government finance for aviation, but this should not be allowed to prejudice judgement of what he did as Secretary of State for Air in 1919–21.[19]

In fact, some indirect subsidies were already operating in 1920 in the form of aerodromes, meteorological services, and R. & D. Regarding the latter, for example, early in the year a White Paper on education and research in aeronautics was published recommending the expansion of research and teaching at centres such as Farnborough and the National Physical Laboratory.[20] Nor should it be forgotten that it was Churchill who had asked the Weir Committee to look into the matter of how the government could help with the further development of civil aviation.

The Weir Report was ready by April 1920 and it favoured a £250,000 subsidy for civil carriers over a two-year period. Lord Inchcape dissented from the majority and advised against subsidies because of the country's lack of finances; and Trenchard issued a separate report declaring against direct subsidies and recommending that the money would be better-spent on design and research. On 7 May Churchill made his views known in a paper for the Cabinet and he did not appear to be at all ill-disposed to the subsidy recommended: a position somewhat at variance with that expressed by him in the House two months earlier, if one were only to pay attention to his remark that the government should not hold civil aviation up in the air.

> In the present Majority Report is a proposal for a modified form of subsidy, by which approved aerial transport companies, operating over approved routes, shall be granted a subsidy equal in extent to 25 per cent of their gross takings. This sum will be limited to £250,000, half of which may be earned in each of the next two years. If the whole sum is earned, it will mean that within two years aerial transport companies will have extracted by genuine business from the pockets of the public

[19] Hansard, 11 Mar. 1920, vol. 126, col. 1622; W. J. Reader, *Architect of Air Power: The Life of the First Viscount Weir of Eastwood 1877–1959* (Collins, London, 1968), 92–3.

[20] Cmd. 554. 1920, 'Education and Research in Aeronautics'.

£1,000,000 in payments for the conveyance of passengers and goods, and I am of the opinion that should companies succeed in doing this, civil aviation will have established itself on a commercial basis.[21]

Unfortunately, when the Cabinet discussed the Weir Report on 29 July various factors worked against immediate acceptance of its recommendations. Finances were still a major constraint: the Treasury had already come out strongly against subsidies, and Trenchard's influential views against them on both military grounds (i.e. he was fearful subsidies would make inroads into resources which could otherwise be used for the RAF) and commercial grounds were noted. But there was something else which was even more decisive. Since the Report had been issued, a representative of one airline had stated that his company was paying its way on a turnover of £100,000 per annum. It was in the light of this that the Cabinet decided to postpone a decision on subsidies, pending further investigation.[22]

While the British government hesitated, the need for subsidies continued to increase. On 28 September Lord Weir wrote to Churchill saying that he strongly favoured them for a two-year period. He was very critical of the Treasury, which he claimed was treating civil aviation as if it were a well-established industry. In his view, this was clearly not the case: it needed government support in order to thrive commercially. In particular, Weir resentfully noted that Britain had 'lost out' in the motor-car industry and he did not want civil aviation to suffer the same fate. Sykes, while not as forceful, also recommended temporary subsidies for civil aviation to Churchill.[23]

On 12 October Churchill made a luncheon speech to the first Air Conference organized by the Air Council, held at the Guildhall in London, in which he announced that the government intended to help civil aviation by every means in its power. By November, in response to various pressures including arguments from Weir and Sykes, clamour in the press for government aid for civil aviation, and the deepening financial

[21] Cmd. 770. 1920, 'Government Assistance for the Development of Civil Aviation'; CAB 24/105, CP(20)1265, 7 May 1920, Churchill on Advisory Committee report.

[22] CAB 23/22, 42(20)12, 29 July 1920; Reader, *Weir*, 95.

[23] CAB 24/116, CP(20)2225, Nov. 1920 with copy of Weir to Churchill, 28 Sept. 1920.

crisis in British aviation companies because of their inability to compete with their subsidized French counterparts, Churchill circulated the arguments of Weir and Sykes to the Cabinet and specifically drew their attention to the 'almost universal expression of opinion in the newspapers in favour of some aid being given to civil aviation'. These were not the actions of someone hell-bent on refusing subsidies.[24]

By the end of the year British aviation companies were failing and Churchill was clearly concerned; however, the RAF was still under threat and continued to have first call on resources, which the Treasury under Austen Chamberlain repeatedly tried to cut down. In the Cabinet Finance Committee on 4 January 1921, Churchill argued that, 'the reduction suggested [in funding] would shatter the whole structure of the Air Force, which, he was convinced, had a great future before it and was of vast importance from an Imperial point of view.' He went on to say: 'The Estimates had been most carefully scrutinised and cut down in the Air Ministry, and he doubted whether it was possible, compatible with the views he had expressed, to reduce them further, but at the most he could not hope to cut more than, say, £500,000.' In fact he shaved nearly £1.25 million off the estimates, producing a new total of £18,411,000—the vast bulk of which was for the RAF, as always his priority and main concern in the Air Ministry. (There were also considerable sums earmarked to settle interdepartmental wartime debts.)

On 4 January, corresponding with Prime Minister Lloyd George, who three days earlier had asked him to relinquish the posts he then held in favour of becoming Secretary of State for the Colonies, Churchill asked to talk things over with him, particularly 'the Air Ministry, which I have shielded from the assaults of the two great military Departments during the whole of the last two years'. Even though safeguarding the RAF's financial status was uppermost in his mind, the effects of the spirited rearguard action he fought against Treasury parsimony in the closing weeks of his time at the Air Ministry extended to civil aviation.[25] He managed to persuade Austen Chamberlain

[24] Ibid.

[25] Gilbert, *Companion*, 1287–88, quoting source CAB 27/71, Cabinet Finance Committee mins., 4 Jan. 1921 and Lloyd George Papers, Churchill to Lloyd George, 4 Jan. 1921.

to grant it a modest subsidy, 'provided that it did not exceed £60,000 from now till March 31st 1922, and that we were not committed to any increase over £60,000 in any subsequent year'. Churchill informed the Cabinet Finance Committee, 'I propose to announce this decision at once, in order to encourage civil aviation before it dies.'[26]

He was almost too late. In February 1921 there were no British companies left operating cross-Channel services. It took a long time for the British civil-aviation industry to pick up from this collapse, but, with the need for subsidies now more obvious than ever before, things began to take a promising shape during the latter part of 1921 and during 1922.

The introduction of operating subsidies coincided with Churchill's departure from the Air Ministry: he was replaced by Captain Frederick Guest. Guest did not have a seat in the Cabinet, which was unfortunate politically for aviation because the respective futures of the RAF and of civil aviation, notwithstanding the new subsidies for the latter, were by no means yet assured. 1921 and 1922 were difficult years for British aviation. Britain's economic difficulties meant that direct subsidies continued to be inadequate, and unfortunately, unlike in the United States, airmail subsidies did not fill the gap that existed between private companies' revenue and their funding requirements. The successor to Weir's Advisory Committee on Civil Aviation, chaired by Lord Gorrell, issued a report (its only one), which recommended the development of a subsidized imperial airmail service, but it was not adopted by the British government, and carriers continued to get a strictly commercial fee for the actual mail carried. (It was not until 1937 that the Empire Airmail Scheme came into operation.) Despite the financial difficulties, including cut-backs for civil aviation in 1923, British aircraft companies did establish a more stable existence during 1921–2. Competition was controlled more, monopolies, so far as British operators were concerned, were established on some routes, and the subsidy system was gradually expanded in operation and increased in terms of its funds. However, it was not until the Conservative Party came to power in 1922 and Sir Samuel

[26] Ibid. War Office Papers 16/73, Churchill memo for Cabinet Finance Committee, 5 Jan. 1921; Cmd. 1170, 1921, 'Air Estimates Explanatory Memorandum'.

Hoare was appointed Air Minister that the future of both the RAF and Britain's civil-aviation industry took on a more permanent and secure appearance.[27]

In 1922 the Conservatives broke away from the coalition that had been formed with the Liberals during the war and successfully fought the general election under the leadership of Bonar Law. As Prime Minister, he appointed Hoare to the Air Ministry on 2 November, with the ominous comment, 'I must tell you that the post may be abolished in a few weeks. Sykes tells me that the Independent Air Force and the Air Ministry cost too much, and that there is everything to be said in peacetime for going back to the old plan of Navy and Army control.' For a short time it looked as if Churchill's and Trenchard's battles had been in vain—that was until Hoare emerged not only as a champion of an independent RAF, but also of a government-supported civil-aviation industry. He saw the RAF as his main priority, but he had more time and energy to spend on the Air Ministry than Churchill had had, he was able to be more effective than Guest, whose appointment turned out to be very temporary, and he placed great value on civil aviation and believed that government had to support it more strongly than it had done in the past.[28] In arguing his case for civil aviation before colleagues, Hoare had two lines of attack: one concerned the value of civil aviation in its own right; the other was to do with the defence roles that it could play by supporting the RAF and by helping to bind the Empire together.

Just as the British government recognized how effective air power could be for helping to police the Empire, so it also realized what a dangerous weapon it could be against mainland Britain in the hands of a future European enemy; and Hoare played skilfully on this fear in his battle for the RAF. By 1923 British disarmament had reduced the work-force in the aircraft industry to the paltry figure of 2,500 and there were only a handful of front-line, combat-ready aircraft. The run-down of Britain's armed services was in accordance with the 'ten-year rule', adopted by the Cabinet in 1919, which stipulated that

[27] Cmd. 1739, 1922, 'First Report on the Imperial Air Mail Service'; Higham, *Imperial Routes*, 42–3.

[28] J. A. Cross, *Sir Samuel Hoare: A Political Biography* (Jonathan Cape, London, 1977), 91; Hoare, *Empire of the Air*, 36.

TABLE 1. *Comparative Strengths, French and British Military and Civil Aircraft 1922–1925*

	Britain	France
Military aircraft Dec. 1922		
Home-based	137	946
Abroad	234	232
Total	371	1,178
Est. total 1925	575	2,180
Civilian aircraft Dec. 1922	167	660

defence planning was to assume that there would be no major war for ten years. That rule stayed in force until 1932; nevertheless, the state of the RAF had worried the coalition government of Lloyd George during its last months in office, particularly after it had received a paper from the Committee of Imperial Defence (CID) signed by Lord Balfour. The paper insisted that 'where national security is concerned the unthinkable must be faced', which meant that Britain had to calculate the desirable strength of her air defences in relation to the strongest air power which could mount a strike against her—even though that state was France, nominally Britain's closest ally.

The coalition government responded to this by planning an additional expenditure of £2 million to provide fifteen additional RAF and five auxiliary squadrons. On 14 December, shortly after coming to power, the economy-minded Conservatives announced in the House of Commons that this programme would be cut back by dispensing with the auxiliary squadrons, but two months later the matter of Britain's air power was raised again.

In February 1923 Hoare reminded his colleagues of the views expressed by the CID the previous year and presented them with figures to show the comparative British and French strengths in both military and civilian aircraft. (See Table 1.)

'The Cabinet', wrote Hoare, 'should realise that, if we cannot at present compete militarily with the French programme, we must give constant attention to the possibilities of Civil Aviation, if for no other purpose than to assist in keeping the aircraft industry alive.' He acknowledged that this was no substitute for RAF squadrons, but 'Civil Aviation, can . . . be a useful and necessary supplement, and it is on this account that it is an essential factor in our air policy. If the industry is to be firmly established the Treasury will have to find the money and will have to take some risks.'[29] Hoare was right to point to the still-enfeebled state of Britain's civil aviation, but in the long term it is doubtful that he could have remedied much there if he had been unable to cope with the more pressing problem of the RAF and Britain's air defences.

On 9 March 1923 Law appointed a subcommittee of the CID, chaired by Lord Salisbury, to review Britain's air power. He was prompted to do this by Hoare, in order to try to resolve what was now a battle royal between, on the one hand, the Navy, led by Admiral Beatty, and, on the other, the defenders of an independent RAF. Fortunately for the RAF, the working subcommittee (of the subcommittee) had Lord Weir as one of its members, and he liaised closely with Trenchard and Hoare to ensure that the interests of an independent air-force were nurtured and promoted. In the course of the summer the Salisbury Committee and its subcommittees recommended that an additional thirty-four squadrons be created, bringing total strength to fifty-two by April 1928, and that the RAF continue, at least for the time being, as a separate entity. Stanley Baldwin, who had succeeded Law as Prime Minister in May, stated in the House of Commons: 'British Air Power must include a Home Defence Force of sufficient strength adequately to protect us against air attack by the strongest Air Force within striking distance of this country.' The hope, long cherished by Churchill, Trenchard, and now Hoare, of maintaining an independent air-force in Britain seemed certain of fulfilment with the obvious priority which had been accorded to air power. For a brief period beginning in 1925, however, that priority was threatened when the government accepted recommendations from a Cabinet Committee on Air Force Expansion for Home Defence, chaired by Lord Birkenhead, that the programme for a fifty-two-squadron RAF should be stretched out, with the target being reached

[29] Ibid., 67–8; CAB 24/128, CP(23)88, Feb. 1923, memo by Hoare, 'Air Policy and a One Power Air Standard'.

in 1935/6. This decision was taken in the light of improved Anglo-French relations and in an atmosphere of international optimism following the signing of the Locarno Treaty on 1 December 1925, which gave force to various European security-pacts. Even so, the need for the RAF's independent existence was never seriously challenged and its expansion was eventually re-accelerated in response to the threat from Germany.[30] Hoare's original initiative in prompting a review of the position of Britain's air power brought highly satisfactory results, and these were complemented by achievements of a similar order in the civilian sphere, though the idea that there was such a clear-cut division between the military and the civilian is misleading. Results Hoare achieved in the latter were partly a consequence of the success of his arguments regarding the former.

Describing the start of his own career at the Air Ministry, Hoare wrote: 'I knew nothing about the technical problems of air transport services, but as a Conservative who had been brought up in the days of Rudyard Kipling, Joseph Chamberlain and Milner, I saw in the creation of air routes the chance of uniting the scattered countries of the Empire and the Commonwealth.' As always, there was a political perspective to civil aviation.[31] However, Hoare also wanted to get aviation on to a viable commercial footing and had a more realistic view of the industry's financial needs than his predecessors. He realized that existing subsidies were woefully inadequate and that the industry had to be given long-term security if it were to flourish and become independent of government.

It was with these convictions that Hoare appointed a committee in January 1923, chaired by Sir Herbert Hambling, Deputy Chairman of Barclays Bank, with the brief, 'To consider the present working of the scheme of Cross-Channel Subsidies and to Advise on the best method of subsidising Air Transport in the future.' Its unanimous recommendations, reported on 15 February, were well received by the press and immediately accepted by the Cabinet.

[30] Hoare, *Empire of the Air*, 67–8; Cross, *Hoare*, 93, 98; H. Montgomery Hyde, *Baldwin: The Unexpected Prime Minister* (Hart-Davis McGibbon, London, 1973), 161–2; CAB 24/201, CP(29)4, 14 Jan. 1929; Hansard, 26 June 1923, vol. 165, col. 2142.

[31] Hoare, *Empire of the Air*, 90.

The Hambling Committee Report was a turning-point in government policy towards civil aviation. It won acceptance for the notion that government support was needed for aviation, and that was something which was not overturned until the 1980s. The Committee proposed a ten-year subsidy-programme of £1 million payments to diminish as the years went by from £137,000 to £32,000 p.a., with the hope that at the end of the scheme British civil aviation would be self-supporting. This in itself was radical, being a significant departure from the previous *ad hoc*, hand-to-mouth schemes, but something even more startling was proposed. Part of the justification for a long-term subsidy-scheme was that the British government should create a large corporation, enjoying privileged status under government control: this was the really radical aspect of the Committee's report. In effect, the proposal was for a publicly controlled monopoly, or near monopoly. The new corporation would be the 'chosen instrument' for carrying mail and passengers overseas and as such would, it was hoped, thrive commercially: instead of government competing against itself by subsidizing a number of companies, competition was to be supplied by foreign carriers.[32]

On 14 March Hoare announced the new subsidy-scheme in the House of Commons and over the next few months the Committee's proposals gained even stronger support in the government, with Stanley Baldwin taking over from Law as Prime Minister and with the subsequent elevation of Hoare to Cabinet rank. Just over a year later Imperial Airways (IA) was formed by the amalgamation of the British Marine Air Navigation Company, Daimler Airways, Handley Page Transport, and Instone Airlines. Even so, it was hardly a giant of the skies: its fleet consisted of seven DH34s, two Sea Eagles, three Handley Page W8bs, and one Vickers' Vimy. Nevertheless, its Chairman, Sir Eric Geddes, who was advised on finance by his friend Sir George Beharrell, and the strong team at the Air Ministry led by Hoare and Sir Sefton Brancker, Controller-General of Civil Aviation, ensured that IA would at least have a more distinguished career in commercial civil aviation than previous British companies had had.

[32] Ibid., 92–3; Cmd. 1811, 1923, 'Government Financial Assistance to Civil Air Transport Companies'; CAB 24/188, CP(27)238, memo by Hoare, 6 Oct. 1927.

TABLE 2. *Imperial Airways Routes 1927*[33]

	Summer	Winter
London–Paris	3 per day	1 per day
London–Paris–Basle–Zurich	1 per day	—
London–Brussels–Cologne	2 per day	1 per day
London–Ostend	1 per day	—
Southampton–Channel I.	1 per week	1 per week
Cairo–Basrah	1 per week	1 per week

In its early years there was little that was actually imperial about IA. Most of its routes continued to be from Britain to European destinations. In 1926, however, there was a sign of things to come when the government, prompted by Hoare and the Imperial Conference of that year, introduced a five-year subsidy-scheme of £93,000 p.a. (maximum) for a route linking India and Egypt (because of difficulties in its early days with Persia it only ran between Cairo and Basrah): this was inaugurated in January 1927 and the shift of emphasis away from Europe to the Empire was now gathering momentum, but IA's route configuration was still overwhelmingly European. (See Table 2.)

Unfortunately,the European routes did not yield profits, and although IA made some headway in its first three years of operation—most notably it maintained a British presence in civil aviation and began the development of Empire routes—its overall commercial achievements were modest. This was partly to do with shortcomings within the company itself, which will be considered shortly, but also judgement has to be relative to what other countries' airlines were achieving, and the most obvious cause for the discrepancy between theirs and IA's performance was money—to finance subsidies, an infrastructure, and the wherewithal for R. & D. All of these things were necessary to provide a sound springboard for IA to take off as a commercial and competitive airline.

By international standards, funding was still stringent.

[33] Hoare, *Empire of the Air*; Geddes had been the first Transport Minister and was a very capable man, but when involved with IA he also had a job with Dunlop which took much of his time; Beharrell was a pre-war colleague and an excellent statistician.

Money for civil aviation had to be fought for against the priority claims of the RAF. Also, the decision to go ahead with an airship scheme did not help matters. It was developed originally by Hoare, and then modified and put into operation during the brief life of the Labour government in 1924, when Lord Thomson was Secretary of State for Air. Some £2 million which might otherwise have been spent on civil aviation was ploughed into the development of the R100 and the R101. When the R101 crashed at Beauvais on 5 October 1930, the programme came to an abrupt and tragic end and all the investment had to be written off without any concrete results to show for it. And finally, Britain's economic performance did not generate enough wealth for the demands of the new industry: in particular the General Strike of 1 May to 19 November 1926 severely damaged the government's finances. In April 1927 Churchill, then Chancellor of the Exchequer, announced a budget deficit of £36.5 million for the previous year, £32 million of which was due to the General Strike. The consequent lack of finance for civil aviation compounded the other problems IA had to deal with and the company began to slip further and further behind its counterparts in other countries. By October 1927 Hoare was once again deeply concerned about the future of British civil aviation, not least, he informed his Cabinet colleagues, because of 'the dynamic state of commercial air transport abroad'.[34]

In a Cabinet paper dated 6 October, Hoare argued two basic points: firstly, that British civil aviation was underfunded compared with that in other countries; and secondly, that Britain, ironically, had the most to lose from this situation because of the need for Empire communications and the commercial gains that they could yield. Leaving the United States aside for the moment, even in the European context Britain was being left behind in civil aviation development. In the year 1927–8 the British government's expenditure on the industry was £230,000; Germany's was £1.2 million and France's £4.5 million. As a result, IA's operations were too limited. The hope of the Hambling Committee that a £1 million subsidy spread over ten years would be sufficient to put IA on to a firm commercial footing could now be seen as too optimistic. And yet the value of

[34] Ibid.; H. Pelling, *Winston Churchill* (Macmillan, London, 1974), 317.

getting IA on to such a footing had, if anything, become greater. In 1926 the Imperial Conference had given express and emphatic recognition to the importance of developing imperial air-routes; Hoare strongly called for them, and, furthermore, he believed that for IA to become a commercial success it had to move out more energetically on to them and away from the unprofitable European ones. Invoking a maritime analogy, he said that IA could no more be commercially viable by simply plying across the Channel than could Britain's merchant marine and passenger fleets.

He suggested that a small Cabinet committee should be set up: 'To review the present position of civil aviation in the British Empire with particular reference to recent developments abroad and to consider and report what modifications of our present policy are desirable and practical.' His proposal was accepted and a committee was appointed under the chairmanship of Cunliffe-Lister (who later became Lord Swinton), President of the Board of Trade.[35]

Just before Christmas 1927 the Committee produced its report and it was considered by the Cabinet a month later, on 25 January 1928. The Committee identified four priorities: funding; stability through monopoly; the expansion of imperial routes—if necessary at the expense of European ones; and re-equipment of IA. In fact, the relationship between manufacturers and operators was belatedly recognized as being of great importance. One of IA's greatest weaknesses later on in the 1930s was the non-existence of a British-made aircraft which could successfully ply the Atlantic, and this problem remained to plague its successor, the British Overseas Airways Corporation (BOAC), well into the post-war period.

There were five detailed proposals:

1. the concentration of Britain's overseas air services in the hands of IA should continue
2. existing agreements between IA, the Air Ministry, and the Treasury should be modified, in order that
   (*a*) the company have security
   (*b*) Empire routes, beginning with the London–Calcutta

[35] CAB 24/188, CP(27)238, memo by Hoare, 6 Oct. 1927.

mail-run could be developed in view of the less remunerative European routes
(*c*) IA's planes could be renewed
(*d*) the British government could secure more favourable participation in IA's profits
3. the Post Office should promote the London–Calcutta mail-route
4. sufficient government money should be made available to achieve the goals set out in (i)–(iii)
5. machinery should be established to facilitate the closest possible co-operation between the Air Ministry, IA, and manufacturers.

Churchill, who as Minister for Air had fought against Treasury cuts affecting his ministry, now sounded a word of caution as Chancellor of the Exchequer. He said that he would not oppose the proposals, 'which made no immediate addition to Government expenditure. He wished it to be understood, however, that the financial details must be settled between the Treasury and the Air Ministry, and he gave warning that it would be necessary for him to press for a diminishing element in the cost of any new arrangement.'[36]

In the House of Commons on 26 July Hoare gave an outline of the new arrangements with IA, which was in accordance with the Cunliffe-Lister Committee report. IA's monopoly position was reaffirmed (though Hoare explained that in exceptional cases other companies might be subsidized), emphasis was given to developing Empire routes, and another subsidy-scheme, involving in excess of £2.75 million over eleven years, was announced.[37] However, despite these promising plans, by the end of the year the government was set to implement a reduction in the Air Estimates because of the overall economic constraints it had to contend with. Hoare complained of this in Cabinet in December, pointing out that Britain was reducing her expenditure at a time when other countries were increasing theirs. In Cabinet on 14 January 1929 Churchill argued for a

[36] CAB 24/190, CP(27)327, 'Report of the Committee on the Future of British Commercial Air Transport', chaired by Cunliffe-Lister, President of the Board of Trade; CAB 23/57, 3(28)5, 25 Jan. 1928; ibid., 15 Feb. 1928.
[37] Hansard, Hoare, 26 July 1928.

TABLE 3. *Air Estimates 1921–1924, 1928–1931, 1936–1939 (£ million)*[38]

	Total	Civil aviation
1921[a]	18.411	0.88
1922	10.895	0.364
1923	12.011	0.287
1924	14.511	0.355
1928	16.25	0.415
1929	16.2	0.450
1930	17.85	0.5
1931	18.1	0.470
1936	39[b]	0.760
1937	56	2.315
1938	73.5	2.925
1939	66.561	4.787

[a] Civil expenditure for 1921 was on infrastructure and meteorological services.

[b] Double the previous year's total.

reduction in air expenditures and Hoare opposed him, pointing out among other things that in the United States, federal expenditure alone on aviation was set at £30 million—twice that of Britain's. Hoare, perhaps realizing the pressure that the air estimates were under, said that he did not want a decision from the Cabinet then, but only after they had considered things carefully. In the event there was a slight increase in the civil estimates for 1929. (See Table 3.)

By the 1930s Britain's civil-aviation industry, although it had made progress, still had serious defects. Hoare had established a better institutional framework for the industry, had managed to establish a chosen-instrument status for IA, had had more success than his predecessors in extracting government financial support, and had done much to publicize the industry by his frequent travels by air. IA pioneered imperial routes, particularly in East Africa and on to South Africa, and surmounted many difficulties in doing so—including political ones—with

[38] CAB 24/201, CP(29)4, 14 Jan. 1929; *Parliamentary Sessional Papers—the Air Estimates.*

the able help of Hoare. On the negative side, IA's management was somewhat autocratic and its planning and R. & D. were often found wanting. The subsidy schemes were never substantial enough to put British civil aviation on a par with that of the United States, or indeed of most European countries. IA had to make do with poor equipment and thus came to emphasize its high standards of catering rather than speed and long-range non-stop flights. In the long run this had damaging consequences for the company and its competitiveness. The lack of funds available to IA meant that the company only placed small orders for aircraft, which in turn restricted the R. & D. of British manufacturers. The result was a series of British planes that could only fly relatively short ranges at low speeds. The tendency to develop routes consisting of numerous short hops that this encouraged was also emphasized by the way the air-mail service was required to make frequent mail-drops. The existence of IA was assured because of the privileged status established for it by the government, but this did not provide immunity from criticism, and the defects in British civil aviation catalogued above gave rise to considerable concern, publicly voiced in the 1930s.

By the end of the 1920s there was a marked contrast between the fortunes of Imperial and PAA, chosen instruments of Britain and the United States respectively for overseas air-carriage. The contrast was the result of the different ways that the two countries had dealt with problems which universally afflicted civil aviation in its early days.

Both countries had recognized the need for temporary subsidies in order to put civil aviation on a viable commercial footing; however, in the United States this resulted in large amounts of money being pumped into civil aviation by both federal and municipal government in the form of indirect subsidies; whereas in Britain much smaller and inadequate amounts of money were provided through direct subsidies to offset operating-costs. The importance of the connection between air forces and airline operators on the one hand and aircraft manufacturers on the other was also appreciated, notably by the Morrow Board in the United States and by the Hambling Report in Britain. But once again it was in the United States that effective action was taken: the federal government introduced a long-term procurement-programme which helped to strengthen the R. & D. component in manufacturing companies, and men such as Trippe in the private sector had the courage and foresight to commission ever larger, faster, and higher-performance passenger-planes. In Britain manufacturers only received orders for small production-runs from IA, and even military orders were chopped and changed, contracted and expanded in numbers, which resulted in unsettling uncertainties that damaged R. & D. By the time that the British became fully aware of the commercial consequences of this, the international situation had deteriorated so much that they were forced to concentrate almost all their available resources on the development and production of military aircraft, leaving IA stranded without modern equipment. The links between civil and military aviation had helped the cause of both British and American civil aviation during the 1920s, but as the next decade progressed, Britain's greater proximity to the threat of European totalitarianism and her more limited resources meant that military priorities squeezed resources for civil aviation sooner and more damagingly than was the case in the United States. These circumstances were more than enough of a handicap for IA on the eve of being confronted with the prospect of competing with US enterprise in the form of PAA, but worse was to come.[39]

During the fifteen months or so between June 1929 and October 1930 there were a number of incidents and developments which adversely affected British civil aviation. On 8 June 1929, with the coming to power of Ramsey Macdonald's Labour administration, Hoare, who had achieved much against heavy odds, was once again succeeded by Lord Thomson. This loss to the industry was followed in January 1930 by another: Trenchard, his beloved independent RAF secure, resigned as Chief of Air Staff. Ten months later the industry lost two other important figures under saddening circumstances: Sir Sefton Brancker and Lord Thomson were both killed in the R101 disaster. Meanwhile, in October of 1929 the Depression had begun, following the Wall Street Crash. This was to have major implications for Britain's civil aviation not only in terms of government financial

[39] M. Smith, 'Planning and Building the British Bomber Force 1934–9', *Business History Review*, 54 (1980), 35–62.

difficulties which restricted developments, but also because the economic crisis caused defaults on war-debt payments to the United States. These in turn led to calls for reducing armament expenditure and the convening of the Geneva General Disarmament Conference which then raised important questions about the future of national airline companies and the possible internationalization of civil aviation. Notwithstanding all these inauspicious auguries for British civil aviation, in 1930 Woods Humphrey, who had been General Manager of IA since 1925 and who became Managing Director in July 1930, left Britain for talks with Juan Trippe in the United States to discuss the future development of transatlantic air-services. As we have seen, on a purely company-to-company basis, IA would have been at a disadvantage in negotiations with PAA, which had better management, was commercially much more successful, and was in the process of acquiring aircraft which would revolutionize civil aviation. However, the political relationship between the United States and Britain at this time was more symmetrical, and thus the political perspective helped to even out the disparity in commercial strength between the two companies.

Trippe and Woods Humphrey had to conduct their talks in a kind of structural vacuum, for there were no formal arrangements to govern links between British and American aviation in 1930. The only exception to this was the Warsaw Convention.[40] It was in this context that the most important international air-route in the world was about to be considered, and the inauguration of Anglo-American civil-aviation relations was now truly about to begin.

[40] CAB 23/67, 32(31)7, 10 June 1931. For a fascinating account of IA's routes and anecdotal pictures of the role played by Hoare in popularizing flying, see A. Frater, *Beyond the Blue Horizon* (Penguin, London, 1987). In 1934 a bilateral agreement was made between Britain and the United States by an exchange of diplomatic notes to the effect that they would give reciprocal recognition to each other's standards of flying-competence and airworthiness. See editorial comment, *FRUS*, 1929, 1, 539.

3
Disarmament and Civil Aviation

BEFORE there could be significant developments in the national policies of Britain and the United States, or on the transatlantic route, civil aviation became of interest to a new multilateral arena—the Geneva General Disarmament Conference. Important questions were raised there about civil aviation, and for a short period in 1932 it even looked as if the development of national aviation policies might be rendered redundant.

The delegates at Geneva considered a number of proposals for internationalizing civil aviation because of its military potential. Many thought that it had to be controlled in order for air disarmament to be effective. In some plans this meant bringing aviation under international controls; in others, that no country could be allowed its own civilian carriers. Instead, an international organization would operate a world airline. If the first of these two types of plans had come to fruition, then the history of both British and US civil aviation would have been very different. If the second type of plan had been implemented, then the present story would end with the 1930s. As it turned out, neither of these eventualities came to pass, because the conference was a failure. Some of the proposals were made simply to gain tactical negotiating-advantages. There were also many practical obstacles to disarmament and often a lack of political will to tackle them energetically, but the debates at Geneva were important in themselves and had consequences in terms of subsequent ideas and plans for international civil aviation. It is for these reasons that the Disarmament Conference needs to be considered.

The priority of disarmament had been set by the Peace Conference of 1919, which tried to prevent the carnage of the Great War recurring. The delegates in Paris committed their countries, subject to ratification by their respective governments, both to disarming and to establishing a system of collective security. Article 8 of the Peace Treaties stated:

> The members of the League recognise that the maintenance of peace requires the reduction of national armaments to the lowest point consistent with national safety, and the enforcement by common action of international obligations.[1]

The general process was to begin with the disarmament of Germany, with other countries then following suit. The undertaking by League members to disarm was expressed in part in a communiqué to Germany stating that German disarmament was to be a preliminary for a 'general reduction and limitation of armaments which they [the Allied and Associated Powers] seek to bring about as one of the most fruitful preventives of war, and which will be one of the first duties of the League.'[2]

In the following thirteen years, apart from unilateral disarmament, such as Britain's run-down of the RAF, and the notable exception of international agreements at Washington and London in 1922 and 1930, which limited the naval strengths of the major powers at set ratios, there was no progress on international agreement to disarm. Indeed, many countries, most notably France, took to building up their armed forces.

France was the most security-conscious of all states in the 1920s. She had suffered two devastating invasions within half a century and was understandably wary about the possibility of yet another onslaught from a revived Germany. Her fears were compounded by two post-war developments. First, the retreat from European security-affairs by the United States: the New World, which had stepped in to redress the power imbalance of the Old in 1917, made it clear that it would not commit itself to a long-term solution of Europe's security problems. Secondly,

[1] Quoted from J. W. Wheeler-Bennett, *The Disarmament Deadlock* (Routledge & Kegan Paul, London, 1934), 2. For the broad aspect of the Geneva Conference, I have liberally drawn from the above and from the following books: E. H. Carr, *International Relations Since the Peace Treaties* (Macmillan, London, 1937); E. Bendiner, *A Time for Angels: The Tragicomic History of the League of Nations* (Alfred Knopf, New York, 1975); and C. Thorne, *The Limits of Foreign Policy: The West, the League and the Far Eastern Crisis 1931–33* (Macmillan, London, 1973). I am also indebted to Dick Richardson, author of *The Evolution of British Disarmament Policy in the 1920s* (Frances Pinter, London, 1989), and 'Process and Progress in Disarmament: Some Lessons of History' in V. Harle and P. Sivonen (eds.), *Europe in Transition* (Frances Pinter, London, 1989). He read this chapter, and I have amended it in accordance with a number of points he made; however, there remain a number of differences of interpretation between us.

[2] Wheeler-Bennett, *Disarmament*, 3.

world opinion became increasingly equivocal about placing war guilt solely on Germany's shoulders. Such opinion was encouraged by the French and Belgian military move east of the Rhine in order to occupy the Ruhr, in January 1923. This was, supposedly, to secure German reparations, but some suspected that it was also motivated by a French desire to weaken Germany permanently by establishing French control over a major part of her heavy industry. Before that could happen, the US-sponsored Dawes Plan produced a compromise solution for reparations, and France and Belgium withdrew their troops. Nevertheless, the invasion of the Ruhr was regarded as highly provocative, particularly by many in the United States, where voices were raised on Germany's behalf. Sentiment continued to shift in Germany's favour during the 1920s. The electoral gains by the Nazis in September 1930 made British opinion less sanguine about meeting German demands and more understanding about France's security needs, but even so, along with American opinion, it still regarded aspects of the Versailles settlement as harsh and unjust and many people were sympathetic to revision. Among other things, there was injustice in that, while Germany had been disarmed, other powers had not kept their pledge to follow suit. The net result of all this was a political and security conundrum that demanded attention, but was perhaps already unsolvable by the time that the General Disarmament Conference convened in Geneva in February 1932.

On the one hand, Germany felt that it had the right to demand equality of status. In particular this meant either that all states should disarm to Germany's level, or, a more likely scenario, that Germany should be allowed to rearm to 'the lowest point consistent with national safety', while other states disarmed to an equivalent level. Germany's position might have had more integrity if she had not already by 1932 exceeded the armaments limit imposed by the Versailles settlement—a fact which alarmed the French. Also, as the Conference progressed, German demands were made in an ever more strident fashion and, despite most of her arguments being couched in terms of the injustices laid upon Germany, she was not herself free of self-serving demands which undermined the possibilities for disarmament.

On the other hand, France continued to agonize over her

ability to resist a rearmed Germany, which had both a larger population and a larger industrial potential than France. Under the Locarno Treaties of 1925, Britain, France, Germany, Belgium, and Italy undertook to preserve the peace in western Europe, and Britain and Italy guaranteed the Franco–German and the Belgian–German borders, but France was never convinced that this was enough to preserve her security. In any case, Locarno did not deal with the troublesome eastern borders of Germany, where France had established close ties with countries in an attempt to hem in Germany within the boundaries established at the end of the Great War. France doubted the strength of the British commitment to uphold France's security, and her concern grew as Locarno seemed to fuel German nationalist claims for revision of the Versailles settlement. France wanted to increase her security before accepting any erosion of the military pre-eminence she had achieved in Europe by 1932. The French were aware of the vicissitudes of international relations and knew that their military strength could be challenged in the longer term by a Germany released from the constraints of Versailles.

Locarno facilitated Germany's entry into the League in 1926, but because of French obstructionism she was still not accorded equal status, even though she clearly needed to be accommodated by some means. The only way that an equal military status, or at least some German rearmament, would have been acceptable to France was if Britain were to have given a strong commitment to uphold an enforceable system of collective security for Europe. Even better would have been if the United States could also have been associated with European security, for example through a consultative pact, as proposed by the Paul-Boncour Plan in November 1932. Unfortunately, neither the United States nor Britain was prepared to commit such hostages to a future which would be determined by what were considered to be the unreasonably security-hungry French and an unstable Germany stinging from the widely acknowledged injustices of the Versailles settlement. Consequently, the proposals put forward by Britain and the United States always assumed French disarmament at a pace, of a kind, and to a level that the French would not accept.

In December 1925 the Council of the League appointed a

preparatory commission for a disarmament conference. It met in May 1926, but it was not until the combination of German nationalism and the Depression highlighted the problems of arms and their cost that the promise of convening a disarmament conference began to look likely to be realized.

The Depression had a twofold effect on the prospects for disarmament. Firstly, it emphasized the desirability of reducing arms expenditure as an economy measure: a way of cutting back government expenditure or of liberating resources for more productive work. Secondly, it made Britain and some European powers eager for progress on disarmament, in order to improve the prospects for American economic help. This was particularly important regarding war-debt repayments.

Since the Dawes Plan, there had been an intricate and delicate relationship between American dollar investment in Germany, Germany's ability to pay reparations to Britain and France, and their ability to pay war debts to the United States. While the source of this circular money-flow continued in operation—namely the export of US dollars—the situation was relatively stable. But when the prospect of making large speculative gains on Wall Street started to choke the dollar flow and attract money back to the United States, the structure of international payments started to wobble. The 'Crash' on Wall Street ended the system.

In 1931 President Hoover proposed and got accepted a one-year moratorium on international debt-payments, including reparations. This provided a breathing-space and temporarily averted outright default by European countries on their war debts to the United States. But while the reparation problem was eventually put to rest at the Lausanne Conference in June 1932, with Germany agreeing to pay one last nominal reparation of £150,000, the United States would not absolve the Europeans from their obligations. Thus, with no reparations to finance payments to the United States, France and Britain were confronted by the prospect of having to default once the moratorium ended in July 1932.[3]

[3] For more detail see Carr, *International Relations*; A. A. Offner, *The Origins of the Second World War: American Foreign Policy and World Politics 1917–41* (Praeger, New York, 1976).

In addition to reducing the risk of war, the British believed that it was necessary to make progress on disarmament so that if the worst were to come, and Britain had to default on war debts, the situation would not be aggravated by US criticism that she had done so while still spending large amounts of money on armaments. If disarmament could be achieved, then this would constitute at least a minimum necessary prerequisite for the Americans to be helpful on war debts.

The auguries for the success of the Disarmament Conference were not good. Apart from the conflicting aims of the main protagonists regarding armaments, and the economic complications, there was a series of other matters which cast a baleful pall over the Conference. The Japanese were waging an undeclared war against China. The Germans announced in January that they could not and would not pay further reparations. The main initial preoccupation of the American delegation, led by Hugh Gibson, US Ambassador to Belgium, was whether or not they would be funded by Congress. The economic problems of the world took up the time of most politicians and distracted them from disarmament, and even when they did pay it attention, it was often with less than sanguine hopes of achieving any success. The President of the Conference, Arthur Henderson, appointed the previous year, was no longer on speaking terms with Prime Minister MacDonald, because of the latter's expulsion from the Labour Party and leadership of the National Government. Henderson was further handicapped as he had lost his seat in Parliament, and so took up his duties with the status of a private, even though distinguished, individual.[4]

The American delegation went to the Geneva Conference with no obligation to disarm, as the United States had not ratified the Treaty of Versailles nor the League Covenant. Nevertheless, the United States had a long-standing preference for disarmament and hoped to use leverage, arising from her creditor position, to push the Europeans down the disarmament road. Unfortunately, the US delegation was ill-prepared for the Conference; American policy on some specific issues, for

[4] For the MacDonald–Henderson relationship, see A. Thorpe, 'Arthur Henderson and the British Political Crisis of 1931', *Historical Journal*, 31 (1988) 117–39.

example air disarmament and the problem of civil aviation, hampered progress; and the general American position as stated by President Hoover in January 1932 meant that it would be extremely difficult to meet French demands for security and Germany's for equality of status. As one historian of the League has put it:

> President Hoover had chilled the ardour of the disarmers by declaring that the Conference 'would be of something less than primary interest to the United States.' The American delegation would be instructed, he said, to make no promises about reducing US land forces, it was to offer no security guarantees and to stay clear of the much dreaded 'entanglements'.[5]

For the most part the US delegation settled for urging disarmament on the basis of high-sounding principles, without providing the necessary practical proposals to reassure a country like France.

The position of the British government was rather similar. Like the United States, it was not prepared to commit itself to a system of collective security for Europe that could drag Britain into a conflict which national interest dictated she should avoid, but she would have been happy to see the United States make such commitments. On the matter of air disarmament and civil aviation, Britain was prepared to be more adventurous and more 'internationalist' than the United States in trying to find solutions. On this she was closer to France than the United States, and so when the former took an initiative on air disarmament, while there was considerable Anglo-French co-operation, the United States was somewhat of a passive bystander.

During the early 1930s the British Secretary of State for Air was Lord Londonderry. His relations with Baldwin, the Lord President, who chaired Cabinet Disarmament Committee meetings during MacDonald's frequent absences, were uneasy (later Baldwin as Prime Minister dropped Londonderry from ministerial office). Londonderry was considered by a number of his contemporaries as a political lightweight and below par for ministerial appointment; nevertheless, he put up a spirited

[5] Bendiner, *Angels*, 276; source, *The Times*, 3 Feb. 1932.

defence of the status quo against air disarmament and the internationalization of civil aviation.

In early December 1931 Londonderry pointed out some of the problems of air disarmament. The crucial point was that Britain ranked only fifth in terms of air power. France, for example, had a 2 : 1 superiority, which meant not only that France would have to be persuaded to accept some disarmament, but that Britain also might have to effect changes to 'perhaps the excessive moderation—of [her] air policy'. During the course of the Conference, the British became acutely conscious of how vulnerable they and the Empire had become because of 'excessive moderation' in armaments and the distinct lack of moderation in the policies of some other countries.[6]

British ministerial views both on air disarmament and on the way civil aviation complicated things had fluctuated rather erratically since the Great War. At the Washington Naval Conference in 1921–2, Foreign Secretary Arthur Balfour had indicated that Britain would not disarm in the air, largely because of the practical difficulties involved with civil aviation. In June 1923 Baldwin amended that policy, stating that Britain would be prepared to talk with others about air disarmament, but he failed to give any attention to the complications arising from civil aviation. However, two years later, in talks with the French in Geneva, the British, for commercial and communications reasons, tried to separate civil aviation from controls that might be applied to military aircraft. The French were unhappy at this. They had feared the bombing-potential of civil aviation as early as the Versailles settlement, where they had unsuccessfully tried to get British and US agreement to a ten-year ban on German civil aviation. In 1926 Sam Hoare, in response to prods from Lord Cecil—Britain's representative to the League for much of the 1920s and a man strongly committed to air disarmament—added a further reason for isolating civil aviation from air disarmament. Invoking the support of the Chief of the Air Staff, he wrote: 'Trenchard and I . . . fear that to devise a means of

[6] CAB 23/69, 86(31)6, 9 Dec. 1931 and memo from Londonderry, CP(31)296; H. Montgomery Hyde, *Baldwin: The Unexpected Prime Minister* (Hart-Davis McGibbon, London 1973); K. Middlemas and J. Barnes, *Baldwin: A Biography* (Weidenfeld & Nicolson, London, 1969).

limiting civil aviation will introduce complications which will make any real progress with air disarmament impracticable.'[7]

Hoare and Trenchard were correct about such complications; however, the difficulties caused by civil aviation in 1932–3 have still not always been sufficiently recognized. Consequently, the problems confronting the Foreign Office, which wanted disarmament and whose job it was to push the issue in the face of understandable opposition from the Service Departments and the Air Ministry, have sometimes been underestimated. Perhaps criticism that Foreign Secretary Simon did not act energetically enough is partly justified, but judgement must be tempered by knowledge of the whole constellation of complications surrounding disarmament, of which international control over civil aviation was an eminent one.

An episode involving Simon and Lord Cecil just as the Disarmament Conference was getting underway illuminates the tangle of problems affecting air disarmament. Cecil, an acknowledged veteran of the cause of disarmament, was offered the part of British representative to the Disarmament Conference. Cecil, however, was unhappy with what he considered to be the British government's ill-prepared position. He sent a critique of it and proposals of his own, accompanied by an offer to elaborate, to Simon for consideration by the Cabinet. The view of its members was rather negative. They had no clear plan of their own, but were cautious about Cecil's suggestions for qualitative disarmament and his comments about civil aviation. The Cabinet wanted a more detailed, practical plan before they would make a judgement. Cecil was not satisfied with this. To him it seemed improper that the British government, while professing to favour disarmament, had no concrete plan of its own and seemingly contented itself with waiting upon other countries to come forward with schemes.

Cecil refused to be the British representative at Geneva; furthermore, he also refused to elaborate on his ideas about civil-aviation controls for Simon unless he could do it in an official capacity as the chairman of some kind of interdepartmental

[7] D. Carlton, 'The Problem of Civil Aviation in British Air Disarmament Policy 1919–34', *RUSI Journal*, 664 (1966), 307–16, and in particular 311, quoting *Cecil Papers*, add. 51083, Hoare to Cecil, 23 Dec. 1926; M. C. Pugh, 'Lord Davies and the British Debate in the 1930s', *International Relations*, 9 (1988), 335–51.

committee. Otherwise, he feared that any plan would simply draw criticism which he would be unable to deflect without some form of official status. One author's view of these exchanges is that: 'By making this suggestion [i.e. that he should chair an official committee] Cecil successfully called Simon's bluff, since with the bulk of the Cabinet plainly determined to maintain its initial, essentially negative policy on civil aviation—"they have no scheme to put forward themselves"—the Foreign Secretary could not take up Cecil's offer.'[8]

Why Simon did not take up Cecil's offer is not altogether clear: to impute the above reasoning to him does not necessarily follow from the evidence. The Cabinet certainly soon had second thoughts about their 'essentially negative policy on civil aviation'. Also, the Cabinet's views on disarmament, and on air disarmament in particular, were not the result of total lack of thought or concern. The intractability of the problem and the myriad of conflicting factors involved created a form of paralysis among members of the government which made decisive action difficult, and undoubtedly some of them were highly sceptical of the whole business of disarmament, but some minds were focused on the problem. A considerable amount of ink was spilt over the following months, and efforts were made by the British at a number of points during the Conference to try to make a success of disarmament.

Britain, however, not immune to infection from the atmosphere of growing political mistrust and fear, looked to her own security first and wanted other countries to reduce their strength while she herself retained as much as possible. Unfortunately, the reasoning of other states was similarly self-interested. Britain wanted France to reduce her land and air arms, but did not want to cut back on the Royal Navy. She wanted the United States to support the European security-system, but would not go any further than Locarno in committing herself to France. French hopes for an enforceable system of collective security had received a severe blow with the Japanese attack against the Chinese in Manchuria. More than ever, the British now believed that collective security was not possible while both the United States and the Soviet Union remained outside the League. The

[8] Carlton, 'Civil Aviation', 314.

British government believed that if League sanctions resulted in war with Japan, Britain would be militarily outdone in the Far East.[9] Britain wanted other countries to disarm in the air, but she was disadvantaged in negotiations because the RAF had been greatly reduced at the end of the Great War and had never been fully restored; furthermore, the success of 'control without occupation' meant that Britain would not give up totally the ability to bomb. It was too effective in controlling the Empire for that and also it was cheap—a vital factor in the years of the Depression. In addition, Britain was wary about controls over civil aviation for commercial reasons, and also because of the importance of imperial communications. Finally, as the problems of controls were considered, it became clear that Germany would oppose them until adequate air-disarmament proposals had been agreed, which looked unlikely. More importantly, the Americans would not have any international regime applied to the United States: they regarded internationalization essentially in terms of Europeanization.

If the Geneva Disarmament Conference that began in February 1932 was to have any chance of success it had to emanate from one or more of the three leading powers; France, Britain, and the United States. The French were the first off the mark. On 5 February they presented the Tardieu Plan, which proposed that all major armaments be handed over to the League, and that there be compulsory arbitration, the results of which would be enforceable by a League police force. There was little that was novel. The proposals reaffirmed a well-known French position, but they also put the problem of civil aviation unambiguously on the disarmament agenda, which was something of a new departure.

Subjects of signatory States would be allowed to construct non-military machines, of a tonnage below a figure to be agreed upon; machines of a heavier tonnage would be confined to continental, inter-continental, and inter-colonial organizations under the auspices of the League of Nations. Only the League should have the right to dispose of heavy bombing machines. In case of 'flagrant aggression', a state that was the victim of an aerial bombardment should have the right, upon the sole

[9] Middlemas, *Baldwin*, 729.

condition that the League be notified, to use all its air forces, even those earmarked [for] the League.[10]

The official British response was low key. Simon avoided offending the French and pushed for qualitative disarmament. The following day, 9 February, Hugh Gibson echoed Simon's general position and then made the specific proposal that security should be enhanced by dividing weapons into defensive and offensive categories and by concentrating efforts on abolishing the latter. Reaction to the French plan in London was divided. In the House of Commons, Sir Philip Sassoon, Under-Secretary of State for Air, asked, with rhetorical flourish whether the British had sufficient faith in an international body to trust it with such powers as the French were proposing. He then answered his own question in the negative. The Foreign Office was more sympathetic. Simon's Under-Secretary of State, Anthony Eden, wanted Britain to be more positive and to stop qualifying her proposals by making self-serving reservations. He expressed such opinions to Baldwin, who was the key figure in the National Government and someone who favoured disarmament if it were practical. The interest generated in air disarmament prompted Baldwin to get military staff in Britain to investigate the likely effects of bombing. As he gained more information about the dangers involved, he became convinced that a serious attempt had to be made to control air armaments.[11]

While a head of steam was gradually building up in London for a detailed consideration of air policy, the Disarmament Conference in Geneva referred the problem to one of its subsidiary bodies, the Air Commission. A series of exchanges between the General and the Air Commission about questions of principle and procedure were followed by desultory and inconclusive negotiations. The Air Commission issued its report on 8 June, but there was little of substance in it.

In London, although the Cabinet had concluded in March that internationalization of civil aviation along lines proposed by the French was impracticable, Baldwin had decided that something

[10] Wheeler-Bennett, *Disarmament*, 14–15.

[11] Middlemas, *Baldwin*, 731; Carlton, 'Civil Aviation', 314, quoting Hansard, 15 Mar. 1932, vol. 263, cols. 207–8.

had to be done as the Disarmament Conference was failing to make any headway. He took action which was supported by Prime Minister MacDonald—frequently absent at this time because of ill health—and aided and abetted by John Simon, who used his considerable intellect to explore some of the implications of Baldwin's ideas. By mid-May skirmishes were underway between those favouring action along lines proposed by Baldwin, and those led by the Secretary of State for Air, Lord Londonderry, who were sceptical of anything other than qualitative air-disarmament. Baldwin and Simon now worked closely together and produced three papers for the Cabinet which established the context for what was the main government debate on air disarmament.[12]

By 26 May the Cabinet Papers were completed. There was one under Baldwin's name which proposed the abolition of military aircraft and then went on to argue that if that were done then 'some form of control of civil aviation must at the same time be initiated'. The other two bore Simon's initials, but they were also at least partly attributable to Baldwin. In his first memorandum Simon urged that the Disarmament Conference be vitalized. In his second he put forward a possible means of doing that. Responding to Baldwin's ideas, and wishing to give them more concrete form, he had drawn up a 'Draft Convention for the Abolition of Military Aircraft and the Internationalisation of Civil Aviation'.

The Draft Convention proposed that military aircraft should be destroyed by the end of 1936; that if civil aviation were used for bombing it should constitute a crime; that there should be internationalization or co-ordination by an elected international body to control all existing airlines; that all other planes in private hands should be limited in number; and that licensing of pilots and export and manufacture of planes should also be controlled by international authority.[13]

These disarmament proposals prompted a number of comments from the departments most directly involved in defence.

[12] CAB 23/69, CP(32)164, 26 May 1932; CAB 24/230, CP(32)181, memo by Londonderry, 31 May 1932. My view of Simon has been influenced by my benefiting from a paper—then unpublished—by David Dutton which was part of his larger study of Simon.

[13] CAB 23/69, CP(32)164, 26 May 1932.

The War Office and Eyres-Monsell, First Lord of the Admiralty, favoured the abolition of military aircraft, as this would restore the sea as Britain's first line of defence; however, there was concern about some of the practical problems involved. For example, Eyres-Monsell was clearly worried by the possibility of civil aviation being used for military purposes, as he wanted more emphasis on the outlawing of bombing.

Londonderry's views were rather different. He believed that there were arguments of principle against air disarmament and therefore that technical questions were of only secondary importance. The main difficulty lay with civil aviation, for if military aircraft were abolished, then an overwhelming advantage would accrue to those nations with a large civil fleet. The only way to obviate the military threat from civil aviation would be to impose crippling restrictions, because there was a danger of bombing, he argued, even from small planes.

> I am convinced [he wrote] that even if we advocate the total abolition of air forces on these conditions there is but little chance of their acceptance. Leaving out of account the French attitude, I cannot believe that America, who sees in aircraft not a threat to cities, but a means of solving one of the greatest difficulties in the government of a Continent, will accept the necessary restrictions upon civil flying . . . I ask my colleagues to agree with me that the virtual suppression of civil aviation, without which it is admittedly impracticable to abolish air forces, is too high a price to pay for the illusion of security.[14]

Londonderry proposed, as an alternative, limitations on the size and scale of armaments and a prohibition on the bombing of civilians. He was against the idea even of publicly mooting the possibility of abolition of the RAF, for fear of the effect on morale in what was already a relatively weak branch of the armed services compared to its continental counterparts. He concluded rather ingenuously that they should not propose abolition of military aircraft anyway, just in case France and the United States were to agree to it.

A few days later Londonderry circulated a memorandum from the Chief of the Air Staff, Sir John Salmond, who made

[14] Ibid., CP(32)181, memo by Londonderry, 31 May 1932; CP(32)176, memo by Chief of the Imperial General Staff; CP(32)182, memo by the First Lord of the Admiralty.

similar observations regarding the problem of civil aviation. He also emphasized Britain's need for bombers in order to keep the Empire under control, and added that it would be easy to recreate a military air force and that the advantage would then lie with the aggressor, as it was easier to drop bombs than to train pilots to shoot down bombers.[15]

On 6 June matters were put before the Ministerial Committee on Disarmament, chaired by Baldwin in MacDonald's absence. Also present were representatives of the Dominions and Eire, who had been invited to attend some days earlier in order that they could express the views of their governments. The meeting began with Baldwin explaining that the Cabinet had yet to discuss the proposals and that they would probably do so the following day. He went on to make his position clear, that was to say that he had originated the proposals because of the lack of progress at Geneva and because of the growth of arms and their cost. In the course of the meeting it transpired that the representatives from the Dominions and Eire, although unable to give authoritative views, believed that their governments would probably go along with whatever the British government decided.

The next development in the discussion was a strong intervention by Samuel Hoare, a long-serving predecessor of Londonderry's at the Air Ministry and now Secretary of State for India. Air power and the tactic of control without occupation by large land-forces on the North-West Frontier was an important matter for the British in India; however, Hoare dwelt on other factors. He argued that internationalization of civil aviation was impractical; that it would not be acceptable to other countries; and that the proposals in general would have a bad effect on the morale of the RAF.

Shortly after that, tension in the meeting rose perceptibly, when Londonderry raised the possibility of resignation: 'His personal position was that he would of course acquiesce in any decision of His Majesty's Government, but if this proposal was put forward seriously at Geneva, his position would become untenable.' For a while after that, the meeting wandered off the main points, but then Simon refocused things, even though,

[15] CAB 23/69 CP(32)183, memo by Salmond, 3 June 1932.

with the pusillanimity typical of him when it came to making decisions, he both proposed action and prepared the ground for inaction.

Simon's legal training and his keen intellect made him adept at presenting arguments both for and against proposals which were brought before him. Unfortunately, to the exasperation of some colleagues, he often failed to realize that political responsibility involved more than preparing briefs: it also involved the courage to take difficult decisions on the basis of incomplete information and incomplete knowledge of what the consequences would be. Simon's capabilities in these respects were deficient.

He reminded the Committee that the proposals had been mooted as a possible way of moving forward in the stalled Disarmament Conference. He remarked on London's vulnerability to bombing and pointed out that if these or other aerial disarmament proposals were not put forward, then members of the British government might have to resign themselves to the wider problem of the failure of disarmament in general. Furthermore, progress at Geneva was important for the imminent reparations-conference at Lausanne. Failure to disarm would prejudice the chances of solving the problem of economic recovery and would have an adverse effect on 'our future relations with the United States'.

Simon thus wanted to go ahead with disarmament proposals which he and Baldwin had produced. However, intellectually sensitive to the arguments put forward by Hoare and Londonderry, and no doubt concerned about the latter's talk of possible resignation, Simon side-stepped the challenge of Britain championing these proposals at Geneva in an effort to win over support. Instead, he suggested that Britain should first approach France and the United States in order to see if the proposals had any chance of success. If they did not, then they should drop the proposals without ever making them public.

Despite Simon striking this note of caution, he, Baldwin, and the Prime Minister (not present), were supported in their wish to promote disarmament by Home Secretary Samuel; Viscount Hailsham, the Secretary of State for War; Viscount Snowden, the Lord Privy Seal; and Eyres-Monsell, who all favoured going ahead with Simon's proposals. But it was the Cabinet meeting on the following day which was to take the final decision.[16]

At the Cabinet meeting on 7 June the arguments which had come to light since Baldwin's and Simon's Cabinet Papers had been circulated in mid-May were once again rehearsed. The Cabinet, with the exception of Londonderry and Hoare, was well disposed to Simon's draft proposals. Sentiment favoured disarmament, but calculation—perhaps insufficient in its range—dictated the kind of prudence Simon had mentioned the day before.

The situation was complex and difficult. The government's desire for disarmament was necessarily constrained by its primary duty to safeguard its people, which involved assessing the threat from possible foreign aggressors and being aware of Britain's military weakness. A further complication was the fact that the British never wanted to get rid of all military aircraft. Some were to be retained for what was euphemistically referred to as 'police actions': the policy of control-without-occupation in the Empire. Finally, there were undeniably immense practical difficulties involved in aerial disarmament—not least because of civil aviation—and men like Baldwin had to weigh up the likelihood of the success of proposals against the damage that there would be to RAF morale if it came to light that the government were contemplating its abolition.

Apart from the more obvious military considerations, there was the question of civil aviation. It was a joker in the disarmament pack, which, depending on how it was played, could help disarmament to succeed or fail, not only in the air but across the board. Hopes that it might be brought under some kind of international regulation, so helping the cause of disarmament, were challenged by numerous political, commercial, and practical considerations. In the case of Britain, she needed a large civilian fleet to help unite the Empire. There was also reluctance even to countenance a restriction on the size of civil aircraft, especially as Britain was contemplating a transatlantic air-service which would require large planes: the kind which had the greatest potential for conversion to military use. And yet it seemed that in order to guarantee an acceptable level of secur-

[16] CAB 23/71, 30(32)4(a), 1 June 1932; CAB 24/230, CP(32)192, 4th meeting of Ministerial Committee on Disarmament, 6 June 1932.

ity, the restrictions on civil aviation would have to be Draconian, so much so that, according to Londonderry, the civil-aviation industry would be crippled. Even if a plan were agreed, there would be problems with its implementation, not least because of Germany's refusal to accept controls over civil aviation until a plan for the abolition of military aircraft had been agreed. Furthermore, knowledge that the United States would not enter into a scheme for the internationalization of civil aviation seemed to doom such plans to failure. And if civil aviation could not be internationalized, then, as the Air Ministry had pointed out, overwhelming military advantage would lie with the country with the largest civil-aviation fleet once military aircraft had been abolished.

Finally, there was Londonderry. His remark that his position would become untenable if the proposals were to be put forward seriously at Geneva was yet another factor in influencing the Cabinet to caution.

Consequently, there emerged a 'general agreement that the proposals for abolishing military and naval aviation, and for international supervision of civil aviation, could not be submitted to the Disarmament Conference before the attitude of at least some of the principal Powers concerned had been ascertained'. It was decided that the French and the Italians should be consulted and if there were no hope of the proposals being accepted, the Cabinet should then decide whether or not to table them at Geneva. (In fact, it transpired that the decisive talks were with the French and the Americans.) Suggestions were made that if broad measures of air disarmament could not succeed, then the British government should consider more limited forms of disarmament to control bombing.[17]

On the following day the Air Commission in Geneva issued its report on air disarmament. It was bland and largely composed of such platitudes as: the effectiveness of military aircraft depended on their size and range. It solved no problems, but it confirmed concerns of the British Cabinet by highlighting the issue of civil aviation. Distinguishing between defensive and offensive weapons in the air was not possible, according to the Commission: 'All aircraft, without alterations of any kind and

[17] CAB 23/71, 31(32)1, 7 June 1932.

whatever their tonnage, may constitute a danger to civilians or against military objectives.'[18]

Over the following two weeks it became apparent that the problem of controlling civil aviation was the major stumbling-block preventing advance in air disarmament. Britain, France, and the United States could not reach agreement, even though relations between them were good—the former two signed a pact of friendship on 13 June, and Prime Minister MacDonald was strongly pro-American. There was an irritant which caused friction between France and Britain on the one hand and the United States on the other, namely the war-debt problem, but Britain and France alone had difficulties on air disarmament.

On the 14 and 15 June Britain and France discussed the future of the Disarmament Conference between themselves. It soon became clear that there were differences between them on air disarmament. The French, as always, were concerned about enforcement, on this occasion in relation to civil aviation. There was also the complication of French disarmament-proposals which had been brought forward on 14 April and which were now taken up again in so far as they provided for air disarmament.

By the 20 June things looked bleak indeed. On that day there was a meeting at Geneva between the British, the French, and the Americans. Herbert Samuel set the tone of the meeting with his opening statement.

> If it were possible to propose an effective scheme for the entire abolition of military and naval aviation, His Majesty's Government would not have opposed such a scheme in principle if there were any likelihood of its acceptance. But there appeared to be no practicable scheme taking into account the menace of civil aviation; if total abolition were not likely to receive a large measure of acceptance His Majesty's Government would not themselves wish to propose it.[19]

The British had adopted the fall-back position envisaged by the Cabinet on 7 June; however, they also had to deal with the French proposals on air disarmament. Progress had been made with the idea of prohibiting bombing and limiting the size of

[18] Wheeler-Bennett, *Disarmament*, 37.

[19] E. L. Woodward and R. Butler (eds.), *Documents on British Foreign Policy*, 2nd ser., vol. 3 (HMSO, London, 1948), 540–4, meeting of US, British, and French delegates, 20 June 1932.

aircraft, but an agreed formula for controlling numbers of aircraft had not emerged from the French plan, nor were there adequate safeguards, in Samuel's view, to prevent the use of small planes for military purposes, nor provisions allowing for the air-policing actions required by Britain in her Empire. There also remained the problem of civil aviation.

Regarding that, Samuel suggested that there were two possible courses of action: to prohibit fittings in commercial planes which would facilitate their conversion to military use; or to impose general controls over civil aviation. On the latter option he commented: 'He would not be against this idea if it was an essential condition of progress, but it was very difficult to realise it in practice.'[20] These comments related not only to the ideas the British had had on civil aviation, but also to the French plan for its internationalization.

Later, in a summary of these talks for the Cabinet, Samuel (along with Londonderry and Simon) elaborated on the problems they saw with the French plan. After consideration, it seemed that the word 'internationalization' was not really appropriate for the French scheme. They no longer wanted to place planes in the hands of the League, and regulations were only to apply to those of three tons and heavier. They wanted to prevent the creation of large national civil-aviation fleets and, if this problem could not be solved, then they would not destroy their own bomber fleet. The French suggested a 'Wagon-Lit' type of company to run civil aviation as sleeping-car trains were operated. Samuel and his colleagues thought that the plan was too complicated and were sceptical about its chances of success, but they were reluctant to oppose it outright, among other reasons because they thought that it might be possible to amend the scheme and reintroduce the League as a monitor.[21]

In fact, much of the debate about internationalization was rendered academic by Norman Davis in the meeting on 20 June. He had indicated the likely position of the United States on air disarmament two days earlier, but he now elaborated. Davis thought that the numbers of military aircraft ought to be regulated and that, at this point, provision could be made to meet

[20] Ibid.

[21] CAB 24/231, CP(32)222, annex I, 23 June 1932.

the British reservation concerning the need for military aircraft for policing-actions in the Empire. He then went on to indicate that the United States saw internationalization of civil aviation in terms of Europeanization. He said:

> As regards civil aviation, that was such a different problem in the United States that the United States Government had not attempted to deal with it, but they would have no objection to any solution that European nations might find.[22]

The snag was that the United States would not participate in any scheme, she would simply be a benign onlooker. The United States would not entangle herself in any kind of international arrangement which involved enforcement, nor would she hamper the growth of her burgeoning civil-aviation industry, which had immense commercial and political value for the United States. Furthermore, America would have additional problems implementing internationalization because, unlike her European counterparts, American civil aviation was made up of a number of private companies, and not of directly subsidized state-controlled operators.

The representatives of the three governments met again the next day, in both the morning and the afternoon, and the French sought support for their air-disarmament plan, but made it clear to the Americans that any proposals concerning civil aviation would not apply to the United States. Such an exception, especially as the United States had the world's leading civilian air-fleet, was hardly calculated to recommend the proposal to the Disarmament Conference. For the time being the British simply said that they would not oppose the proposals in principle, though they were highly sceptical of them succeeding.[23]

Before any further progress could be made with either British or French thoughts on disarmament, the Americans took a dramatic initiative. 1932 was the year of a presidential election, and Herbert Hoover, the incumbent standing for re-election, was seriously handicapped because of the Depression. Largely motivated by the need to boost his electoral chances, he in-

[22] Woodward, *Documents*, 2nd ser., vol. 3, 541, meeting of US, British, and French delegates, 20 June 1932.

[23] Ibid., 544–4, two meetings of US, British, and French delegates, 21 June 1932.

structed the American delegation in Geneva to put forward new disarmament proposals which became known as the Hoover Plan.

The Plan's basic theme was the strengthening of defensive and the decreasing of offensive capabilities; its sub-plot involved both drawing attention repeatedly to the economic savings which could be made if the plan were adopted, and impressing the US domestic peace-lobby. Its main proposals were that arms should be reduced by approximately one-third, and that existing ratios between states should basically be retained. The provision made for air disarmament was typical of the plan as a whole—apparently simple and morally correct in tone, but inadequate and impracticable. 'All bombing planes to be abolished. This will do away with the military possession of types of planes capable of attacks upon civil populations and should be coupled with the total prohibition of all bombardment from the air.'[24] It was as if the long debate about the danger from civil aviation had never taken place; neither was any deference shown to the French insistence that provisions for disarmament had to be enforceable. The French motto of no disarmament without enhanced security was totally ignored.

Even pro-American members of the British government were bitter and unhappy about the Hoover Plan, because of the US domestic political motives behind it, because of the way it was presented without any real prior consultation, because of the way it challenged Britain's image as the leader of the disarmament movement, and because of its contents. The immediate reaction of the British in Geneva was to inform the Foreign Office that: 'Certain of the naval proposals in United States plan would be unacceptable to us.' A run-down of the Royal Navy on the scale proposed would have jeopardized Empire security in the British government's opinion. This might appear a patently self-serving position, but the British could argue with some force that naval armaments were primarily defensive, and, in any case, Britain, of all the great powers excepting Germany, was the least well armed. Any further reduction in her main line

[24] Ibid., vol. 4 (HMSO, London, 1950). app. 5, 606–68, Statement of the Instructions Issued by President Hoover to the American Delegation: 'The Hoover Plan'.

of defence, the Royal Navy, was going to be difficult, if not impossible, for her to accept. Baldwin and others, although desirous of disarmament, were becoming aware of how vulnerable British defences were; and Japan's activities in China had exposed the impotence of the League in upholding collective security as an alternative to national defence.[25]

From the British and French perspectives, the US position seemed replete with moral humbug. The Americans were happy to propose some quantitative reductions in naval armaments, but were unhappy about British qualitative counter-proposals, which would have reduced the effectiveness of US cruisers in the vast reaches of the Pacific. They urged both repayment of war debts and disarmament on the grounds of responsible economic policy, but refused to act responsibly themselves: the Hawley-Smoot tariff had raised American economic protectionism to its highest-ever level. The Americans urged Britain, and more especially France, to behave responsibly on disarmament and to accommodate German demands, but were unwilling to take risks themselves. They would not countenance any entanglement in the security affairs of Europe, not even to the extent of pledging not to help an aggressor. When difficult practical problems of disarmament arose which directly affected their interests—for example, the military potential of civilian aviation and hence the need to control it in any scheme of air disarmament—they simply side-stepped the issue as if they did not have anything to do with it. Internationalization of civil aviation was for them Europeanization.

Despite the widespread anger with the Americans in the British government, there was great reluctance to antagonize them deliberately. The British still sought America's help with the problem of European security, even though hopes of success were rapidly fading, and also did not wish to alienate her from attempts to concert action on economic problems. Thus the British publicly welcomed the Hoover Plan as a basis on which to build new attempts to disarm, and as their contribution to that building-programme the British Cabinet decided that it must put forward proposals of its own to the Geneva Conference.

[25] Woodward, *Documents*, 2nd ser., vol. 3, 548–54, Patteson to Vansittart, 22 June 1932; Thorne, *Limits*, 315–18.

By the 27 June, when the Cabinet met to discuss proposals laid before it by John Simon, its sights had been lowered since early in the month, and the target now was quantitative and qualitative controls throughout, including in the sphere of air disarmament.

The Cabinet was determined both to make a show of Britain's concern over disarmament and to achieve the semblance of at least some progress before the delegates at Geneva took recess for the summer; but there was also deepening pessimism concerning the eventual outcome of the Conference. Members of the Cabinet disliked the Hoover Plan so far as land forces were concerned, strongly opposed its provisions for naval reductions, replacing them with a scheme of qualitative rather than quantitative controls, and amplified the American suggestions for air disarmament.

The Cabinet agreed that all bombing should be prohibited except in internationally defined battlefield areas; that the size of aircraft, except for seaplanes and troop-carriers, should be regulated; and that military aircraft should be limited in number. Even these rather timid proposals were anathema to Londonderry, who believed that Britain needed a strong bomber-force, especially as she only had a small army. And others, such as Baldwin, could not have been sanguine about the likely effectiveness of such proposals, given their views about the dangers from civil aviation and the proposals—or rather lack of them—which the Cabinet now favoured on that aspect of air disarmament.

It was decided that no reference should be made to the question of the internationalization of civil aviation. The Cabinet minutes add: 'It would be necessary, if the subject was mentioned in the declaration, to explain what was meant and how the proposal was to be implemented. In any case the U.S.A. would never consent to participate in any internationalisation scheme.'[26] In short, the Cabinet had concluded that there were insurmountable practical problems with internationalization and that even if someone did come up with a workable idea there would not be much point to it, because the United States would not take part.

[26] CAB 23/71, 39(32)1, 27 June 1932; Middlemas, *Baldwin*, 734.

The absence of provisions to deal with civil aviation was an obvious flaw in both the British and American proposals for disarmament. The resolution adopted by the Disarmament Conference on 23 July, largely as a result of British and American efforts to prevent the disarmament talks from expiring, was an anodyne amalgam of generalities culled from the Hoover Plan and the proposals agreed by the Cabinet on 27 June. The provision for air disarmament followed the British line almost word for word. The only major change was to do with civil aviation, which, contrary to Cabinet specification, made vague references to international control. They in no sense dealt with the practical problem of implementation or with US determination not to involve itself in enforceable international regulation—except by providing a reservation which would allow it without any difficulties to remain outside an international regime. II (1) b, of the resolution read as follows.

> Civil aircraft shall be submitted to regulation and full publicity. Further, civil aircraft not conforming to the specified limitations shall be subjected to an international regime (except for certain regions where such a regime is not suitable [i.e. the Americas]), such as to prevent effectively the misuse of civil aircraft.[27]

The resolution kept the disarmament movement alive, but only just. Hopes that proposals on air disarmament might have revived the fortunes of the Geneva Conference had been disappointed. The practical difficulties involved prevented agreement about controls over civil aviation among the European powers, and the United States retained its total opposition to subjecting its own industry to international control. While the will and resolve of the Western powers faltered, their security dilemma worsened. Their initial reluctance to sacrifice their own particular military strengths in order to achieve disarmament increased as the international political situation deteriorated following the Japanese successes in China and the growth of nationalism, most worryingly in the form of National Socialism, in Germany.

Germany opposed the July resolution. Her representative, Herr Nadolny, declared that it did not meet Germany's demands

[27] Woodward, *Documents*, 2nd ser., vol. 3, app. 6, 609–13, Declaration of British Disarmament Policy, 7 July 1932.

for equality of rights and so Germany would no longer collaborate with the Conference. Over the following months British diplomacy, largely on the initiative of the Under-Secretary of State at the Foreign Office, Anthony Eden, tried desperately to bring the Germans back to the Conference. Finally, by December 1932 a declaration was composed which the two main antagonists, France and Germany, could accept. The Germans agreed to participate once more when the Conference reconvened, on the premise that its aim was to give Germany equal rights within a system which would provide security for all states.[28]

Although Britain invested time and energy in attempts to rescue the Disarmament Conference from failure during the first half of 1933, leading ministers were disturbed by Britain's military vulnerability and pessimistic about the likely outcome of their efforts. On 9 November 1932 Baldwin made a famous speech in the Guildhall in London about the 'bomber always getting through'. He commented also about the problem of civil aviation: 'No one could prohibit flying and it was impracticable to prohibit bombing without controlling civil aviation as well.' Nevertheless, as one of his biographers has put it, he tried again in the first half of 1933 'with steadily diminishing conviction to see his scheme for disarmament through'.[29]

During the latter part of 1932 and in early 1933 Eden played a key role in the disarmament saga. Much of the momentum for further attempts to unravel the deadlock at Geneva came from him. When the Conference reconvened in late January, Eden presented and explained on behalf of the British government a programme which would, it was hoped, move the Conference forward. And once again air disarmament emerged as the key area where it was hoped that a major breakthrough might be made. However, there were two intractable problems connected with the British position. The first and most difficult one was to find an acceptable method of dealing with the military potential of civil aviation. The second, which was strongly objected to by others at the Conference, was the reservation to allow bombing in 'outlying areas'—that is to say, in the Empire. Eden

[28] Wheeler-Bennett, *Disarmament*, 68–89; A. Eden, *Memoirs: Facing the Dictators* (Cassell, London, 1962), 26–8; and Viscount Simon, *Retrospect: Memoirs of the Right Honourable Viscount Simon* (Hutchinson, London, 1952), 185.

[29] Middlemas, *Baldwin*, 735 and 737.

himself was unhappy about this reservation, but the insistence of Londonderry, Hoare, and the RAF among others (Baldwin also had this reservation in his plan for disarmament, which he was still nursing in February 1933) ensured its retention.

The proposals which the British put to the Conference in January 1933, in order to move things along, included the establishment of a committee to examine the possibility of abolishing military and naval aircraft and to see if it were possible to effectively control civil aviation. The Conference's Air Commission took up these tasks, but soon ran into difficulties. It could not decide which matter to deal with first; abolition of military aircraft, or international controls for civil aviation. On 20 February the Commission decided on the latter by a margin of one vote, with six countries abstaining, including the United States, which by such inaction declared its lack of interest. Despite the vote, the wranglings continued, with the Germans refusing to consider international controls over civil aviation until the problem of military aircraft had been resolved. Again there was deadlock, partly disguised, as was so often the case at the Conference, by referring matters to subcommittees.[30]

Looking at things on the level of the Air Commission, there was little prospect for advancing the cause of disarmament, but turning to Eden's discussions with the French and the Americans, matters were slightly more hopeful. Eden's position in Geneva was difficult. He had to juggle with two possible courses of action, namely abolition of military aircraft along with controls over civil aviation, and quantitative and qualitative air-disarmament. In neither case was he able to put forward fully fledged plans. And in both cases he had difficulties. In the former the British Air Ministry (and many in the Cabinet) did not believe that an international regime for civil aviation was possible; and in both cases there was the problem caused by the reservation concerning a bombing capability for Britain in the Empire.

On 10 February Eden wrote to Baldwin with some optimism after talking with the French.

The most hopeful sphere is in the air, in respect of which Paul-Boncour told me yesterday that he hoped something might be done. This is the

[30] Woodward, *Documents*, 2nd ser., vol. 4, 492–4, Draft Proposals, 30 Jan. 1933; Wheeler-Bennett, *Disarmament*, 88–96.

only sphere where the French do not tightly link disarmament with security.[31]

However, Eden was also angry with Londonderry and Simon, who had been urging him to mention Britain's need to reserve the right to use bombers in the Empire. Eden tried to avoid this issue while there was still even the slightest hope for abolition of military aircraft. His irritation spilt out in the latter part of his letter to Baldwin.

> I do hope that we shall be able to continue to press for total abolition of military and naval aircraft as the only real solution to the problem. . . . I know that you will appreciate how difficult it will be for us, however, to maintain a lead in air disarmament . . . if at every stage we are to make technical reservations which will encumber our own footsteps and cast grave doubts, however unjustified, upon our sincerity.[32]

Unfortunately, the French position was subject to fluctuation, because of frequent political changes at home and the growing threat from Germany. Hitler became Chancellor on 30 January and there followed in quick succession the Reichstag Fire on 27 February, Nazi gains in the elections of early March, and, on 23 March, the granting to Hitler of dictatorial powers by the Enabling Laws. With these developments, France's worst fears began to be confirmed and more than ever she demanded enhanced security before disarmament.

On 16 February a letter from Eden to John Simon thus told a rather different story than his letter to Baldwin of only a few days earlier. No doubt another reason for the difference was the fact that Eden now reported not so much the views of Paul-Boncour, but those of Londonderry's French counterpart, M. Cot of the French Air Ministry. Eden wrote:

> As regards air M. Boncour seemed to want to press to give effect to resolution of July. I explained the position of His Majesty's Government and M. Cot who was also present said that France was quite prepared to say total abolition of military and naval aircraft was ultimate aim but that it must be made subject to two conditions (1) Effective control of civil aviation and (2) Establishment of International Air Police force.[33]

[31] Eden, *Dictators*, 29.

[32] Ibid.

[33] Woodward, *Documents*, 2nd ser., vol. 4, 496–7, Eden (via Patteson) to Simon, 16 Feb. 1933.

The French had put their finger on the twofold character of the Achilles' heel of air disarmament. Not only were they insisting that international controls had to be introduced—something which many in the British government thought impractical—but also, contrary to what Eden had thought some days earlier, they were saying that any such system had to be enforceable via an international air police force. But the British were set against enforcing sanctions in this, or indeed any other, way.

The effect of the French position was to turn British thoughts once again away from the abolition of military aircraft (which then made the reservation about the right to bomb in the Empire more acceptable to Eden) and the internationalization of civil aviation and towards more piecemeal quantitative and qualitative controls. But even here Britain's ideas were uncongenial to the French. Eden had talked to them in terms of other countries reducing their air armaments to Britain's level and then all states cutting what remained by a third. Cot's response to this was to say it was rather like them asking the British to reduce the Royal Navy to the French navy's level before then going on to make further reductions.[34]

On 22 February Eden wrote again to Baldwin, but this time, despairing of any advances in the Conference unless further initiatives were forthcoming from the British, he suggested that they should put forward a fully detailed plan. Eden wrote first to Baldwin, because of his influence in the Cabinet and because he had some sympathy for the disarmament cause. A few days later he wrote a similar letter to John Simon, also sympathetic to disarmament, but indecisive and too willing, in the view of some, to acknowledge the cogency of the arguments against disarmament. Eden now went ahead, helped by Sir Alexander Cadogan, chief Foreign Office adviser to the British delegation at Geneva, and produced a detailed draft convention. After some considerable hesitation, it received both MacDonald's and Baldwin's support, and on 16 March the former presented it to the delegates at Geneva.[35]

In a rambling speech, MacDonald nevertheless spoke frankly of some of the problems—notably concerning air disarmament—

[34] Woodward, *Documents*, 2nd ser., vol. 4, 496–7.
[35] Eden, *Dictators*, 29–37.

which had troubled his government. He gave a dramatic, if rather fanciful, rendering of the possible dangers from civil aviation. He said he feared that if there were no effective controls and military and naval aircraft were abolished, then civil aviation, 'in the twinkling of an eye, on the receipt of a telephone message, could be transformed into a fighting force'. He reported his Cabinet's views that it would be unfair to retard or penalize the commercial possibilities of civil aviation, and also that it had not been possible to arrive at a satisfactory plan for international controls, having taken both the commercial and the military perspectives into account. As a result, British proposals, while still mentioning abolition of military aircraft and controls over civil aviation, now concentrated primarily on the alternative of quantitative and qualitative controls.

A weight limit of 3 tons was to be placed on military aircraft, except for flying boats and troop-carriers. Numerical limits on military aircraft were to be imposed in accordance with a nation's size and status: the major powers—the United States, Britain, France, the Soviet Union, and Italy—were all to be allocated a maximum of five hundred each. A timetable was given for the abolition of aircraft in excess of the limits laid down. And finally, as a double insurance against the military threat from the air, under article 34: 'The High Contracting Parties accept the complete abolition of bombing from the air (except for police purposes in certain outlying regions).'[36]

The MacDonald Plan was a brave attempt to enact the spirit of the December 1932 declaration concerning disarmament and security for all states. Unfortunately, the international situation was deteriorating rapidly, with Hitler gaining dictatorial powers on 23 March and with Japan announcing on 27 March its intention to withdraw from the League of Nations. The Germans baulked at the manpower limit proposed for their army, and in particular at the insistence that the Nazi paramilitary forces should be included in the calculation of numbers. The French were also increasingly reluctant to countenance disarmament as Germany became more assertive, and accelerated her armament programme.

[36] Woodward, *Documents*, 2nd ser., vol. 4, 558–65, MacDonald: Speech Introducing Draft Convention Plan; text is in Wheeler-Bennett, *Disarmament*, app. II, 267–92.

The last ray of hope for disarmament came in May, from a somewhat unexpected quarter. On 16 May the new President of the United States, Franklin Roosevelt, made a speech calling for restraint in the field of armaments, for a universal non-aggression pact, and for disarmament on the basis of the MacDonald proposals. This was followed on 22 May by a statement by Norman Davis to the General Disarmament Commission which seemed to indicate a slight shift in America's policy of refusing to be drawn, in any way, into Europe's security affairs. For a short while it appeared that the United States might give some practical support to the task of maintaining European peace. This would have reassured the French somewhat, for they always insisted on enhancing their security before undertaking disarmament.

> . . . we are willing to consult [with] the other states [Davis said] in case of a threat to peace with a view to averting conflict. Further than that, in the event that the States, in conference, determine that a State has been guilty of a breach of the peace in violation of its international obligations and take measures against the violator, then, if we concur in the judgement rendered as to the responsible and guilty party, we will refrain from any action tending to defeat such collective effort which these states may thus make to restore peace.[37]

The air of optimism this created was short-lived. Within days the US Senate amended legislation before it to mandate that any US embargo against belligerents had to be impartial. No distinction was to be made between aggressor and victim. In the end this bill was lost in the House-Senate Conference Committee some time later, but it had already deflated European hopes about the possibility of the United States making a practical contribution to the security of Europe, and was in any case a good indicator of the direction in which the United States was heading. Her first inter-war neutrality-law was passed in 1935.[38]

The final vestige of hope for sweeping measures of air disarmament disappeared at the end of May 1933. After further talks in Geneva, Eden recounted to Simon that the Americans had made strong representations to the British to abandon the

[37] *FRUS*, 1933, 1, 154–8, Norman Davis to General Commission, 22 May 1933.

[38] Bendiner, *Angels*, 289; J.M. Gabriel, *The American Conception of Neutrality After 1941* (Macmillan, London, 1988), 31.

caveat about the use of bombing in the Empire. American concern on this point was emphasized a few days later in a conversation between Davis and Londonderry. Davis said that Roosevelt sympathized with the British position, but felt that other states would claim exceptions for bombers on similar grounds. Even on the 27 May it was clear from Eden's letter that air disarmament was a lost cause. He bluntly told Simon that Britain's proposals for air disarmament had received a hammering. He concluded: 'Altogether this was most damaging day our Draft Convention has suffered.'[39]

Any kind of air disarmament was now highly unlikely, and a major breakthrough was no longer possible. On 29 May Captain Babington of the British delegation wrote to the Deputy Chief of the Air Staff:

> It should be realised that there is no prospect of agreement upon abolition of airforces except as a distant ideal to be reached by stages. Nor is there any possibility of agreement on the allied question of internationalisation of civil aviation and international air police force both of which under repeated examination in the United Kingdom have so far been shown to be impracticable.[40]

During the following weeks attention shifted to the World Economic Conference in London, where there was a further blow to internationalism when Roosevelt refused to co-operate in stabilizing the international currency-system and declared that the United States was going to concentrate on domestic problems as her first priority. Talks on disarmament did continue but no headway was made. In early July, in answer to cirticism of Britain's reservation concerning bombing in the Empire, Eden stated in the House of Commons that if it had been the only obstacle to disarmament, then things might have turned out very differently. Sadly it was not, and after the delegates took recess for the summer, the situation went from bad to worse.[41]

German rearmament was now proceeding apace and the French became even more obsessed with ensuring that any collective security measures could be enforced. They proposed a

[39] Woodward, *Documents*, 2nd ser., vol. 4, 279 and 303–4, Eden to Simon, 27 May 1933, memo of conversation between Londonderry and Davis, 8 June 1933.

[40] Ibid., 279–80, Babington (via Patteson) to Simon, 29 May 1933.

[41] Hansard, 5 July 1933, vol. 280, col. 371.

four-year supervision period, to be followed by disarmament. Italy and Britain went along with this, but in mid-October the final crisis of the Geneva Conference came, with Germany declaring that as the other heavily armed states had no intention of disarming, her demand for equal status could not be met and therefore she was leaving the Conference. Simultaneously, it was announced in Berlin that Germany would withdraw from the League of Nations. Two days later Norman Davis in effect said that as any further talks could no longer be about world disarmament, and as the United States was not allied to or connected with the European states, she would have nothing more to do with disarmament affairs: the US delegation thereon packed and left.

There was now no more talk in the British government of air disarmament. Even before the announcement of the Eden-MacDonald Plan on 16 March 1933, the Cabinet Disarmament Committee had started to hedge its bets. Baldwin, speaking to the Committee on 7 March, said that Britain's priority now must be parity in the air with other powers. A year later, on 8 March 1934, eleven years on from making an almost exactly identical statement in the Commons, Baldwin said that the government 'will see to it that in air strength and air power this country shall no longer be in a position inferior to any country within striking distance of our shores'.[42] Shortly thereafter the Geneva General Disarmament Conference petered out. It was never actually brought to a close: instead, it inappropriately faded away like old soldiers.

Civil aviation was of major concern at the Disarmament Conference. If its non-commercial significance needed any confirmation by the 1930s, then the Geneva Conference certainly provided it. Especially because of its post-war developments, no nation could ignore the importance of civil aviation in terms of its role in intelligence operations and communications: the flying-skills that it produced; the technology which it promoted; and the physical capacity which it had for conversion to military purposes.

Germany's stance on air disarmament provides ample testimony to the importance of these factors. At Versailles in 1919

[42] Hansard, 8 Mar. 1934, vol. 286, col. 278; Middlemas, *Baldwin*, 738–9.

the French, perceptive as ever, had realized the possible military potential of civil aviation and had tried to put a ban on Germany's for ten years, but the British and the Americans would agree only to a much shorter period. Thus, within a few months of the end of the Great War, Germany was able to begin developing aircraft and technology under the aegis of civil aviation. By the 1930s she had one of the most technologically advanced civil fleets in the world. Its potential contribution to her military power in the air was immense. Not surprisingly, therefore, the Germans were loath to forgo their freedom of action in an area that was unfettered by the Versailles settlement and which could contribute to German military power. Their inequality of status would have been increased if they had accepted international control of civil aviation before a system of air disarmament had been agreed.

Germany was not the only power whose perceived national interest, regarding civil aviation, conflicted with the position of others at the Disarmament Conference in ways which undermined its chances of success. The United States would have nothing to do with international controls over civil aviation. Her justification of this had two themes. The first was her refusal to become entangled in any international arrangement involving enforceable regulations and European countries. The United States rejected involvement in anything which could conceivably drag her into a European conflict. Since 1929, measures which would have taken the United States into the Paris Air Convention had languished in the Congress. A similar fate had afflicted government attempts to join the Permanent Court of International Justice. On both counts, one of the factors which prevented the measures succeeding was the fear of being implicated in the work of the League of Nations, even though the Court and the Air Convention were supposedly independent bodies. Given that the United States was cautious of being dragged into Europe's security affairs by such circuitous routes, she was hardly likely to submit her civil aviation to international controls, overseen and enforced by the League, as part of a disarmament programme.[43]

[43] See ch. 2; and M. Dunne, *The United States and the World Court 1920–1935* (Pinter, London, 1988).

The second theme consisted of the political and economic value of civil aviation to the United States. By the 1930s American operators in civil aviation were poised to emulate British dominance of maritime travel and commerce and US plane makers were prepared to achieve a supremacy in the air similar to that which her automobile manufacturers enjoyed on the roads. Politically, civil aviation was important domestically in the task of uniting the country by a swift, efficient network of air routes. In foreign policy it was important both as a potential adjunct to the military and naval air-forces, and because it established staging and refuelling posts—particularly important were those in the Pacific—which could be used subsequently for military purposes. It was also diplomatically important, especially in Central and South America, where PAA showed the flag, facilitated commerce, and helped to counteract an undesirable European influence on civil aviation.

British reasoning ran along similar lines regarding defence, the importance of communications—though in an imperial rather than a national context—and the commercial prospects of civil aviation. However, unlike the Americans, the British tried to make such factors in their national interest compatible with comprehensive controls over civil aviation—at least while there was still some prospect of abolishing military aircraft.

After detailed consideration, the British concluded that abolition of military aircraft would not enhance security unless there were controls over civil aviation as well. Civil aviation thus became the key to air disarmament, which in turn was seen as a possible catalyst that could activate disarmament across the board. Unfortunately, no practical scheme of control could be agreed, and so the British government turned away from abolition and instead concentrated mainly on piecemeal qualitative and quantitative controls for military aircraft. Once it was apparent that military air forces would most likely continue to exist, then Britain's particular vulnerabilities as the defender of a far-flung Empire had to be taken into account. The result was a number of obviously self-serving reservations. For example, the exemption of flying boats and troop-carriers from weight restrictions and the assertion of the right to bomb in 'certain outlying areas'. With other countries also determined to protect what they saw as their particular vulnerabilities, the whole disarmament movement became deadlocked.

Of course, well-founded political distrust was the main reason for the deadlock at Geneva, but recognition of civil aviation's importance and the failure to devise acceptable controls for it helped stymie attempts at air disarmament and prevented the much-sought-after (even though rather fanciful) breakthrough to disarmament on a broad front.

In the end, civil aviation, like armaments, was untouched in practice by the Geneva Conference, but the Conference left a legacy of ideas which lived on for some years. There now appeared to be two impulses favourable to the acceptance of an international regime for civil aviation: the need for uniformity in technical and safety standards and other requirements of flying dealt with by the Paris and Havana Conventions; and the need for controls so that an effective system of air disarmament could be devised.

During the Second World War the latter impulse diminished in force, and it later expired, when cold war deterrence replaced disarmament as the main hope for security. Before that happened, two other internationalist impulses developed: a preference for internationalization over what was feared would otherwise be Americanization; and a desire to facilitate the expansion of international routes and traffic.

The first of these impulses originated from the British, who sought the survival of their own civil-aviation industry through international safeguards, even if that meant the loss of some sovereignty. Their position on sterling and what they would have ideally liked the International Monetary Fund (IMF) to be was strikingly similar. The second of these impulses came from America, which embraced internationalism in the Second World War and sought to expand her civilian aviation by gaining routes, and landing, embarkation, and disembarkation rights through an internationally accepted set of rules and code of conduct. Various possibilities for internationalizing aviation which had been discussed at Geneva were considered again during the Second World War, but in very different circumstances and for different reasons. However, these impulses were still far away in the early 1930s. The immediate concerns for Britain and the United States were the reorganization of their respective civil-aviation industries, and negotiations to establish a transatlantic commercial air service.

4
Brief Encounters 1930–1939

BETWEEN 1919 and 1930 Britain and the United States, while recognizing the need for air sovereignty, supported the principle of easy access for foreign airlines, and at the 1929 talks to revise the Paris Convention they both advocated a liberal regime. Unfortunately, their efforts were in vain and an important opportunity was lost, for as the 1930s progressed both governments intervened more in civil aviation, and became more protective and competitive when negotiating air rights.[1]

So far as strategic considerations were concerned, it was easy for Americans to espouse liberal principles, because no great power existed within air-striking distance of the United States: their only worry was the vulnerability of the Panama Canal. However, commercial considerations had a more protectionist influence, and as a result there was reluctance to grant foreign countries rights of entry to the United States unless a very favourable quid pro quo could be obtained. If international agreement had created an environment which encouraged states to grant easy access for foreign aviation, then US policy might have been different. But that was not the case, and the United State pursued its own self-interest with unsurpassed vigour. As the 1930s progressed, that policy was strengthened by isolationism, the economic nationalism of the New Deal, and strategic considerations in the Pacific. In 1934 the US government abandoned its attempts to persuade Congress to join the Paris Convention; it would have nothing to do with plans for internationalizing civil aviation which were mooted at the Geneva Disarmament Conference; it would not permit foreign entry into Hawaii; and in 1938 the Civil Aeronautics Act created a system whereby all domestic and foreign routes had to be approved by government. There was thus a contrast between rhetoric and performance.

[1] Ch. 2 above; J. C. Cooper, 'Some Historic Phases of British International Civil Aviation Policy', *International Affairs*, 23 (1947), 193–7.

Britain's position was even more complex. Ideally, it favoured and continued to advocate a liberal system during the 1930s. However, practical considerations and changing economic circumstances caused policy to fluctuate in a way that made the British government appear to contradict itself. Strategic considerations, involving possible air-attack from Europe, were of immediate and direct concern and emphasized the value of controls and air sovereignty. The British also wanted to develop a system of imperial communications, which for political reasons had to be operated by IA and other airlines of the Empire. The plan was assisted by fostering imperial cabotage, which understandably caused resentment among other countries, even though the British government was willing to grant them reciprocal rights for entry into Britain.

These restrictive tendencies were counterbalanced by various factors which depended upon a more open system. Access to the Empire, for example, could be (and was) impeded by France, Italy, and Persia, which lay across the direct route to the Middle East, India, and beyond, so care had to be taken not to invite retaliatory protectionism. British thinking on the matter of granting foreign aviation rights was also influenced by her longstanding attitude towards maritime commerce, the free-trade tradition of thought which was bound up with that, and the derivative conviction that free commercial access for international aviation was morally correct. In the nineteenth century, it made eminent sense for Britain, as the leading industrial and maritime power, to advocate freedom of the seas and free trade. In the 1930s the commercial reasons for wanting greater freedom for commercial aviation were not as compelling as they had been for maritime trade a century before, because Britain had declined in relation to other powers. But it was still hoped that IA would reap substantial profits in the long term, despite the commercial deficiencies of the company, which became ever more evident as the decade progressed.

The tension between liberal and protectionist tendencies in Britain was increased by the experience of the Depression, which brought forth arguments for greater imperial unity and economic co-operation—in some cases economic autarky—which turned people's thoughts even more to the need for imperial co-operation in aviation. The fear of cutthroat competition, particularly in the light of IA's limited ability to cope with it, also modified the favourable British disposition towards granting liberal rights of access to foreign aviation.

Thus British policy clearly contained contradictions, but in principle it did not deviate so sharply as America's from the idea of a liberal international regime. At the Geneva Disarmament Conference and after, the British professed a more internationalist position than the United States. And when pursuing the expansion of their own civil-aviation industry, they had to be more sensitive than the Americans to the interests of others in the world's aviation community because their domestic situation alone could not support a viable system of commercial aviation.

These British and US attitudes help to explain changes in their respective policies and some of the reasons behind the bargaining that occurred between the two over the Atlantic route. But before turning to those negotiations, it is important to have a general picture of how government policies for civil aviation developed in the 1930s.

RESPONSIBLE CAPITALISM AND CONTROL OF CIVIL AVIATION IN THE UNITED STATES

In the deep depression year of 1932, the Democratic contender for the presidency, Franklin Roosevelt, beat the Republican incumbent Herbert Hoover. He became President on 4 March 1933 and committed himself to imaginative government action. There followed a hundred days of frenetic activity variously aimed at alleviating the worst effects of the Depression, stabilizing the banking system, and responsibly regulating capitalism. Roosevelt's New Deal had diverse and contradictory features, but at the heart of its pragmatism was faith in free enterprise, providing that it did not ignore humanitarian values: it was government's job to ensure that capitalism behaved responsibly. In 1933 this referred to domestic capitalism; in the Second World War the principle was internationalized.

Given the political disposition of Roosevelt's regime, it was not surprising that Brown's airmail 'spoils system' was criticized. A political furore erupted when a special Senate investigation led by Hugo Black, later of the Supreme Court, publicized the fact that airmail contracts had not been exposed to effective competition. A series of ill-judged government actions followed which kept aviation in the public eye during a long debate that determined the relationship between airlines and the government for decades to come.

On 9 February 1934, under instruction from Roosevelt, Postmaster-General James Farley cancelled all existing domestic airmail contracts; foreign mail was excepted because there appeared to be no alternative carrier to PAA. The Army Air Corps took over deliveries, but disaster followed, with loss of life in bad weather conditions, and it soon became apparent that the army was not capable of operating the system. In May temporary airmail contracts were reissued to private operators while further action was contemplated by the government.[2]

On 12 June the 1934 Airmail Act, jointly sponsored by Senators Black and McKellar, provided for the Post Office to continue granting contracts and set up a holding operation for the control of civil aviation. It marked the beginning of legislative attempts to encourage controlled competition in the industry. The Act prohibited unfair commercial collusion, helped separate manufacturing from airline operating, and reduced subsidies. Under the 1934 Act, the granting of mail contracts soon stabilized, for although they could only be awarded initially for one year (altered to three in 1935), once an airline had demonstrated competence, it could then be given a permanent contract. However, the increased competition that the Act fostered, along with lower subsidies, undermined the financial stability of the industry and caused bankruptcies and difficulties that did not disappear until the war. These changes had implications for the broader question of how civil aviation ought to be controlled, and it was with regard to this matter that the Act had its most important impact, through the enabling power that it granted to the President to appoint a five-man Federal Aviation Commission.

[2] R. E. G. Davies, *Airlines of the United States Since 1914* (Putnam, London, 1982), 153–64 and 194–203; R. Daley, *An American Saga: Juan Trippe and His Pan American Empire* (Random House, New York, 1980), 219–21; and J. A. Farley, *Jim Farley's Story* (McGraw Hill, New York, 1948), 46–7. For a concise account and review of the immense literature on Roosevelt, see M. Simpson. *Franklin D. Roosevelt* (Basil Blackwell, Oxford. 1989).

Journalist and leading Democrat Clark Howell was appointed Chairman of the Commission, with Edward P. Warner, a widely acknowledged aviation expert, as the Vice-Chairman. It reported on 22 January 1935, recommending that competition should be encouraged, that the Post Office should have a free hand in choosing its airmail carriers, and that a new agency ought to be created to oversee the industry. Just over a week later Congressman Clarence Lea of California presented these proposals to the Congress, and from this point onwards the controversy that had first arisen because of the Black Senate investigation gained a new political dimension.

Roosevelt did not want a separate agency. Instead, he preferred to expand the existing powers of the Interstate Commerce Commission (ICC) and turn it into an instrument of control over all aspects of transportation which fell under the jurisdiction of the federal government. There now followed two years of hearings in the Senate Committee on Interstate Commerce, with various proposals being periodically put to the Congress which reflected the positions on civil aviation of contending factions both in government and on its periphery.[3]

A crucial decision which Roosevelt had to make in the midst of increasingly contentious arguments concerned the extent to which the government should exercise control over aviation. Such a decision had implications which went beyond the industry itself and affected the way the public viewed the overall political disposition of the Roosevelt regime. It is therefore instructive to look at letters on aviation received by the White House, which give an impression, albeit rather subjective, of the mood of the public and of the industry itself.

Not all correspondence merited sober attention; for example, in February 1935, a Mr Guiliano railed at Roosevelt: 'Your clerks who do not inform you about my discoveries are traitors, to you, to God to mankind and to me!' He claimed to have invented 'the perpetual motor'.[4] Fortunately, most of the letters had a more serious message, or rather messages, for it is possible to see five points emerging between 1934 and 1938.

[3] F. D. Roosevelt Library (hereafter FDR), OF 2955, box 1, folder: 1936–June 1937, Truman to Roosevelt, 1 June 1937.

[4] Ibid., OF 249, box 2, folder: Aeronautics 1935, Guiliano to Roosevelt, 18 Feb. 1935.

First, there was the view that civil aviation needed rationalization and control through government action which would prevent cutthroat competition. That argument was reinforced both by the need to protect employment—a poignant matter during the Depression—and by the value of developing civil aviation for strategic reasons. Fourthly, there was a fear that the United States might lose her technological lead to unfriendly powers if the industry were not nurtured by government. And finally, there was a general feeling that the cancellation of airmail contracts in 1934 had damaged the industry and that therefore there was a moral obligation on government to rectify matters. These factors had significant impact on the various views on civil aviation that existed within the Roosevelt Administration and they help to explain why the debate about reforms lasted from 1935 to 1938.[5]

The debate on what was eventually to become the 1938 Civil Aeronautics Act soon turned acrimonious. There were interdepartmental and agency squabbles, which were complicated by considerations of what the overall character of the federal administration should be. This was no small matter, because many of the early New Deal measures creating new agencies, e.g. the National Industrial Recovery Act, had been struck down by the Supreme Court as unconstitutional. Also, there was a bitter dispute between PAA and the Maritime Commission which involved criticisms of PAA's status and its plans with IA for a transatlantic air-service.

At the start of 1937 Roosevelt was still keen to expand the power of the ICC over civil aviation, and he worked in tandem with Representative Lea and Senator Pat McCarran, who was an aviation enthusiast and much-committed to US strength in the air. Lea introduced an Air Transport Bill early in 1937. Subsequently, in May, he submitted a new draft, after amendments to his original had been put forward in the Senate by McCarran, but even then it soon ran into difficulties. On 3 June Roosevelt wrote to Lea:

> I have had some very hurried protests from Assistant Secretary Johnson of the Commerce Department and Mr Joseph Kennedy of the Maritime Commission. Their objections are strong and vigorous, and before

[5] Ibid., boxes 1–8.

anything further is done in the matter, I think it would be wise to contact them and talk the matter over.

I also understand the Post Office is opposed to the bill.[6]

The objections of Kennedy were mainly directed at the proposed provisions for regulating overseas routes and they led him into direct confrontation with PAA. By 1937 Trippe had come to accept the inevitability of some form of government control—public and government demands for it were irresistible—but he was determined that it should be of a kind which would help and not hinder the fortunes of PAA. Above all else, Trippe was worried that his monopoly of foreign air-routes would be ended and that airmail contracts, which were about to expire, would not be renewed with his company. In order to prevent this, he had worked hard to get a so-called 'grandfather clause' inserted into the Lea-McCarran proposals, which gave preference to the continuation of existing contracts. Trippe, knowing that some form of regulation was inevitable, wrote to Commissioner Eastman of the ICC on 20 July arguing that it would be a mistake not to include overseas and foreign operations under the aegis of the measures before Congress. If there were to be controls, then he wanted PAA to have the benefit of the 'grandfather clause'.[7]

Joe Kennedy, founder of the Kennedy political dynasty, was a powerful man by the 1930s and an important contributor to Democrat coffers. His views about aviation controls were coloured by his chairmanship of the Maritime Commission and by the views of his aeronautical adviser, Grover Loening. As head of the Maritime Commission, he had direct interest in aviation because of the then pre-eminent position of flying boats on foreign routes and the expectation that they would take over the sea-borne passenger market. For these reasons Kennedy wanted to separate control of foreign from that of domestic air-services and vest authority over the former in the Maritime Commission. According to Trippe, he was summoned to the Kennedy home at Hyannis Port, Massachusetts, for a weekend stay to talk matters over. Things did not work out as Kennedy

[6] FDR Library, OF 2955, box 1, folder: 1936–June 1937, Roosevelt to Lea, 3 June 1937.

[7] Ibid., OF 2875, Trippe to Eastman, 20 July 1937; Daley, *American Saga*, 219.

hoped and Trippe was sent packing prematurely when he refused to agree with the views put to him.

The other line of attack from Kennedy was authored by his adviser, Grover Loening, who had been a business associate of Trippe but had now turned against him. Loening attacked with venom what he described as the *de facto* monopoly of PAA on foreign routes. Worst of all, Trippe had signed an agreement with Woods Humphrey of IA to divide the Atlantic between their two companies to the exclusion of others. So the hurried protests that Roosevelt had received from Kennedy were in fact well-thought-through and involved both a desire that the Maritime Commission be the organ of control over foreign air-routes and that PAA be divested of its monopoly.[8]

While Kennedy mounted his threat to PAA, disagreements between the Post Office, the Commerce Department, the ICC, and the Maritime Commission became more involved and heated and threatened to prevent progress. By the summer there seemed to be insurmountable problems involved with the two main proposals that had emerged in Congress: one was the Post Office-backed Mead-McKellar Bill, which had no support elsewhere in the government; the other was the Lea-McCarran Bill, which was the nearest to Roosevelt's original idea of expanding the authority of the ICC, but it had defects and was strongly opposed by many. A government memorandum commented on it:

> Definitely premature, undesirable and unworkable as to foreign lines and creates a monopoly by law. Post Office opposes it due to being out in the cold. Department of Commerce objects to having many regulatory functions taken away or duplicated. Maritime Commission objects to premature legislation on foreign lines and freezing a monopoly.
>
> All airlines . . . are for it—chiefly because they think they will get a valuable non-competitive franchise.[9]

Clearly the situation was becoming deadlocked. Roosevelt, confronted with these difficulties and aware that some of the Lea-McCarran provisions were incompatible with new plans he

[8] Ibid., 219–21; Library of Congress, 'US Maritime Commission: Aircraft and the Merchant Marine'. 1937—the Grover Loening Report; FDR OF 2955, box 1, folder: July–Dec. 1937, Loening to Kennedy, 20 July 1937.

[9] Ibid., undated memo, 'Pending Aviation Legislation'.

had developed for an overall reorganization of the federal bureaucracy, now changed his mind and decided that a new agency would have to be created for civil aviation. In 1938 proposals providing for a Civil Aeronautics Authority (CAA) were put forward by Lea and McCarran which became the 1938 Act.

After four years of political controversy it was something of a damp squib, for no major changes were effected to either the domestic or the foreign operations of American airlines. On the contrary, it confirmed the status quo of the route system. For the longer term, however, it provided the government with the potential to make important alterations. The Act authorized the President to appoint (i) a three-man safety-board, (ii) an aviation authority of five members to deal with the legislative side of the industry and who could only be dismissed for good cause, and (iii) an Administrator in charge of executive matters who could be removed at will by the President. All appointments were subject to approval by the Senate. Any commercial aviation route had to be approved by the CAA, and in addition the President could veto the granting of foreign ones. For the future, these measures gave the government the ability to determine the configuration of routes, but, so far as immediate policy was concerned, the 'grandfather clause' resulted in the approval of all existing routes, including PAA's. With regard to the question of monopolies, the Act exempted the CAA from antitrust legislation and it was not until the 1970s that this was challenged. In the interim, monopolies could be condoned, and indeed for some years PAA's was. However, as witnessed by Kennedy's attack and also by subsequent criticism from American Airlines, which wanted a part of the transatlantic market, there was growing opposition to Trippe's empire.

Despite the specific intent of the Roosevelt Administration to defuse the controversy about which institution should control aviation by setting up a new agency, problems continued. In 1940, therefore, Roosevelt, acting under the broad powers conferred upon him by the 1939 Reorganization Act, abolished the Air Safety Board and assigned its previous duties and authority over the economic regulation of the industry to a new independent agency, the Civil Aeronautics Board (CAB). And along with the CAA—which kept control over licensing aircraft and over navigational and some safety matters—it was placed under the umbrella of the Commerce Department. That set-up remained in force until 1958, and even then the changes wrought by the Federal Aviation Act did not directly alter the foreign civil-aviation operations of the United States.

By 1938 government had directly intruded into civil aviation in the United States. The form that it took was different from that in Britain, but there was little difference during the 1930s in terms of the end result, which was that the character of civil aviation was determined not only by the workings of the commercial market-place, but also by government policies.

The Civil Aeronautics Act of 1938, by basically ratifying previous practice, bridged the gap between civil aviation's performance and government rhetoric. The United States now seemed to have abandoned, at least temporarily, the position she had upheld at the Havana Conference and in international talks in both 1919 and 1929, which favoured free and easy exchange of commercial rights with other countries. Now all commercial rights had to be processed by the CAB, which suggested that a much higher level of government control was to be exercised. Unless and until a multilateral international agreement came into being, each state would have to negotiate with the United States for commercial rights as best it could, in order not only to strike a commercial deal, but also to gain the imprimatur of the government as well.[10]

IMPERIAL AIRWAYS AND THE RESPONSIBILITIES OF EMPIRE

Decadence is often a characteristic of imperial decline, and so perhaps there is a moral to be drawn from the dominance of the Short 'Empire' Flying Boat on IA's routes in the late 1930s. These planes were the last word in luxury in the inter-war period, but their name and their technical performance both say a lot about what was wrong with British aviation. To get some idea of their technical standard, it is instructive to note that their American

[10] Cooper, 'Historic Phases', suggests that a dramatic change from a liberal policy to a policy of government regulation was wrought by the 1938 Act. There is something to this, but it overlooks the longstanding difference between US rhetoric and ideals on the one hand and the workings of both the industry and the government on the other.

contemporary, the Martin 130, had the same cruising speed, carried nearly twice as many passengers, and had a range of over 3,000 miles, compared with the 1,300 miles of the Cabot and the Caribou S.30 Flying Boats, which were meant for the North Atlantic service but could only cope with the distance involved by having in-flight refuelling.

Concentration on the Empire meant IA did not compete with other airlines, and while this was by no means the only reason for the company's modest commercial performance, it was a significant factor. Also, IA's dominant position with regard to making specifications for new planes must also be held partly to blame for the failure of Britain's aircraft industry to produce successful long-range passenger-airliners. The story of British aviation is not without successes in the 1930s, but in relation to what happened in the United States, it does not compare well.

In Britain, as elsewhere, the Depression encouraged protectionism. This manifested itself clearly in the 1932 Ottawa Conference, whence came the system of Imperial Tariff Preferences, which became a symbol of Britain's wavering commitment to the free market (especially for people in the United States like Cordell Hull, Secretary of State 1933–44). The emphasis on economic co-operation within the Empire helped strengthen the 1920s' policy of developing imperial air-routes: it also encouraged the British government to favour the development of those routes to the exclusion of foreign operators. But imperial cabotage conflicted with avowals by the British that they favoured a liberal exchange of air rights, and it was soon questioned on these and on more practical grounds.

In April 1933 Londonderry produced a note for the Cabinet about a report from Sir Eric Geddes, Chairman of IA, concerning how IA should develop. Geddes's views had important consequences. First and foremost, he wanted more development of imperial routes in co-operation with the Dominions. Secondly, he wanted to bridge the Atlantic in order to bring Canada into the planned round-the-world imperial route and to open up the lucrative US market. Unfortunately for Britain, as Geddes pointed out, the carriage of mail would be important for defraying the costs of the transatlantic route, but, as the United States controlled 85 per cent of west-to-east mail whereas Britain only controlled 30 per cent of the east-to-west mail, she would lose out to the United States unless there could be an agreement to divide the carriage of mail more evenly between the two. Geddes explained in his report that one of the main reasons why IA had kept on good terms with PAA was because he knew that they would have to strike a deal with Trippe on this matter. The British, rather belatedly, were beginning to appreciate the importance of airmail to civil aviation. But, with regard to finances, Geddes did not just single out airmail as a necessary source of funds, he wanted more direct subsidies from government as well. Finally, it seemed to make sense to him, given the vast tracts of ocean to be negotiated, that IA should concentrate on the development of marine aircraft. In the long term this was a mistake, but at the time it is difficult to see what grounds there were for recommending otherwise. The problem for Britain was not that she developed flying boats, but that these were inferior to American ones and unable to service the Atlantic; also, unlike the United States, she did not have the resources to develop land planes at a similar pace.[11]

The Cabinet were allowed to ruminate at length during the summer over the report from Geddes. It was not until November that Londonderry brought it to the attention of ministers once again and tried to bring about some decision. By this time the self-satisfied opinions he had expressed about the performance of IA in April were replaced by concern stimulated by public criticisms that 'the United Kingdom has not to date pursued, and is not today pursuing a sufficiently forward policy; but [he informed his colleagues] I have been, and remain reluctant to sponsor any proposals for substantial fresh expenditure.' Nevertheless, his summary of what he took to be the four important points of Geddes's report included matters of finance, which would require Cabinet decisions. (i) Was the British government going to introduce new subsidies when the existing ones expired? (ii) If it did, what relationship should there be between government and IA—should chosen-instrument status continue? (iii) If the answer was yes, should IA be reconstituted on a broader basis, involving the Dominions? (iv) Was it possible to extend greatly the use of airmail to help IA become commercially self-supporting?[12]

[11] CAB 24/240, CP(33)110, 'Future of Civil Air Communications of the Empire', note by Londonderry, Apr. 1933; CAB 23/76, 48(33)8, 26 July 1933.

[12] CAB 24/243, CP(33)249, 29 Nov. 1933.

The last question provoked argument between ministers. Kingsley Wood, the Postmaster-General, unlike Londonderry and Geddes, was not enthusiastic about an airmail scheme. He estimated that its minimum cost would be £600,000 and that even if IA cut her costs by 25 per cent, it would still have to charge twice the rate for surface mail. The Cabinet meeting on 6 December 1933 decided that 'large issues of policy' were at stake in the disagreement between Londonderry and Wood, and it therefore appointed a committee chaired by Walter Runciman, President of the Board of Trade, 'To review the present position of British commercial air transport with special reference to the further development of Imperial air routes; and to make recommendations as to future policy, and, in particular, as to the relations between His Majesty's Government and Imperial Airways.'[13]

In July 1934 the Committee on Commercial Air Transport issued its report, which was approved almost in its entirety by the Cabinet. The British government agreed to continue subsidizing IA, which was to remain its chosen instrument. Measures were to be taken to develop an Empire Airmail Service (EAMS) and to expand imperial routes further, but it was thought unwise to give the Dominions any say in the operations of IA as it needed to retain maximum freedom in its commercial operations.[14]

The decisions arising out of the Runciman Report augured well for the future of IA. There was a long-term government commitment to subsidize the company: it had retained its chosen-instrument status, and the announcement of the EAMS on 20 December looked promising. Nevertheless, criticism of the company continued to strengthen. In October 1934 a specially built DH88 Comet won the first 'trans-world' air-race from London to Melbourne. It was a triumph for British engineering, at least within the category of small powerful racing aircraft. However, the race was also notable for the fact that second place went to a DC-2 passenger transport flown by the Dutch KLM airline. Its performance was a revelation to the public of what

[13] CAB 24/243, CP(33)286, 1 Dec. 1933, memo by Wood; CAB 23/77, 68(33)6, Dec. 1933.

[14] CAB 24/250, CP(34)190, July 1934; CAB 23/79, 30(34)5, 25 July 1934.

American industry had achieved in civil aviation. Geddes now came under pressure from public opinion, and he defensively announced that he was about to place orders for new planes. They soon came, for a staggering twenty-eight Short Flying Boats and fourteen Armstrong Whitworth Ensigns: the order was given to Short's before a prototype had been produced, and it was an enormous gamble on the part of Geddes to try to close the gap between the equipment at his disposal and that of PAA. Among other things, this was also the consummation of Geddes's conviction that IA should concentrate on marine aircraft.[15]

The performance of IA caused increasing concern as the military threat from Europe grew, particularly after the breakdown of the Geneva Disarmament Conference. The 'ten-year rule' had been abandoned in March 1932, and even while the Disarmament Conference continued, the British government became concerned about how to achieve defence parity with other European states. Among other things, this led to plans for expansion of the RAF and a greater willingness by government to give attention and support to civil aviation because of its strategic and communications value. IA's lamentable record in Europe could now no longer be ignored. Unlike its continental counterparts, IA did not have fast modern aeroplanes, nor did it conduct night flights. Public criticism and the strategic and defence implications of IA's poor performance moved the British government to review its existing policies.

In May 1935 the government established the Interdepartmental Committee on International Air Communications (ICIAC), chaired by the Permanent Under-Secretary of the Treasury and Head of the Civil Service, Sir Warren Fisher. It spent many of its early days considering problems with the Atlantic route, but it was also troubled by the situation of British aviation in Europe and wanted IA to relinquish its subsidy monopoly, in order to allow other companies a chance to show what they could do with government help.

At the same time as these ideas gained currency, a new company, British Airways (BA), came into being through a

[15] 841.796/329, Atherton to Secretary of State, November 1934; Davies, *Airlines*, 189.

series of mergers. It had sound financial backing, good management, and an able parliamentary spokesman in the shape of Arthur Balfour, later Under-Secretary of State for Air (1938–44). After some hesitation on the part of both IA and the British government, the necessary changes were made to allow subsidies to be given to companies other than IA, and in early 1936 BA was awarded a modest amount and gained mail contracts for northern Europe.

The company performed well, and while IA had to buy British, it was able to buy planes from the Dutch and the Americans. Indeed, there appeared to be little alternative to buying abroad for BA in 1936 because contracts for the RAF and IA had taken up available British manufacturing-capacity. It was unfortunate that British companies had difficulty in buying domestic manufacture, because the government was now clearly trying to stimulate more growth in civil aviation. In accordance with the Runciman recommendations and as part of the government's determination to strengthen British aviation in response to the deterioration in world affairs, the Air Navigation Bill of 1936 increased subsidies from £1m. to £1.5m. p.a., and in 1938, in the aftermath of the Cadman Report, subsidies were increased again, this time to £3m. It was unfortunate that at the same time as a more competitive situation arose in Britain's foreign airline operations (not only from BA, but also because of the intent to open the Atlantic route), and as more government money became available, British aircraft-manufacturers and designers became overloaded with rearmament orders and were unable to respond to the new demand for civil aircraft.

Partly because of its freedom to buy aircraft such as the Lockheed Electra, but also because of its more energetic management and competitive spirit, BA soon increased its status in the eyes of the government. Between March 1936 and March 1937 the Fisher Committee was involved in drawing up plans and in requesting schemes from airlines for a route to South America. When no submission was deemed to be adequate by the Committee, it then scaled down its specifications to a route to West Africa only, with a prospect of later building up a South American route from that basis. On 3 March 1937 the Cabinet accepted the recommendation from the Secretary of State for Air that BA was the only capable operator for the West Africa route.

In some ways, more important than that was the Air Ministry's wish to build up BA as a second string to IA: there were now to be two chosen instruments, admittedly one much more junior than the other, but the failings and inadequacy of IA were being acknowledged more and more by the government.[16]

While questions continued to be asked about IA's performance, the government also found itself having to deal with Britain's domestic airlines. These were decidedly 'small beer' compared with the American domestic carriers, but their plight in the mid-1930s is worth noting, if for no other reason than that official recommendations echoed many of the attitudes that had come to prevail in the United States in the controversy that followed the cancellation of domestic airmail contracts.

On 10 July 1935 the Cabinet agreed to the appointment of Sir Henry Maybury as Chairman of the Civil Aviation Committee. Its brief was 'To consider and report upon measures which might be adopted by His Majesty's Government or by Local Authorities for assisting in the promotion of civil aviation in the United Kingdom and their probable cost.' The work of the Committee was delayed because of illness, but in 1936, when it reported, there was increasing concern as domestic-route mileage decreased and companies made losses because of excessive competition. The Maybury Report recommended that 'cut-throat competition must be eliminated and indiscriminate multiplication of services must be avoided'. It suggested that route monopolies should be granted for limited but renewable periods, and that all radio and traffic-control facilities should be government-operated. In Cabinet on 27 January it was agreed that the government should act in accordance with the recommendations. As in the United States, the idea of responsible capitalism, regulated in order to avoid cutthroat competition, seemed to be the order of the day.[17]

Government activity was not restricted to the problems of domestic aviation. There was a counterpart to Maybury in the

[16] CAB 22/87, 10(37)5, 3 Mar. 1937; CAB 24/268, CP(37)76; *The Economist*, 21 Nov. 1936; R. Higham, *Britain's Imperial Air Routes 1918–39* (Shoe String, Hamden, Conn., 1961), 242–58.

[17] CAB 23/34, 42(36)6, 17 June 1936; CAB 23/87, 4(37)5, 27 Jan. 1937; CAB 24/267, CP(37)25; P. and G. Ford, *A Breviate of Parliamentary Papers 1917–19* (Basil Blackwell, Oxford, 1951), 292, Cmd. 5351, Jan. 1937.

sphere of Britain's international civil aviation—namely the Cadman Committee, which was established as a result of criticisms of IA. The Committee brought problems into clearer focus and recommended sweeping reforms.

1937 was an unhappy year for IA. In June its much-respected Chairman, Sir Eric Geddes, died, and his successor, Sir George Beharrel, and the Managing Director, Woods Humphrey, were not well equipped to deal with the difficult and sensitive problems that soon arose. Public attention was focused on the company by questions from Robert Perkins MP in the House of Commons. He kept up a steady stream of pointed but well-measured enquiries about IA in the House. Matters then became more heated towards the end of the year because of industrial troubles. The British Air Line Pilots' Association objected to the dismissal of pilots by IA, and their complaints were given added poignancy by large salary-increases for management and handsome dividends for stockholders. On 17 November, Perkins launched into a broad attack, criticizing the company's industrial relations, its commercial performance, its lack of modern aircraft, deficiencies in its operating-practices, and its poor technical achievement. When he called for a public inquiry, the Under-Secretary of State for Air, Colonel Muirhead, had little option but to accede to the demand.

After some controversy about its composition, a committee was set up under Lord Cadman, head of the Anglo-Iranian Oil Company, composed of leading industrial, commercial, and banking figures; the only effective limit to its brief was that it should not reopen matters dealt with by Maybury.

The Cadman Report was received by the Cabinet in February 1938 and placed in the hands of a specially created subcommittee under Sir Thomas Inskip, Minister for Co-ordination of Defence. It needed careful consideration because it confirmed many of the criticisms made by Perkins. However, in the view of one historian of IA, the criticisms were not always well-founded or accurate. As IA claimed in its own defence, arbitrary reductions by the Air Ministry of authorized subsidies, and delays by the government which obstructed important developments such as the EAMS—decided on in 1934, but not begun until 1937—hampered IA's performance, and thus government itself was partly responsible for some of the deficiencies pointed out by Cadman. Wherever the blame might be placed, in a sense, it was of secondary importance: more important was the fact that IA and the government framework within which it had to work both needed a shake-up, and that was precisely what the Cadman Report achieved.

There should be an additional Parliamentary Under-Secretary of State solely concerned with civil aviation, and a Permanent Under-Secretary to take charge of research and production and to co-ordinate military and civil policy. . . . Imperial Airways should operate Empire Services, British Airways the European services, and a joint organisation the London to Paris service. The management of Imperial Airways has been seriously defective and in its relations with the Air Ministry has been intolerant and unyielding. Immediate reform and some change in personnel was required.[18]

The government moved quickly. It raised the subsidy for civil aviation immediately to £3 million. In the Commons on 16 March Prime Minister Chamberlain made clear his belief that the Cadman Report had been right to emphasize the importance of producing modern airliners, and there were significant developments from this: the appointments of C. J. Stewart and Sir Donald Banks respectively as Director of Civil Research and Production and Permanent Under-Secretary for Air; and the decision of the Secretary of State for Air to appoint a committee under Harold G. Brown to look into 'The Production of Civil Aeroplanes'. In June of the following year the Brown Committee made its report and bluntly stated what had been said mutedly in various ways before: 'Civil aviation in this country will need generous assistance from public funds for many years to come.' It recommended that higher priority be given to the development of civil aviation, that the Air Ministry should not be responsible for making specifications for new aircraft, and that the RAF should use civil aircraft for transport purposes. Awareness of the inadequacy of Britain's civil-aviation manufacture was now becoming all too apparent. By 1939 the public knew that the Empire Flying Boats could not cope with a transatlantic

[18] CAB 23/92, 5(38)14, 16 Feb. 1938 and 11(38)11, 9 March 1938; CAB 23/93, 19(38)12, 13 Apr. 1938; Higham, *Imperial Routes*, 271–309; for the US Embassy view of things, see 841.796/387. Counsellor H. Johnson to Hull, 8 Nov. 1937, and 10 and 14 March 1938; Ford, *Breviate*, 293, Cmd. 5685, 1938, Cadman Report.

passenger-service, and the futures of both of Britain's most modern land-planes—the Armstrong Whitworth Ensign and the De Havilland DH91 Albatross—were in question. The Ensigns tired pilots because of their stiff controls, were underpowered, and were said to 'weave' in flight; the DH91 fared little better. At the outbreak of the Second World War Britain still lagged a long way behind the United States in terms of designing and producing an airliner of competitive specifications.[19]

A new post of Under-Secretary of State for Civil Aviation, contrary to Cadman's recommendations, was not created, but Colonel Muirhead was released of responsibilities for the RAF and so in effect became just that. William Hildred was appointed Deputy Director General of Civil Aviation, and Lord Reith was made Chairman of IA. Also, in June 1938 Kingsley Wood replaced Lord Swinton, who had been at the Air Ministry since June 1935.

These changes of personnel had important consequences. Woods Humphrey, whose job as Managing Director had been superseded by the appointment of a full-time Chairman of the company, decided to resign, and Lord Reith, now in full charge, wanted to develop IA along very specific organizational lines. Using the recommendation that a joint company should be set up to run the London-to-Paris route, he developed that idea and argued for a merger of IA and BA to form a public corporation, along the same lines as he had experienced as the first head of the BBC. Kingsley Wood was hesitant at first, but Reith's idea gained support, and in July 1939 legislation to create the British Overseas Airways Corporation (BOAC) was passed. In August 1940 the company took over from IA and BA, but by then everything was provisional because of the outbreak of war.

IA's performance and the role of government in civil aviation were interlinked during the 1930s. As IA faltered in its attempts to achieve goals expected by the government, so the government decided that it had to take a more positive line of action. Once the military threat from Europe became the British government's main concern, then the poor performance of the country's civil aviation could no longer be tolerated. In the

[19] Cmd. 6038, June 1939, 'Production of Civil Aeroplanes'; 841.796/421, Johnson to Hull, 24 Jan. 1939.

United States the main reason for the intrusion of government control into civil aviation had been the need to make the industry conform to a model of responsible capitalism; in Britain controls had come for different reasons and in two stages. The first stage had been in the 1920s, when IA had been formed and accorded government subsidies for fear that foreign companies would be the only ones to provide services to and from Britain. The second stage came in the 1930s and was a response to the inadequate performance of IA.

Why British commercial aviation in the shape of IA only had limited success from 1924 to 1939 is difficult to explain. It is easy to indicate the factors involved, but less easy to assign relative importance. By shifting the emphasis of development from European to imperial routes, the British government directed IA away from a highly competitive to a largely non-competitive arena, until the development of the Atlantic route began to change things. However, there was little competition for PAA on the US foreign routes, but its performance was much more impressive than IA's. This is attributable partly to better management and partly to a different outlook on the industry itself. Americans placed more emphasis on commercialism and, by the mid-1930s, on the prospect of carrying passengers in large numbers. Ironically, just as the United States was reducing mail subsidies, thus encouraging US airlines to develop ways of making the carriage of passengers more profitable—which was where the future lay—Britain introduced the EAMS. Although there was always a great deal said in Britain about making IA self-sufficient commercially, the manner of realizing that goal was compromised by strategic considerations and matters of imperial communication. Furthermore, the élitist character of British society may also be seen in the emphasis IA gave to comfort and luxury, at the expense of speed, efficiency, and volume traffic. The style of IA drew upon the experience of the luxury passenger-liners, which were dependent upon the patronage of the well-born and the well-to-do and which only thrived in an age of slower pace. The speed of communication now possible through aviation required a new attitude towards travel, commerce, and eventually society itself, and the Americans adjusted to those requirements more quickly than did the British.

British technology did not respond well to the needs of civil aviation. This was not because it was incapable—it produced world-beating racing aircraft—but it turned out little of which Britain could be proud in the class of large civil airliners. Aircraft ordered by IA were rarely of a specification which was attractive to other airlines. Production runs were thus smaller than they might otherwise have been, and consequently the stimulus for R. & D. was only modest, unlike in the United States, where competitive domestic carriers and PAA produced a demand for ever more advanced aircraft. IA concentrated on flying boats, which were limited in their operations by weather conditions and had to disembark passengers in harbours which were often some distance from final destinations; also, the performance of the Empire Flying Boats was greatly inferior to that of their American counterparts, the Martin and Boeing Clippers. When Britain did turn to land planes, they were either of poor design, like the Ensigns, or not commercially attractive, like the Albatrosses. And finally, there was a certain precariousness about British commercial aviation in its early days which prejudiced its growth. Throughout the inter-war period, the British government laboured under stringent financial constraints and this, perhaps more than anything else, explains Britain's poor performance. When the government finally took a more energetic line, military demands meant that it was not possible for Britain to allocate sufficient resources to civil aviation in order to make up the deficiencies that the industry had accumulated. And even when money was available to order new planes, the manufacturing capacity was not.[20]

During the 1930s there was a sharp contrast between the performance of PAA and IA. The former was not without its difficulties, particularly towards the end of the decade, when criticisms were made of its monopoly. Also, in March 1939 there was a palace coup which toppled Trippe from power. But the new regime of Sonny Whitney did not last long; Trippe was back by January 1940. One of the reasons for his return was the incompetence of Whitney; the other was that by 1939 Trippe's

[20] For IA's record, see Higham, *Imperial Routes*; and especially Peter Fearon, 'The Growth of Aviation in Britain', *Journal of Contemporary History*, 20 (1985), 21–41; R. Miller and D. Sawers, *The Technical Development of Modern Aviation* (Routledge & Kegan Paul, London, 1968), 71.

management had made PAA the world's largest international operator, and in that year it declared a company profit of close on $2 m. The contrast with IA needs no underlining.[21]

Although American and British airlines in general performed very differently, their experience of the growth of government control was similar. This was despite the fact that, as has been noted, the respective stimuli to the intrusion of government into aviation in Britain and America was different. The one really major difference in the experience of the two countries came in 1940, with the effective nationalization of BOAC, but the consequences of that were not felt until after the war. In the unregulated international aviation market, despite the two countries' protestations of principle to the contrary, their governments used their increasingly institutionalized power to practise restrictive policies with regard to the granting of aviation rights to foreign countries. However, as the decade advanced, the attitude of the British government began to be influenced by factors which inclined her to practise more liberal policies once again.

The Ottawa Agreements of 1932 strengthened imperial economic ties and encouraged the idea of imperial cabotage. It was hoped that such a policy would help to give the airlines of the Empire unity of purpose, which would strengthen their bargaining-hand when negotiating commercial rights with other countries; and there were sound political and strategic reasons in favour of it as well. As late as the London Imperial Conference of 1937 there were still widespread hopes for a coherent imperial policy. One historian of the conference records that:

> The 'answer' to American and European competition [the British government] believed, could be 'the establishment of a trunk route right round the world with arterial and subsidiary services radiating in all directions from important points.'[22]

However, in London the more restrictive views on granting commercial aviation rights to foreigners was already under

[21] Daley, *American Saga*, ch. 32; IA's profits in 1937 were returned as £97,267, but they included a subsidy of £380,000.

[22] David Mackenzie, 'Canada and the Civil Aviation Discussions During the 1937 Imperial Conference', *British Journal of Canadian Studies*, (1987), 97–109, quoting source Public Archives of Canada, e(37)4, Feb. 1937, 'The Commonwealth Air Route Round the World'.

pressure before the Imperial Conference of 1937 got underway. In 1936 an issue arose which occasioned fresh thoughts about the wisdom of excluding other countries' aviation from parts of the world where Britain wielded influence. On 17 June Cabinet Ministers were troubled by the possibility of German aviation penetrating Egypt and Greece, but they were also concerned about the costs involved if IA's operations were to be extended in order to keep the Germans out. There was no commercial justification for such a policy, indeed it would involve probable annual losses for IA of £20,000.

The government subsequently decided on economic grounds to allow Germany into Egypt, but the wider implications of the matter rumbled on and fell into the lap of Fisher's ICIAC. Eventually the Committee produced a report that prompted Swinton to review British policy. In the Cabinet on 2 June 1937, he noted that Britain had failed to get a liberal regime adopted for civil aviation at the Paris Convention, and as a result had decided to use the geographical advantages of Empire 'to ensure the fullest reciprocity and the best bargain in each case' of negotiations for commercial aviation rights. This policy was subject to three conditions: cutthroat competition had to be avoided; routes of strategic importance had to be protected; and British interests in important foreign airlines had to be maintained, though not necessarily by denying other foreign operators commercial rights. Out of this practice Britain had done rather well; however, the time had come to change, and to adopt a more liberal line. He felt that this was dictated by self-interest, because imperial routes were so dependent upon transit rights from others that they could not afford to alienate states by continuing with restrictive policies. Furthermore, there were delicate political problems involved in opposing the expansion of German aviation by the means that had been used previously. Samuel Hoare expressed general concurrence, saying that in the past it had made sense to develop an exclusive policy for the Empire, but he now thought that air routes should be developed in a manner similar to 'the case of the merchant marine'. This more liberal, though no less self-interested, approach gradually gained momentum. In May 1938 a problem of further German penetration was resolved when the Cabinet decided that it would be 'impolitic' to obstruct German access to the Near and Far East; instead, reciprocal rights should be sought. And that same month Kingsley Wood announced in the Commons that landing-rights were being granted to PAA in the West Indies without receipt of reciprocal rights.[23]

The German problem had prompted thoughts about altering Britain's more restrictive policy on granting commercial air rights because of the costs involved, but there was also the wider problem of transit rights from other countries to facilitate imperial communications. This was a more important factor, and it generally disposed Britain to be liberal in granting transit and commercial rights, not only at this time, but on many occasions in the future as well.

In addition to matters of cost and transit rights there was a third factor which influenced the British government. The policy of an exclusive imperial civil-aviation network was not working because members of the Empire would not commit themselves wholeheartedly to it. The fact was that they often had interests which conflicted with policies devised in London. In 1935 New Zealand granted rights to PAA without reciprocity, because it was the only airline offering a service to New Zealand. This weakened the British government's hand at a time when there was much conflict in the Pacific with the United States. However, there was a much more serious failing of British policy at the London Imperial Conference in 1937.

Although the British themselves were beginning to question restrictive policies while the Conference was in session, its outcome helped further to convince them that the only practical course was to develop a more liberal policy. The British convened the Conference hoping to get co-operation for a round-the-world Empire route and for united action in negotiating commercial air agreements with non-members of the Empire; they also wanted the Empire to adopt a 'buy British' policy for civil aircraft. Canadian involvement in trade with her southern neighbour resulted in her opposing the 'buy British' policy and it was soon dropped. However, initially there was considerable support for Britain's other two aims, but as the Conference progressed, it became clear that Canada would only commit

[23] CAB 23/84, 42(36)6, 17 June 1936; CAB 23/88, 23(37)4, 2 June 1937; CAB 23/93, 26(38)5 and 6, 25 May 1938; 841.796/406, Johnson to Hull. 20 May 1938.

herself in very general terms. The outcome was a declaration of willingness 'to co-operate with each other to the greatest possible extent' regarding the establishment of a round-the-world aviation route and a commitment by members to do their best to get reciprocal rights in any negotiations with foreign governments. Dominions Secretary, MacDonald, later reported to the Cabinet that 'a definite and satisfactory agreement for co-operation' had been achieved, but that was a little optimistic when Canada did not seem prepared to participate in the Pacific leg of the imperial round-the-world route, and had 'demurred' regarding the idea of pooling imperial bargaining-assets.

If governments really wanted to act independently, as New Zealand had done, in granting rights to PAA, then there was really nothing to stop them doing so. Britain's restrictive policy on granting commercial aviation rights was thus placed in question by her vulnerability concerning transit rights; by the costs involved in pre-emptive action by IA to keep foreigners off certain routes; by her long-standing disposition to grant foreigners easy access to trade and commerce; and finally by the unwillingness of the Empire itself, or at least one important member within it, to accept imperial cabotage and full co-operation on the granting of commercial rights.[24]

On the eve of the London Conference, Ray Atherton, Counsellor at the US Embassy in London, sent some perceptive comments to Washington about Britain's emerging dilemma and official British views about commercial air rights. He reported that Britain and Australia still favoured the idea of imperial cabotage (in fact, as has been noted, the British government was about to question the wisdom of that), but there were obviously problems. For example, the continuation of the Britain-Australia route was dependent upon use of the Dutch East Indies. Up to this time British pressure to persuade Australia to deny landing-rights to the Dutch had been successful, but as Atherton remarked,

> It is recognised [by the British government] that a certain measure of reciprocity may be essential. Moreover, there is the established precedent of foreign ships being allowed access to Empire ports. If the

[24] See Mackenzie, 'Canada and Civil Aviation'; CAB 24/270, CP(37)161, memo by MacDonald, 25 June 1937.

Dutch request is granted . . . the United States claim to similar facilities across the Pacific could not be resisted.

Britain's position on granting aviation rights to foreign countries was thus complicated by a series of factors which often conflicted with each other. Her policy of allowing foreign operators into and out of Britain was generally very liberal, though influenced by fears of cutthroat competition.[25] So far as the Empire was concerned, particularly in the aftermath of the Ottawa Agreements, she nurtured ideas of developing a system of imperial cabotage and a united imperial position for negotiating air rights with foreign countries, but Canadian unwillingness to give support, and the need for transit rights from other countries, meant that those ideas had to be modified. However, the goal of a round-the-world imperial route remained, and that, in addition to the fear of competition, influenced the British and tempered their liberalism in the negotiations with the Americans for the creation of the Atlantic route.

ATLANTIC CROSSINGS

Planes and bases were at the heart of both the conflict and the need for co-operation between Britain and the United States in aviation, and nowhere was this more evident than on the Atlantic route. By the mid-1930s the Americans had taken a massive lead in the design and production of planes which could bridge the Atlantic and reap commercial rewards. Britain lacked such equipment, and this was a problem which continued into the post-war period and got worse before it got better. However, the British Empire controlled a vast network of bases, to which the United States needed access not only for transit and technical stop, but also for trade, otherwise many of their routes would be commercially unviable. There were other factors which affected Anglo-American aviation negotiations, but these two were the most important.

Between 1930 and 1934 steps were taken, largely on PAA's initiative, to develop routes across the Atlantic. The first was a joint Anglo-American-French project to go via Bermuda and the

[25] 841.796/370, Atherton to Hull, 15 Mar. 1937; 841.796/32, Atherton to Hull, 5 June 1934.

Azores, but various problems resulted in non-performance and the lapsing of permits granted to PAA and its French counterpart. Also, Trippe thought that the British and the French were slow to make progress, so he began talks with Newfoundland for the short northern crossing. Matters were proceeding well until economic problems led to disorders in Newfoundland, revocation of its Dominion status, and, in December 1933, reversion to being a British Crown Colony. At that point the British government became fully aware of what had been going on and, most importantly, realized that the granting of landing-rights by Newfoundland would not necessarily have been reciprocated by the US government for IA. Up to then exploratory talks on the Atlantic route had been left to Woods Humphrey and Trippe, but now, realizing that things had to be conducted at government level if Britain were to be sure of getting full reciprocity and a good bargain for an Atlantic route, the government took a more active part, and matters were considered in detail by the Fisher Committee and the Cabinet. In future, Woods Humphrey would have to work more closely with the British government.

In November 1934 Vice-President Cooper of PAA went to London for talks with IA to try to overcome the difficulties which had recently arisen with the British government. But despite helpful efforts by IA, it was soon clear that company-to-company talks would not be allowed to continue on their own. The British government, in addition to being concerned about reciprocity, was also worried by the US lead in aircraft and wanted the transatlantic service to begin only when both IA and PAA were ready. After a meeting at the Dominions Office on 23 January 1935, it was clear that the British would insist on there being two sets of talks: one governmental, the other at company level. PAA was not keen to bring the US government directly into the discussions and argued that official US policy was for airlines to obtain necessary permits and facilities on their own initiative. It was also the case, however, that PAA believed that it had a better chance of getting a beneficial agreement from IA if their respective governments were not involved. The delay in the Atlantic was disappointing for Trippe, especially after promising progress had been made and amicable relations established with IA. He now turned his main energy towards the Pacific, where he had spectacular success, though partly at the cost, yet again, of antagonizing and worrying the British.[26]

While Trippe's attention shifted to the Pacific, there was still activity in the Atlantic. In February 1935 officials from the US Commerce Department and France discussed the possibility of opening a route operated jointly by France, the United States, and Britain. In 1935 Trippe, as well as the British, were not keen on this. Trippe explained to State Department officials the delicate nature of the situation, given that the British 'hold the key to the situation to a great extent' because of their control of refuelling-stops. For the time being, little came of these French overtures, but there was now more urgency than ever for the British to formulate their plans clearly. Simultaneously with these developments, PAA and IA proceeded to prepare for a transatlantic route; however, no matter what they did, eventually the impasse would have to be broken at government level.[27]

The problem was taken up by the Fisher Committee, which set about formulating policy in early summer. Reporting on their work to the Cabinet on 1 August Swinton wrote:

> The Committee has taken the view, and I think rightly, that in considering these international routes we should give priority to the establishment, as early as possible, of services between the U.S.A. and the United Kingdom, as this is obviously a route which is destined in the comparatively near future to carry a very large amount of traffic, and has great political value. From the Empire point of view this also completes the projected scheme by the inclusion of Canada.[28]

The British felt that they had to play their hand in the Atlantic very carefully. They were worried about the cost of operating the route, fearful of cutthroat competition, and wary of America's superior equipment and the competitive advantage she held in controlling a much larger proportion of transatlantic mails than Britain. The Fisher Committee proposed action to acquire planes and develop the technical back-up necessary

[26] Trippe Papers, box 20, 'History of Transatlantic Air Services', 17–18; ibid., box 8, folder: 1956 Newspapers and Magazines, draft ch. by Vern Haugland; FO 371/19635, W5479/3218/50, ICIAC mins., 19 June 1935; Daley, *American Saga*, 207.

[27] *FRUS*, 1935, 1, 510–19, Hull to Ambassador Bingham, 24 Apr. 1935 and mins., Moore, Trippe, *et al.*, 6 May 1935.

[28] CAB 24/256, CP (35)164, Swinton memo, 1 Aug. 1935.

for an Atlantic route, and also expressed the hope of sending a negotiating-team to Canada and the United States in the autumn. They believed that the dangers for Britain on the Atlantic route could best be handled by the judicious use of Britain's control over key Atlantic refuelling-stops: Bermuda in the south and Newfoundland in the north. Also, just to make absolutely sure that they could not be outmanœuvred, the Director-General of Civil Aviation, Shelmerdine, had engaged the Irish in successful talks at the end of July about creating a base in Eire at British expense, in return for exclusive landing-rights. With Bermuda and Newfoundland under British control and the possibility of an agreement to close Ireland to competitors, Swinton observed that 'the advantages of such an agreement appear to me to be almost incalculable'.[29]

The British also wanted to route traffic to the United States via Montreal. This would allow them to pick up passengers for onward flights across Canada and eventually on to a transpacific service which would link with Australia and complete IA's round-the-world route. If the service were to fly straight to New York, this would not be possible. When Trippe got wind of these plans, he was much concerned. Among other things, there was the implied threat that Britain might start a transatlantic service to Canada without granting commercial rights to PAA. In fact, there was no real likelihood of that: good political relations with the United States were deemed to be too important in the Foreign Office. Also, the British felt that they needed a slice of US transatlantic mails, and IA felt no little amount of loyalty to PAA, because of the way that the two companies had co-operated in the past. IA reported to Trippe that the British government recognized 'that planning a service to Canada without consideration of the United States' position would be "madness".' The government had no intention of excluding PAA from the Atlantic route, but it wanted to make sure that IA managed to protect itself from other competitors, that it serviced the Empire round-the-world route, and that it got a more equal division of airmail than was prima facie warranted by what each country then generated.[30]

[29] CAB 24/256, CP(35)164, Swinton memo, 1 Aug. 1935.
[30] Trippe Papers, box 20, 'History', 25–6.

On 5 November British Ambassador Lindsay informed Hull that a negotiating-team led by Sir Donald Banks, Director-General of the Post Office, was leaving England on the 13 November for talks about an Atlantic air-service with the Canadians and that they wished to follow those with conversations with US officials. On 12 November R. Walton Moore, Assistant Secretary of State, replied to Lindsay on behalf of his department saying that he and his Interdepartmental Committee on Civil Aviation, appointed by the President as an advisory body on 2 July 1935, would meet with the British delegation.[31] Before those meetings, the British had talks with Irish, Canadian, and Newfoundland officials to try to establish a united position for dealing with the United States.

The Banks Mission to North America included Shelmerdine and Woods Humphrey. There had been some friction between the latter and the government since it had taken centre-stage in the drama of the Atlantic-route discussions. In particular, there had been difficulties for the relationship between PAA and IA. This was resented by Woods Humphrey, but, according to the official record, he played a most co-operative and helpful role during the Mission's time in the United States.[32]

The talks with the Irish during the transatlantic voyage, and the discussions in Ottawa, were not without problems, but in the end what emerged was more or less what the British wanted. It was agreed that British, Canadian, and Irish representatives, who were going on to Washington, should use proposals drawn up by the Fisher Committee as the basis for talks with the Americans.

In July 1934 the Runciman Committee had recommended against the broadening of IA into a Commonwealth airline, for fear of losing control to Dominion governments. Eighteen months later, the British government decided that in order both to help defray the costs of operating the Atlantic route and tie Eire, Canada, and Newfoundland into a scheme which enabled

[31] 811.79640/96, Lindsay to Hull, 5 Nov. 1935; and Moore to Lindsay, 12 Nov. 1935.

[32] Friction between Humphrey and the British government has been exaggerated in Daley's *American Saga*, 207–8. In Swinton's report to the Cabinet he praised Humphrey, saying that he had 'acted throughout in the closest collaboration with his Government colleagues and the British Delegation'. CAB 24/259, CP(36)14, memo by Swinton, 16 Jan. 1936.

Britain to control the main transatlantic refuelling-stops, it was now desirable that a Commonwealth operating company should be set up. However, the British government was still determined to keep control of policy in British hands. That caused considerable difficulties with the Irish, but the final arrangement was that IA should have a 51 per cent controlling share in the Company, and Eire and Canada 24.5 per cent each. There was a sweetener for Eire in the form of subsidies for ground and meteorological facilities, whereas the more prosperous Canadian Dominion was expected to contribute up to 20 per cent of the costs of operating regular services—the contributions of Eire and Newfoundland were left to be decided on at a later date. Experimental flights were to be conducted by IA, and then the joint operating company was to undertake the carriage of mail and passengers twice-weekly—preferably on the northern route, although it was recognized that the Bermuda–Azores route would probably have to be used in the winter.

So much for the formal set-up, but how was this supposed to strengthen the British bargaining-position? First of all, the talks produced a united position to present to the Americans. Some of the British, for example Banks himself, were concerned about adverse American reactions to what might be perceived as a *fait accompli*, but on the whole there was a good deal of optimism and satisfaction. The British believed that the agreement would allow them to exclude or control competitors, achieve agreement involving full reciprocity with the United States, make another important air-link in the Empire, and, finally, enable IA to strike a favourable mails deal with PAA. As Fisher's Committee explained,

> The landing rights of the several Commonwealth air bases would be exclusive to the joint company as against *foreign* companies, except by mutual consent of the partner Governments. It is hoped to secure full American co-operation by judicious use of this situation before landing rights are extended to Pan American Airways, whilst it should be practicable at the same time to prevent other foreign companies operating over the direct route via Ireland and Newfoundland.[33]

[33] CAB 24/257, CP(35)222, joint memo by Chancellor of the Exchequer Chamberlain and Secretary of State for Air Cunliffe-Lister (created Viscount Swinton of Masham during 1935), 2 Dec. 1935, which includes summary of

In other words, PAA and IA were going to divide the Atlantic between them, with foreign operators only being granted access on sufferance, and then probably only on the southern route, which was longer and therefore more costly to operate. Regarding the problem with airmail, the Fisher Committee also believed that they had sighted a solution.

> . . . it is . . . essential to come to some arrangement for full co-operation between the American and the British operating companies. It is hoped that the provisional agreement reached in Ottawa will enable the Commonwealth delegations to present such a united front at Washington that they may be able to bring the negotiations with the U.S.A. Government to an entirely satisfactory issue by virtue of the geographical assets possessed by the Commonwealth Governments at Bermuda and on the direct route via Newfoundland and Ireland.[34]

While the representatives of the Commonwealth countries held council in Ottawa, Woods Humphrey had discussions with Trippe in New York from which it transpired that, unfortunately, the talks with the Americans were unlikely to go quite as the British hoped. According to Trippe (as related by Humphrey),

> In the first place, political considerations (particularly the importance of the large Italian and German votes of the forthcoming Presidential election) would make it quite impossible for the Government of the United States of America to contemplate the conclusion of a formal agreement with any foreign Government on an exclusive basis. Moreover it seemed certain that the United States Postal authorities . . . would be debarred legally from entering into any agreement with regard to the mutual exchange of air mails in advance of the establishment of a service . . . In these circumstances, Mr. Trippe and he [Humphrey] were agreed that the best . . . approach would be to continue negotiations between the two Companies with a view to producing a basis of common agreement.[35]

Fisher's ICIAC report on 'Proposed Commonwealth Agreement For an Atlantic Air Service'; CAB 24/259, CP(36)14, 'Report of the UK Air Mission to North America Nov.–Dec. 1935', 30 Dec. 1935; 811.796040/109, US Minister in Canada to Hull, 2 Dec. 1935; CAB 24/257, CP(35)184, 30 Sept. 1935. Lord Privy Seal Londonderry strongly opposed establishing a base in Eire, which he believed would be both a hostage to fortune and an act of treachery against Ulster.

[34] Ibid.

[35] CAB 24/259, CP(36)14, 'Report of Air Mission', 30 Dec. 1935.

In the talks with Moore and his Committee, Trippe's speculations were borne out. In addition to the factors he had mentioned, there were worries in the administration about unfair commercial collusion and monopolies which strengthened its unwillingness to grant exclusive rights to PAA and IA for either the Atlantic route or for mail carriage. The US government was willing to exchange reciprocal rights with the British government for commercial aviation across the Atlantic, but would take no further steps to protect or promote the positions of PAA and IA. Walton Moore made the position clear in his statement at the end of the talks on 12 December, when he said that agreements with other countries had not been precluded and that 'The matter of the carriage of mails is necessarily postponed for further consideration.'[36]

Although the US government would not authorize exclusive arrangements for PAA and IA in the Atlantic, the British government, by virtue of arrangements with Canada, Eire, and Newfoundland, could and would—at least so far as the shorter, more economic, northern route was concerned. On 30 July, in a statement made to the House of Commons on the outcome of the Ottawa and Washington talks, the Under-Secretary of State for Air, Philip Sassoon, said that Canada, Newfoundland, Eire, and Britain had

> undertaken to grant the necessary landing and transit rights within its own territory to the joint company and to Pan-American Airways. It is contemplated that unless otherwise determined by the consent of the four Governments such rights will be exclusive in respect of transatlantic air services for a period of 15 years . . .[37]

The US government could grant commercial air-rights to as many countries as it liked, but if those countries could not gain access to the refuelling-stops controlled by Britain, then they would be unable to fly the northern route.

Thus, for the time being, the danger of too much competition, feared by both PAA and IA, was taken care of unilaterally by Britain; but other matters involving frequency, carriage of mail, and the way PAA and IA were to relate to each other were left for Trippe and Woods Humphrey to resolve.

[36] 811.79640/120, statement by Moore, 12 Dec. 1935.
[37] Hansard, 30 July 1936, vol. 315, col. 1733, Sassoon.

Within weeks the two men had reached an agreement, which they signed on a company-to-company basis on 25 January 1936. There were to be two flights a week by each airline on the northern route: operations were to begin simultaneously, and there was an understanding that relations should be conducted on the basis of 'a square deal' existing between the two companies. In accordance with that understanding, they later agreed on provisions for dealing with the British disadvantage concerning the likely revenue from the carriage of airmail.[38]

All now seemed to be in place for rapid developments on the transatlantic route, but instead there followed a series of delays before operating-permits were issued between February and April 1937. There were various reasons for the delay, some of which were public and obvious. PAA, for example, came under scrutiny in the general reappraisal of American civil aviation that occurred in the aftermath of the 1934 cancellation of domestic airmail contracts. In January 1935 Farley had criticized PAA's foreign airmail operations and, as time went by, questions mounted about its position and the way it conducted business. In particular, the US government was reluctant to expand PAA's *de facto* monopoly on foreign routes any further, and the company's agreement with Portugal for exclusive use—as opposed to other American companies—of the Azores did not help matters. However, there were other factors at play which were not so obvious and which involved a broad context of Anglo-American commercial rivalry. It was partly as a result of this that the two sides moved slowly on the Atlantic route.

On the American side, there had been periodic worries about Britain developing a route across to Canada which would exclude US operators. There was never any real prospect of this happening, but the Americans could never be absolutely sure of that, and it certainly helped Britain's bargaining-position and encouraged the Americans to be more forthcoming than they might otherwise have been. One aspect of this, which was

[38] CAB 24/259, CP(36)14, 'Report of Air Mission', 30 Dec. 1935 and mins., Humphrey, Trippe, Cooper, and Shelmerdine, 13 Dec. 1935; J. A. Miller, 'Air Diplomacy: The Chicago Civil Aviation Conference of 1944 in Anglo-American Wartime Relations and Postwar Planning', Ph.D. thesis, Yale University, 1971 Univ. Microfilms International, NBA71–22342, 28; Daley, *American Saga*, 208–9.

argued over at length, concerned America's wish that Britain delete Montreal from the northern route in favour of the more direct route from Newfoundland to New York. The British refused and in their turn urged a case for Montreal to be the main stop on the west side of the Atlantic, with a shuttle service to New York. Difficulties over this continued and caused delay, but in the end a solution was reached by which IA flew Bottwood (Newfoundland), Montreal, New York; and PAA flew the more direct route Bottwood, Shediac (New Brunswick), New York.[39]

While the Americans were wary of the British because of their control of bases and their ambitions for the Empire route, the British were worried by America's superior planes and by her commercial aggressiveness. PAA and IA co-operated closely in the Atlantic in attempts to keep other countries' airlines out, but that did not prevent their coming into conflict elsewhere, most notably in the Pacific.

PAA's progress in the Pacific was spectacular. With the strong support of the US Navy, because of the strategic advantages to be gained, PAA routes expanded rapidly. In November 1935 they crossed the Pacific with a mail service to Manila in the Philippines. From there, Trippe wanted to enter Hong Kong, link up with his subsidiary, China National Airways Corporation, and fly on into China. However, the British wanted an exchange of rights involving Hong Kong and Hawaii, but the Americans refused, on the pretext that the 'most favoured nation' principle, at the heart of Hull's policy of trade liberalization, would oblige them to accord similar rights to other countries, including Japan. In fact, although this was a cogent argument, it was also a ploy, because the United States simply wanted to maintain its monopoly of civil aviation in the Pacific against all comers. Faced with this impasse, Trippe devised a way of bringing pressure on Britain. In 1937 he obtained landing-rights from the Portuguese for Macau, which, he pointed out to

[39] FDR OF, box 2, folder: 1937 Aeronautics, *New York Times*, 8 Apr. 1937, statement by Assistant Secretary of Commerce J. M. Johnson. One of the most criticized aspects of PAA's operations was the Form B Contracts, which gave exclusive and discriminatory rights to the company in South American countries. See M. Josephson, *Empire of the Air: Juan Trippe and the Struggle for World Airways* (Arno Press, New York, 1972).

the British, could develop as a major commercial centre by virtue of its air services and come to overshadow Hong Kong. 'As a result', Trippe later explained, 'we were invited to Hong Kong. . . . From that day we stayed there.'

Trippe was equally energetic in sending PAA into the South Pacific. In 1935 he negotiated landing-rights with New Zealand, much to British dismay, and then sparked off a long-running dispute with Britain over the sovereignty of strategic Pacific islands which could be used as air bases. The most celebrated controversy was over Canton Island, but in the end, with war clouds forming in Europe and after the British had taken some defensive action in the Pacific against American assertions of sovereignty, tension subsided, and an arrangement was made for joint Anglo-American control over some of the most keenly disputed islands.[40]

Regarding the Atlantic, it was little wonder that the British had marshalled their bargaining-counters carefully before negotiating with the United States. However, by February 1937 there seemed to be no further reason to delay, and over the following two months the appropriate operating permits were exchanged, which enabled PA and IA to start preparations in earnest.

The months that followed witnessed great activity. Survey flights were conducted, a service between New York and Bermuda was begun, and a series of conferences in Eire, in Canada, and again in Eire helped to establish safety standards and meteorological and communication arrangements. However, political hitches arose, particularly in the United States, and there were also problems with aircraft, both for PA and IA.

Political criticisms of PAA were directed at its monopoly position, and the government was reluctant to grant mail contracts with only one contender for the Atlantic route. In order to bring some remedy to that situation, it encouraged the plans of American Export (Amex), a shipping company, to develop an airline for Atlantic operations. There were also criticisms of PAA by Congress and by the Maritime Commission during the

[40] Trippe Papers, box 1, 24 Feb. 1966, address to American Foreign Service Association; ibid., box 20, Gatty to Trippe, 7 Oct. 1936; M. R. Megaw, 'The Scramble for the Pacific: Anglo-US Rivalry in the 1930s', *Historical Studies*, 17 (1977), 458–73.

preparations for what became the 1938 Civil Aeronautics Act. These developments worried Trippe, and in March he explained to Woods Humphrey how the square deal which divided the Atlantic commercially between them compromised his position politically in Washington. The result was that their agreement was amended and the conditions requiring the simultaneous inception of services by PAA and IA and the pooling arrangements were deleted. Later, on 9 February 1939, in a further attempt to mollify critics, he agreed to waive the exclusive landing-rights he had negotiated with the Portuguese government. These moves helped to dampen down criticism and they also increased PAA's ability to act independently of IA if it became necessary.

While the political controversy in the United States continued to make PAA anxious, there were also problems in Britain. Criticisms were voiced concerning PAA gaining commercial access to New Zealand without reciprocal rights being granted to IA. With the passing of the 1938 Civil Aeronautics Act in the United States, such criticisms mounted, because there were fears that something similar might occur on the Atlantic route, as Britain now had to reapply for commercial entry rights under the new Act. In the end, the CAA did grant Britain reciprocal rights, but by then the aircraft available to PAA and IA respectively had allowed the United States to seize the advantage.

Both companies had experienced difficulties with aircraft. For a short period in 1938, as the delivery of Boeing 314s was delayed for PAA and the company was troubled by aircraft losses, it looked as if Britain was about to take the lead over the Atlantic. On 21–2 July 1938 the Short–Mayo Composite flew the first commercial transatlantic flight from Foynes in Eire to Montreal. However, the success of this strange pick-a-back plane was one of prestige more than anything else, because the small Short S21 carried aloft on the back of an Empire Flying Boat had only a very limited capacity for commercial carriage. Britain's larger planes, however, were plagued with problems. Like PAA, IA suffered aircraft losses (in its case through ice forming on engines), but also the Empire Flying Boats could only cross the Atlantic with in-flight refuelling. Other British plans for transatlantic flights were placed in doubt by the breakup on landing of the DH91 Albatross land plane, which the British had hoped would alternate with Empire Flying Boats in crossing the Atlantic.[41]

After numerous teething problems and over a year's delay in delivery, the Boeing 314s finally began to be handed over to PAA in March 1939. Since the beginning of the year things had begun to develop rapidly for PAA. Trippe was still worried by criticisms that had been levelled against his company and, in spite of striking a deal with Amex to divide the Atlantic routes between them (which was declared illegal by the CAA later in 1939), he wanted to begin operations as soon as possible, to forestall any other possible competitors. Also, he hoped that once the transatlantic route started, that in itself would help to redeem PAA in the eyes of Congress and the public. Trippe no longer had any formal obligation to wait until IA was ready to begin services, and further delay because of the shortcomings of British aircraft would by this time have been irksome to him. However, Britain could still deny him landing-rights and there was the matter of Atlantic staging-posts.

While Britain held the key to transatlantic flights by controlling refuelling-points for aircraft without the range to cross from the New to the Old World, she could still dictate terms to PAA and, in particular, insist that it did not begin transatlantic services until IA was ready. But in January 1939 the United States took the first step to outmanœuvre the British, when it announced that it had been granted landing-rights by France for a temporary, six-month period. That in itself was not enough to undermine the British position, but combined with the range of the Boeing 314, it was. The new Boeings had a range of over 3,500 miles: they could by-pass Bermuda on a single hop from the United States to the Azores, refuel, and fly on to Marseilles. Faced with this, the British realized that it would be pointless to place obstacles in the way of PAA beginning the transatlantic service on its own. The Under-Secretary of State for Air stated in the House of Commons on 1 February,

[41] 841.796/415 and /421, US Consul Southampton to State Department, 5 Oct. 1938, and Johnson to Hull, 24 Jan. 1939, enclosing clippings from Daily Mail, 21 Jan. 1939; Higham, *Imperial Routes*, ch. 9; Daley, *American Saga*, 228–9.

> We hope the start will be simultaneous, but if either country should be ready to start earlier than the other, we should not wish to place any obstacle in the way of doing so.[42]

On 9 May PAA opened the southern route to France; on 24 June the northern route was inaugurated with a Clipper flying into Southampton. All that IA could manage was eight mail flights by in-flight-refuelled Empire Flying Boats during August and September, until the outbreak of the Second World War caused operations to be suspended.[43]

The British lost the race for the Atlantic route to the Americans. Anglo-American rivalry had been keenly felt on both sides, and there had been little evidence of Britain's move back to a liberal policy of granting commercial aviation rights to foreigners, largely because of the fear that US and other competitors would damage IA's fortunes.[44] In the end, superior equipment and commercial aggressiveness of the United States overcame Britain's advantages regarding the control of bases. Although this was only one battle lost, so to speak, the British were not slow to draw conclusions about their future prospects. When Britain's position *vis-à-vis* the United States deteriorated further during the war, because of its inability to develop a machine that could compete with US airliners, it was forced to review its position. As a result, it began to favour greater controls. More or less simultaneously, the Americans realized that they would benefit from a liberal policy for international commercial aviation, and therefore began to pursue such a course. These divergent policies were to lead to controversy and confrontation.

[42] Hansard, 1 Feb. 1939, vol. 343, col. 187, Balfour. FDR, Berle Papers, box 54, folder: Aviation International June 1942–Jan./May 1943, 'National Sovereignty of Air Space', 22 June.

[43] Daley, *American Saga*, 228–9.

[44] Nevertheless, general liberality of British policy was recognized; see, for example, 841.796/32, Atherton to Hull, 5 June 1934, enclosing a report on British civil aviation.

5

The Other Air-Battle 1940–1944

VICTORY in the Battle of Britain meant survival, but, in the continuing struggle that followed, British fortunes were badly damaged. Civil aviation, specifically, had three problems. US airlines expanded their operations with planes that the British could not match and penetrated areas which had previously been their preserve. The British became dependent upon the United States for supplies which made their bargaining-position vulnerable in aviation and other negotiations. And the British government felt obliged to make two agreements with the United States which had important consequences for post-war civil aviation.

When war came, British civil-aircraft projects were cancelled and BOAC was brought directly under the control of the Air Ministry. Maximum resources were devoted to military production and there was no opportunity for Britain to close the gap that already existed between its own and America's civil aircraft. Civil aviation was pushed aside and little thought was given to it from the outbreak of war until mid-1941. During that time PAA continued to operate as normal with neutrals and regularly plied the southern Atlantic route to Lisbon. At the start of the war PAA's fortunes waxed strongly because of demand for transatlantic passage and co-operative ventures of strategic importance with the US government. Also, in June 1941, after talks in London with Churchill about communication problems with his beleaguered forces in North Africa, Trippe established a PAA route from West to East Africa and on to Egypt. This had more serious implications for BOAC than PAA's pre-war entry into New Zealand. Concern grew in Britain and it was not motivated solely by PAA: Eastern, TWA, and others also flew the Atlantic and other foreign routes on war business. Such developments, which would be difficult to reverse, as well as the experience that US operators were getting and their superior aircraft, made the prospects dim for Britain in terms of competing with the United States when peace came.[1]

It was not only aviation that was damaged during the war, Britain's whole economy suffered. On 7 December 1940 Prime Minister Churchill warned President Roosevelt that 'The moment approaches when we shall no longer be able to pay cash for shipping and other supplies.' He hoped that the United States would meet Britain's needs in any case, and indeed it did, but only at a price. The solution to Britain's supply problem devised by the Americans was Lend-Lease. For the twenty-seven billion dollars' worth of goods Britain received as a result of that, she provided six billion dollars' worth in return, and gave the remaining consideration by sharing technological knowledge and by undertaking to co-operate with America in establishing a liberal world-economy.[2] There were direct consequences for aviation. One of the shared technological secrets was Sir Frank Whittle's jet engine, but it was vulnerability to American pressure during the process of economic co-operation that affected British civil aviation the most.

The Anglo-American Atlantic Charter of August 1941 set the broad context for a liberal post-war economy. After the British had been put under considerable pressure, its principles were reaffirmed in the final arrangement for Lend-Lease in 1942. US Secretary of State Hull and his acolytes were determined to take advantage of Britain's wartime exigency, press her to adopt liberal policies, and in particular persuade her to end the discriminatory trade-system of imperial preference. If the latter were allowed to continue, it could revive autarkic tendencies

[1] R. E. G. Davies, *Airlines of the United States Since 1914* (Putram, London, 1982), ch. 11; R. Daley, *An American Saga; Juan Trippe and His Pan American Empire* (Random House, New York, 1980), ch. 41; R. L. McCormack, 'War and Change: Air Transport in British Africa, 1939–45'. *Canadian Journal of History*, 24 (1989), 341–59. See also David A. Day, 'P. G. Taylor and the Alternative Pacific Air Route, 1939–45', *Australian Journal of Politics and History*, 32 (1986), 6–19, which illustrates some of the British imperial concerns about the Pacific (even though voiced by an Australian) and which provides some background for part of the story of ch. 7 below.

[2] W. F. Kimball (ed.), *Churchill and Roosevelt: The Complete Correspondence* (3 vols.; Princeton University Press, New Jersey, 1984), i, 108, Churchill to Roosevelt, 7 Dec. 1940; R. G. D. Allen, 'Mutual Aid Between the United States and the British Empire 1941–45', *Journal of the Royal Statistical Society*, 109 (1946), 245.

which, among other things, could result in a policy of imperial cabotage and exclusion of US aviation from other parts of the world dominated by British political influence. Commitments to economic liberalism were thus important for Americans, not least because they made it difficult for the British government to argue for protection for specific industries such as aviation.

British instinct to resist the more free-market American demands was qualified by desire for co-operation, dread of a renewal of US isolationism, and an acute awareness of Britain's material dependence on the United States. Also, except for ardent imperialists in the Conservative Party, and the Left in the Labour Party, opinion in Britain favoured free trade, provided it was within a framework of responsibly regulated capitalism of a kind advocated by New Dealers and by J. M. Keynes in Britain. In the war Keynes was an adviser to the Treasury and led British teams in most of the wartime economic discussions between the United States and Britain. During those talks, the British became worried by their vulnerability to American pressure and by the speed with which the United States wanted to move to a competitive world-economy: the British felt that they needed a transition period to recover from wartime damage and disruption. Although they never expected to be subjected to as much pressure as they were in 1945, they were wary of American economic ambitions and had learnt through experience that Americans would press their position ruthlessly, irrespective of their professed principles, if convinced it was in their interests to do so. Thus the British had to keep these considerations in mind when dealing with civil aviation. Their aversion to a premature abandonment of controls before the British economy could compete effectively, and their reluctance to abandon favourable discrimination for the Empire without a tangible quid pro quo were both pertinent to aviation because of Britain's lack of modern transports and her hopes of trading access to routes for concessions from the United States. Above all else, they wanted to avoid a system in which airlines operated without any commercial controls, because they feared that this would lead to an American monopoly of international aviation, including vital imperial routes.[3]

[3] Cmd. 6311, 23 Feb. 1942, 'Principles Applying to Mutual Aid'. For details of Lend-Lease see my, *US Wartime Aid to Britain 1940–46* (Croom Helm, London,

In addition to this general state of affairs, expediency forced Britain into two aviation agreements with the United States in 1942. The first of them was prompted by PAA's African route. After much argument with the State Department, there was agreement that its operation should be conducted on a purely military basis and that if commercial advantages were sought, then they should be discussed after the war. Although the United States acquiesced in this, it also sought to pre-empt the possibility of the British government embarking upon a policy which would obstruct America's obtaining foreign aviation rights. The Americans knew that Britain's main strength was her control of bases and they did not want it to be increased during the war. Therefore, on 27 May the State Department wrote to the British Embassy that it hoped 'no attempt will be made by either Government, or by companies acting for either Government, to set up arrangements which would exclude air transport lines of the other', except after diplomatic consultation. On 28 July the Embassy replied, agreeing with the American proposal and suggesting that it should apply worldwide. This was the so-called Halifax Agreement, named after Britain's Ambassador to the United States.[4] PAA's move into Africa made the agreement attractive to Britain, and her greater potential for gaining exclusive arrangements meant that it safeguarded American interests too. The principles involved made it more difficult for the British government to espouse a discriminatory aviation policy, but on the other hand it prevented the United States from taking commercial advantage of wartime circumstances. Also, by stalling things, the Halifax Agreement might make it possible for an international body, advocated by Britain, to allocate routes, set fares, and equitably distribute

1986), and for the broader position my *Politics of the Anglo-American Economic Special Relationship* (Wheatsheaf, Brighton and St. Martins, Brighton and New York, 1988). For Roosevelt's assurances see Kimball, *Correspondence*, i, 357–8, Roosevelt to Churchill, 11 Feb. 1942; and for British suspicions, my articles 'A Mess of Pottage for Your Economic Birthright: The 1941–42 Wheat Negotiations and Anglo-American Economic Diplomacy', *Historical Journal*, 28 (1985), 739–50 and 'The Export White Paper, 10 September 1941', *Economic History Review*, 39 (1986), 59–76.

[4] *FRUS*, 1942, 4, 23, Halifax Agreement: Eden to Hull, 28 July 1942; CAB 87/2, RP(42)48 15 Dec. 1942; Berle Papers, box 55, folder: aviation 1944, Berle to Hull, 31 Aug. 1944.

commercial rights, i.e. in a way that would help Britain gain a substantial share of the post-war civil-aviation market.

The other agreement of 1942 contributed much to Britain's main handicap in civil aviation. On 13 October the Cabinet decided that Oliver Lyttleton, Production Minister, should go to Washington in order to develop plans for an Anglo-American division of labour for wartime production. On the whole, his mission was a great success. Even Roosevelt's Chief of Staff, the anti-British Admiral Leahy, was moved to write in his diary, 'He [Lyttleton] is an exceedingly attractive and plausible advocate of British interests.' However, one of the things agreed upon was that the United States would produce transport planes, as well as other types, and that Britain would concentrate on fighters and night-bombers. This specialization consolidated America's technological lead in civil aircraft, especially as Britain produced no purpose-designed transports in the war.[5]

These three developments—the expansion of US airlines on to foreign routes, Britain's commitment to co-operate with the United States and her dependence on her for economic help, and the two agreements of 1942—weakened Britain's civil aviation and strengthened America's. During the course of the war, the significance of this was emphasized because civil aviation grew in importance for commercial, political, and military reasons.

American commercial interests were most fervently promoted by Hull, who believed that it was imperative to end protectionism and discrimination because they caused friction and war. He and others also feared the return of depression if foreign markets were not opened to the increased capacity now available to US manufacturers because of the wartime expansion of industry, and such concerns extended to civil aviation. The fact that the United States held the best competitive position was another consideration in American demands for the greatest possible post-war expansion of, and freedom for, aviation. On the political front, the spreading of American influence and culture round the world by its airlines was seen as beneficial

[5] Sir Alec Cairncross (ed.), *Sir Richard Clarke, Anglo-American Collaboration in Peace and War 1942–49* (Clarendon, Oxford, 1982), ch. 1; US Library of Congress, Leahy Papers, box 5, 5 Nov. 1942; CAB 65/28, WM140(42)1, 13 Oct. 1942.

and desirable in itself, and it would also help American business and commerce, as well as more sinister things such as espionage. And finally, the importance of aircraft in military operations in the Second World War, and the danger of surprise attack that now existed therefrom—vividly symbolized by the day of infamy on which Pearl Harbor was attacked—resulted in further support for a strong and ubiquitous world-presence for US aviation. This would help sustain America's manufacturing-potential for emergencies and provide world-wide routes and bases and a large fleet of aircraft which could be commandeered for military transport. Such views formed a general consensus in the United States; however, in order that its aviation could spread round the globe, the United States knew that it would have to reach an accommodation with the British government for access to bases which it controlled.

British reasoning about the importance of civil aviation was similar to American, but there was also imperial communications to be taken into account and, given Britain's relative decline, civil aviation was also seen in more sensitive terms regarding its prestige value. Britain was thus no less determined than the United States to secure a major part of the world's civil-aviation business, but she lacked planes and feared that the consequences of untrammelled post-war competition would be an American monopoly in the air.

This was the making of 'the other air-battle'.

BRITISH PREPARATIONS 1941–1943

British civil aviation came to a standstill because of the war. Effectively, BOAC became part of the armed services, engaged in transport duties. In 1940 it lost its Chairman to the Ministry of Information, and Clive Pearson, an oil magnate, took over, with Walter Runciman as the Director-General. In 1943 even BOAC's military role was reduced when the RAF created its own transport command. BOAC's exasperation with government neglect, in particular the apparent lack of planning for peacetime, was made manifest in a mass resignation from the board in March 1943. Thereafter things on the planning front began to improve visibly, but in fact nearly two years earlier, in July 1941, the British government had begun to consider post-war civil aviation.[6]

Propaganda needs and co-operation with the Americans forced British attention to the post-war world. On 30 May 1941 Foreign Secretary Eden described Britain's war aims in a speech at the Mansion House, and three months later came the Atlantic Charter, at the heart of which was Roosevelt's Four Freedoms—freedom of expression and religion, and freedom from want and fear. But the main stimulus for post-war thoughts arose from Lend-Lease discussions and the Anglo-American pledge to craft a liberal international economic system.[7]

In response to these developments, Churchill appointed an advisory Committee on Reconstruction Problems (CRP). For its first year it was chaired by Minister Without Portfolio Arthur Greenwood and thereafter by Sir William Jowitt, who was successively Paymaster-General, from March to December 1942, and then Minister Without Portfolio, until October 1944. Members of the Committee included Clement Attlee, Chancellor of the Exchequer Kingsley Wood, and Transport Minister Moore-Brabazon. The Committee did not achieve much overall, but it played a significant role in civil aviation.[8]

On 11 July 1941 Greenwood established a committee under Sir Francis Shelmerdine, Director of Civil Aviation, composed of representatives from interested departments. Its brief was 'To survey the whole field of Civil Aviation in its international, Imperial and national aspects, and to make recommendations as regards reconstruction, organization and development both during the transitional period from war to peace conditions and thereafter.'[9] Before reporting in April 1942, the CRP was reconstituted, which was important because its political make-up affected the way it reacted to the proposals that were made. Jowitt took the chair, and the Committee was inclined to Labour and the Liberals politically, especially with forceful figures like

[6] A. Sampson, *Empires of the Sky: The Politics, Contests and Cartels of World Airlines* (Hodder & Stoughton, London, 1984), 58–9.

[7] L. Broad, *Eden: The Chronicles of a Career* (Hutchinson, London, 1953), 154–5; Cmd. 6321, 1941, 'Joint Declaration'; Cmd. 6391, 23 Feb. 1942, 'Principles Applying to Mutual Aid'; the Four Freedoms were announced to Congress on 6 Jan. 1941.

[8] CAB 87/1, RP(41)1, 24 Feb. 1941.

[9] Ibid., RP(41)17, 11 July 1941.

Ernest Bevin, Minister of Labour, and Hugh Dalton, President of the Board of Trade, as members.

On 28 April 1942 the CRP considered Shelmerdine's report. Jowitt observed that it proposed the internationalization of civil aviation, but he was not sure that this was practical. All, except Leo Amery, the Secretary of State for India and an arch-imperialist, agreed that internationalization was desirable, but they shared Jowitt's scepticism about practicalities, especially because of aviation's military implications. To anyone involved in the discussion about internationalization at Geneva in 1933–4, the reasoning must have sounded familiar.

Possible difficulties arising from internationalization and US opposition to it prompted Kingsley Wood to observe:

> It is . . . arguable that if we were successful in building up a common front on the question of air services throughout Europe and her Dependencies, we should be in a stronger position to deal with the Americans, and might . . . force them to put forward counter proposals . . . which would not be unreasonable.[10]

He acknowledged that there were dangers involved in this line of thinking, but as a tactic it recurred in various permutations throughout the war, as the British tried to enhance their position by forming blocs with other countries such as members of the Empire, and European and Middle Eastern countries with which they had influence. This approach was actually at odds with pure internationalism, but it had considerable appeal to the British government in civil aviation and in security and defence matters and, regarding the former, it became the fall-back position if internationalism were to fail.

The picture from this CRP meeting is one of Britain very much on the defensive, with internationalization seen as an attractive option in theory, but with serious difficulties in practice. Nevertheless, internationalization had strong political appeal both to Labourites and, though less significantly, to Liberals. It was also attractive to elements within the Foreign Office, which was headed by Eden, who had done much in 1932 and 1933 to try to salvage the Geneva Conference by promoting internationalization of civil aviation as a precondition for air disarmament.

[10] CAB 87/2, RP(42)2, 28 and Wood's letter 25 Apr. 1942.

Political interest was sufficient for things to be taken further. In mid-July Eden, Attlee, and Sinclair, Secretary of State for Air, decided that Lord Finlay, Schelmerdine, and Orme Sargent of the Foreign Office should study internationalization further.[11]

Sadly, Schelmerdine died in the course of the year, but the report was ready by December 1942. In an accompanying letter Finlay wrote: 'the choice before the world lies between Americanisation and internationalization. If this is correct, it is difficult to doubt that it is under the latter system that British interests will best be served.' In the report, Finlay laid before the British government the factors that had led him to this conclusion. These were: PAA's continued expansion, Britain's abandonment of design and production of civilian airliners, America's wealth of pilots and transport planes, and her penetration of places like Africa and Ascension Island. Last but not least, there was the Halifax Agreement. Finlay believed that the British would be unable to hold the Americans to its conditions, because when peace came, they would not have the planes to take over routes being operated by the United States on a wartime basis. The lack of planes with which she could compete with the United States was at the heart of Britain's difficulties in civil aviation, and Finlay recognized that, stating: 'It is of paramount importance that we should be in a position, say two years hence, to produce modern transport aircraft in the few types and sizes required in reasonably large quantities.' Finlay was aware that he had raised questions of high policy, in particular by recommending the full internationalization of all civil aviation. Among other things, such a policy would involve co-operation not competition and it would be incompatible with an exclusive imperial policy.[12]

The reaction of the CRP was rather reserved. On 20 January it noted that internationalization was probably impractical. The British government would not accept such proposals in the analogous case of shipping, where strength alone was sufficient to safeguard British interests, so why should the United States accept internationalization for civil aviation? The matter was

[11] Ibid., RP(42)6, 21 July 1942.

[12] Ibid., RP(42)48, 'Internationalisation of Civil Aviation After the War', 15 Dec. 1942.

passed to a high-powered subcommittee consisting of Eden, Jowitt, Wood, Sinclair, Lord Leathers, Minister of War Transport, and Sir Stafford Cripps, Minister for Aircraft Production, for further consideration and to produce recommendations. In fact, it continued as an important idea for some months and attracted sufficient support for the government to send a letter to the Dominions on 7 April, proposing a joint approach to the United States advocating full internationalization. But this was as far as it ever got.[13]

Before the Cabinet changed their policy, there were two developments which indicated the likely way things were to go. In February Clare Luce, Republican Congresswoman and wife of publisher Henry Luce (famous for his nationalistic statements about the 'American Century' in a 1941 Life Magazine editorial) made some extremely provocative pronouncements in Congress. She advocated the development of overwhelming airpower for the United States and criticized the internationalist ideas of Eleanor Roosevelt and Vice-President Wallace as 'globaloney'. State Department officials dissociated themselves from this policy, but the publicity that had been aroused worried the British and seemed to question the viability of internationalization when it could be ridiculed so effortlessly.[14] But even more worrying was an incident in the House of Commons.

Although the British government was taking action on civil aviation, it was not evident to MPs, who were becoming critical and were disturbed by the mass resignation from BOAC. On 25 February Eden told Cabinet colleagues that he was not ready for talks with the Americans on civil aviation and that he wanted to discuss things with the Dominions first. He thought that an approach to the United States should come later, when British plans were well advanced. The timetable was clearly a lengthy one, but some progress was being made, and on 24 May the Cabinet decided that Attlee should be prepared to defend its policy in a debate in the Commons on 1 June. On the day, there was criticism that the British government lacked a policy. Attlee

[13] CAB 87/3, 1st meeting Reconstruction Committee, 20 Jan. 1943; CAB 65/34, WM77(43)5, 24 May 1943.

[14] H. G. Nicholas (ed.), *Washington Dispatches 1941–45* (Weidenfeld & Nicolson, London, 1981), 13 and 21 Feb. 1943.

explained that the government was convinced of the need for the utmost international co-operation, but that at first Britain was consulting with the Dominions. At that point he was challenged with the charge that there were differences within the Cabinet concerning internationalization. His reply in itself was not that striking, but the House's reaction said much about prevailing attitudes. Attlee said: 'There are various methods by means of which this problem might be dealt with; among other matters some form of internationalization may be considered. (Laughter)'[15]

There were, in fact, considerable differences in official British circles about the future of civil aviation. The Air Ministry, BOAC, and the RAF all opposed internationalization on grounds of practicality and national and/or self-interest. The steamship companies—eager to have a say in post-war aviation—and the Foreign Office both favoured internationalism of some sort, though the Foreign Office was aware of the practical problems involved. At an important Cabinet meeting on 24 June, matters began to clarify, with the help of papers from Churchill, Arthur Balfour, Under-Secretary of State for Air, Jowitt, and Amery. In the discussion, Home Secretary Herbert Morrison disclosed an attitude that said much about the commitment to internationalism in the Labour Party. He remarked that he 'wished that it had been possible for us to put forward proposals for internationalisation, in order that it might be clear that the opposition to such proposals did not come from us. It was explained, however, that the Dominions were not prepared to support a scheme of full internationalisation.' This opposition from the Dominions, along with the public reaction to talk of internationalization in both the United States and Britain, convinced the Cabinet of the futility of pursuing the matter further. The biggest obstacle had always been the opposition of the United States, and now, without hope of a concerted Empire policy, there was no chance of overcoming it. However, all was not lost. As American reports from London accurately observed, Britain's eventual policy would depend much upon where it was decided. In autumn of 1943 decisions on that matter were taken, and in

[15] CAB 65/33, WM35(43)3, 25 Feb. 1943; CAB 65/34, WM77(43)5, 24 May 1943; Hansard, 1 June 1943, vol. 390, col. 99.

what emerged as a consequence there was still a strong element of internationalism.[16]

Already on the 24 June things were taking shape. Cranborne, the Lord Privy Seal, was put in charge of a committee to direct planning, and it was felt that if there could not be full internationalisation, there must at least be an 'enlightened international settlement' and agreement on rates and frequencies arrived at by some form of operators' organization. There must also be co-operation with the Dominions to establish a united front. Impetus for further developments came with a change of personnel. On 24 September 1943 Lord Beaverbrook replaced Cranborne as Lord Privy Seal and assumed the chairmanship of the ministerial Committee on Civil Air Transport. He was a powerhouse of energy, a skilful negotiator, a staunch imperialist, and a man determined that Britain should on no occasion give way more than was necessary to the United States. He wanted to achieve a situation in which British airlines could compete with US operators within a properly ordered system. He brought in Peter Masefield as Secretary of his committee, in preference to using the more cautious Director of Civil Aviation, William Hildred or his deputy, George Cribbett, and he worked mainly in co-operation with Sinclair, Leathers, Cripps, and Cranborne, who was now back in the Dominions Office.[17]

Over the next few months British aviation policy began to take on a more developed and fixed character. The problem it had to address was: how could British interests best be defended, and in particular a US monopoly be avoided, in the absence of full internationalization? The British had to devise a

[16] CAB 65/34, WM88(43), 24 June 1943, considering papers WP(43)251, 257, 259, and 262; FDR, Hopkins Papers, box 336, folder: book 9 Air Conference Postwar Aviation, W. A. H. Burden, Aviation Assistant to the Secretary of Commerce, 'Notes on Present British Opinion on Postwar Air Transport'; J. A. Miller, 'Air Diplomacy: The Chicago Civil Aviation Conference of 1944 in Anglo-American Wartime Relations and Postwar Planning', (Ph.D. thesis, Yale University, 1971, Univ. Microfilms International, NBA71–22342).

[17] House of Lords Record Office, Beaverbrook Papers D/297, WP(43)283, 28 June 1943, appointment of Committee on Postwar Civil Air Transport (CAT), reconstituted Sept. 1943 with Beaverbrook as Chairman, disbanded Aug. 1944 after completing its task of consulting with the Dominions and considering postwar arrangements for civil aviation; ibid., Beaverbrook to Churchill and his reply, 19 July and 23 Aug. 1944. For general attitudes, see A. J. P. Taylor, *Beaverbrook* (Hamish Hamilton, London, 1972); Miller, 'Air Diplomacy', much of which is based on interviews and correspondence with Masefield.

means of allowing civil aviation to flourish whilst protecting British operators from cutthroat competition, especially in the difficult period at the end of the war, when Britain would be disadvantaged because of a lack of suitable aircraft. But they had to take care not to alienate countries by policies which might force them to a form of protectionism that would deny Britain rights of transit and technical stop which were essential for imperial communications. The eventual solution appeared to be the establishment of a powerful international body that would allocate routes, set rates, control frequencies, and oversee the kind of technical matters previously dealt with by the Paris Convention. There would not be full internationalization, but international controls would regulate aviation so that the United States could not monopolize things.

On paper this was all very well, but how were Americans to be persuaded of the wisdom of establishing such a system, and what were the British going to do about their lack of planes?

In December 1942 Cripps appointed Lord Brabazon as chairman of an interdepartmental committee 'to consider the new types of aircraft for post-war air transport, the conversion of existing types as an interim measure, and the possibility of using spare design and productive capacity without interference with war production'. The Committee tried to deal with the problem, so plainly identified in Finlay's report, which was the Achilles' heel of Britain's plans for civil aviation. The committee recommended the immediate design of new transport aircraft and jigging and tooling for the production of transports from existing military aircraft. The Cabinet was sympathetic to these proposals. It was intended that Britain should play 'a big part in post-war air transport' and that she should hold her own against American manufacturers. However, Wood explained that while he generally agreed with the recommendations, he could not authorize expenditure for the production of civilian types of aircraft. In the end, all the Cabinet could do was to resolve that work on new types would begin when it became possible to do so without interfering with the war effort, affirm the principle that Britain would have a post-war civil-aviation industry 'on a scale and quality in keeping with our world position', and accept that the British government had the responsibility for producing a minimum number of essential types of transports.

The spirit was willing, but circumstances of both finance and war prevented any effective action to remedy Britain's greatest deficiency in civil aviation.[18]

Although the equipment problem remained, there seemed to be positive developments in creating a united stance by Britain and her Dominions. On 18 October Beaverbrook wrote to Harry Hopkins, Roosevelt's closest adviser, that British and Dominion agreement had been reached in recent talks about civil aviation in London, and asked whether the Americans would now take part in negotiations about post-war arrangements. The Americans were not ready: there were difficulties in the State Department because of the sudden resignation of Under-Secretary of State Sumner Welles and there was apprehension about dealing with the British, especially if they were backed by a united Commonwealth. Furthermore, after the success of the recent Moscow Foreign Ministers Conference, Hopkins did not want to leave the Soviets out of things and so he told Beaverbrook that talks would have to wait.

In fact, as was reported by US Ambassador Winant in London and by the US Chargé d'Affaires in Canada, the Canadians had only attended the talks in London with great reluctance, and Beaverbrook's so-called agreement was only of the most tentative kind. This eased the tension in Washington, but the Americans knew that demands for aviation talks would not go away and that they needed to put their house in order if their ambitions for post-war aviation were to be realized.[19]

AMERICAN PREPARATIONS 1939–1943

Organizational problems of US aviation were not entirely solved by the reforms of 1938, and one of the more promising government arrangements, the Interdepartmental Committee, was abolished on the request of Chairman Moore because he thought

[18] CAB 65/33, WM35(43)3, 25 Feb. 1943. There were two Brabazon committees, the net result of which were proposals for various types of civilian aircraft, including jets. See Ch. 6.

[19] Hopkins Papers, box 336, folder: Air Conf. 2, Beaverbrook to Hopkins, 18 Oct. 1943 and Hopkins to Winant, 3 Nov. 1943; ibid., folder: Air Conference Book 9 Air Conference, Postwar Aviation, Hopkins to Beaverbrook, 27 Oct. 1943; 841.796/541, Winant to Hull, 27 Oct. 1943; 800.796/472, Clark to Hull, 25 Nov. 1943.

that it had now become redundant. Adolf A. Berle, who had wartime responsibility for aviation in the State Department, later bemoaned the lack of bureaucratic structure to cope with his brief. The CAA itself had an unsettled early life, and it was not until the creation of the CAB and the subsequent appointment of Welch Pogue as its Chairman in January 1942 that a sense of permanence and purpose were achieved.[20]

Both in terms of the US aviation industry and R. & D., worries were widespread. The President of the Air Transport Association, Edgar Gorrell, had complained in January 1938 that American aviation needed sound financing and governmental supervision, and although the Civil Aeronautics Act did much to meet those points, the financial situation of many airlines remained precarious: it was not until the coming of wartime service that they began really to prosper. Americans in 1938 also faced a new challenge from European R. & D., stimulated by the imminence of war. At the end of December 1938 J. S. Ames, Chairman of the National Advisory Committee for Aeronautics, expressed to the President his fear of America slipping behind the Europeans in the field of high-performance aircraft. Three months earlier a Special Committee on Future Research Facilities had been set up, but now Roosevelt pushed more energetically than ever in his support for the aviation industry and in 1939 pressed Congress for more funds. In fact, there was little work on new types of planes during the war, but US production capacity increased enormously, in order to churn out massive numbers of types which already existed, or were in an advanced stage of development when the war broke out, and this was initially fostered by large orders from Britain and France.[21]

With war on the horizon, a further matter for the US government was the role of civil airlines. In the inter-war period their military value had been widely acknowledged and that had been used by government to justify subsidies, but how were the

[20] B. B. Berle and T. B. Jacobs (eds.), *Navigating the Rapids 1918–71: From the Papers of A. A. Berle* (Harcourt Brace Jovanovich, New York, 1973), 81–2, Berle to Hull, 9 Sept. 1942; FDR OF 2955, box 2, folder: 1938, Moore to Roosevelt, 3 Oct. 1938.

[21] Ibid., box 249, folder: Aeronautics 1938 Jan.–June, Gorrell to Roosevelt, 6 Jan. 1938; ibid., box 3, folder: Aeronautics July–Dec. 1938, Ames to Roosevelt, 30 Dec. 1938; and see generally following folders on aeronautics.

airlines actually to be organized by the government? Thanks to the work of Gorrell, and co-operation from Brigadier-General D. H. Connally, Military Director of Civil Aviation, things went remarkably smoothly. The government contracted with the airlines and also bought planes from them and then leased them back, with payments made for wartime services under the overall direction of the Army Air Transport Command. The system worked well and maintained corporate structures—something that was important for later reversion to peacetime work.

PAA was treated on the same footing as other airlines after Pearl Harbor, but long before then the company was involved in covert activities. Mention has already been made of PAA's role in Africa, but there was also the so-called delousing of SCADTA, the Colombian airline secretly owned by PAA. The US government told Trippe to get rid of German personnel in the company, and with some difficulties he eventually complied. The most important service rendered by Trippe, however, was asked of him by Roosevelt in the summer of 1940. The proposal was that he build a large number of land and sea bases for planes in countries which were of strategic importance to the United States. Trippe hesitated: large profits were not in prospect; nevertheless, in the end he decided it would be politically prudent to undertake the project, given the recent criticism of PAA from both Congress and the administration.

Initially, PAA's position was strengthened because of the war, and for a while there was no further criticism of the kind which had worried Trippe in 1937–8. However, a decisive shift of policy was taking place which would eventually end both Trippe's monopoly of America's foreign routes and his private diplomacy, which had produced exclusive agreements with foreign governments. The change of policy was championed by Berle, Welch Pogue, General 'Hap' Arnold, Chief of the US Army Airforce, and ultimately by the President. Its aims were to bring other US airlines on to overseas routes and firmly establish sole authority for the government to negotiate foreign civil-aviation rights.

By 1943 the respite for PAA ended, as it became clear that the government was taking a firmer line against the idea of a single post-war chosen instrument. Berle was willing to promote US civil aviation in any way that would yield it advantage, but even his relatively conservative brand of liberalism soon led him to dismiss the idea of a private-company monopoly. Berle favoured more competition, but also more government regulation, particularly through an international organization that would internationalize technical aspects of civil aviation and oversee multilateral agreement about transit, technical-stop, and commercial rights. Along with General Arnold and Pogue, the State Department began to make it known publicly what they wanted, including the end of PAA's monopoly.[22]

In mid-1943 Arnold moved against PAA. He was determined to see post-war competition, and there was also an element of personal antagonism involved, because he had been in PAA before its take-over by Trippe. Arnold encouraged the formation of the Airlines Committee for US Air Policy in order to lobby Congress and ensure competition by a wider distribution of foreign routes. Of the big companies, only PAA and United Airlines (UA) stayed out of the group. Tactically, PAA was now on the defensive.

Trippe had high-level government contacts, including his son-in-law Edward Stettinius, a man inclined to support the ideas of Henry Luce about 'the American Century', but it was to Admiral Leahy that Trippe turned for help. On 1 July Leahy noted in his diary: 'Lunched alone with Mr. Trippe . . . who spent the lunch hour expressing an opinion that any internationalism of air routes and air facilities would practically destroy American commercial aviation because of our higher production and operation costs.' Trippe's attempt to enlist support from high government echelons had little effect in deflecting the direction of policy which was undermining PAA's position. In October, Welch Pogue announced that from then on the State Department and the CAB would negotiate civil-aviation agreements with foreign countries. The whole matter of international aviation was moving inexorably into the hands of government and away from PAA. The company still had a further card to play—the All American Flag Line Bill—but

[22] For more detail, see Daley, *American Saga*, ch. 39–41; L. C. Gardner, *Economic Aspects of New Deal Diplomacy* (Beacon Press, Boston, 1964), 270–5; Davies, *Airlines*, 266–9.

decisions which now moulded American policy were taken mainly as a result of interaction between the State Department, the Service Departments, the CAB, and the White House. By the end of 1943 PAA's inter-war role in determining much of American overseas aviation policy had been taken over by the US government.[23]

The consensus in government circles regarding PAA did not extend to wider policy. Between March 1943 and the convening of the Chicago Conference in November 1944, there were complex negotiations between the State and Service Departments, the CAB, and the White House as they strove to formulate US policy. Attitudes and ideas of the individuals and departments involved naturally developed and changed over that period, but it is perhaps as well to identify the main configuration of policies advocated by the participants before delving into the details of position papers and negotiations.

All parties involved advocated competition. This was not so much an article of free-enterprise faith as a conviction that it would most benefit and advance US aviation, providing the competition was primarily with foreign, and not between US, airlines.[24] Generally, there was also consensus that there should be an international multilateral agreement that all signatories extend to each other rights of innocent passage and technical stop. The most important differences concerned how commercial rights were to be acquired. The Army, the Navy, and, more importantly for the determination of policy, the CAB, took a more nationalistic line than the State Department and Roosevelt. Pogue wanted to use US strength to obtain commercial rights through bilateral negotiations. He was fearful that international agreements might undermine American supremacy in the air. In the autumn of 1943 he engaged the support of Harry Hopkins in the White House to try to counter what he saw as the naïve internationalist tendencies of Berle, who he believed was not dealing with the British firmly enough. However, as we shall see, Pogue's efforts ran against the wishes of Roosevelt, who, most strongly of all American senior officials, wanted inter-

[23] Sampson, *Empires*, 62; Leahy Papers, Diary 1 July 1943.

[24] Berle Papers, box 54, folder: Aviation International 1942–43, Berle memo, 24 March 1943.

national controls over technical matters and a multilateral agreement on transit, technical, and commercial rights.

When Berle was given the aviation brief in February 1941, he had to contend with PAA at home and with the British abroad–for whom it was well known that he had many criticisms regarding their imperialism. He also had such frustrating organizational problems that in September 1942 he suggested to Hull that aviation should be handled by someone else. He was so convinced of its importance for commerce, defence, and foreign policy that he felt it needed more attention.[25]

Despite misgivings, Berle retained the aviation brief, and early 1943 saw Hull giving the subject more priority. On 9 January he wrote to US Ambassador Winant in London asking for information on all British planning for civil aviation, and Livingston Satterthwaite at the Embassy became the world's first civil-air attaché. Meanwhile, Berle engaged the help of Welch Pogue and also organized an informal advisory group to help develop aviation policy. On 12 March 1943 Berle wrote to Roosevelt asking that the group be given official status. Roosevelt granted his request. The group, chaired by Berle, was known as the Interdepartmental Committee on International Aviation (IDCIA). It had a working subcommittee under the chairmanship of Pogue, and it was soon clear that this set-up would formulate much of US policy.[26]

On 2 March 1943 Pogue sent the first report from his subcommittee to Berle. One of its clearest and most forceful points was that the key to the problem of post-war aviation was Britain's control of bases. Pogue was uncertain how to proceed but felt that it was important to have early talks with the British, because somehow reciprocal rights had to be extracted from them and all members of their Commonwealth. Pogue wanted to use all the bargaining-assets America possessed in order to

[25] Berle, *Rapids*, 481, Berle to Hull, 9 Sept. 1942.

[26] 841.796/463, Hull to Winant, 9 Jan. 1943; Berle Papers, box 54, folder: Aviation International 1942–3, Berle to H. D. Smith, Director BOB, 2 Feb. 1943; FDR OF 2955, box 3, folder: Jan.–Mar. 1943, Berle to Roosevelt, 12 Mar. 1943, Roosevelt to BOB and reply 19 and 27 Mar. 1943, Roosevelt to Hull, 29 Mar. 1943; Beaverbrook Papers D/288, Halifax to Eden, 9 June 1943; for a continuous sequence of mins. of the IDCIA and of Pogue's subcommittee, see US National Archives RG 40, Secretary's Office, Department of Commerce, box 955, folder: 102517(4) and box 956.

promote its aviation interests, and part of the report suggested that overseas bases built by the United States during the war should be used for both peacetime civil aviation and in diplomatic talks about commercial rights; Lend-Lease Administrator Stettinius had pledged his help with this. Also, along with the military, Pogue recognized the potential of such bases for the United States in times of war or international crises. Already in 1943 ideas about integrating America's peacetime economy with her military establishment and needs were taking shape. Pogue's Committee, furthermore, sought to strengthen America's position by controlling sales of US aircraft to possible competitors, in order to help persuade them to America's point of view regarding post-war aviation.[27]

Berle summarized the report for the President. The Committee, he wrote, recommended rights of transit and technical stop, cabotage, limited rights to maintain service crews abroad, and a right to two commercial landings a week in foreign countries, with the possibility of negotiating more.[28]

Pogue wanted to promote American aviation vigorously, but his position was by no means the most nationalistic. Trippe for example believed

> that we [Americans] should keep ourselves free of any general commitments in favour of reciprocity, that we should seek landing rights without offering them, that we should handle requests for landing rights from countries that have granted them to us, on their merits, that in practice . . . we should successfully, and without jeopardising our own position abroad, find plausible reasons to deny most requests and keep our concessions to a minimum.[29]

Berle, however, even before being apprised of these views, had become anxious about America overplaying its hand. Not only did he disagree with Trippe, he also doubted the wisdom of Pogue's more moderate nationalism. Like Pogue, as he explained to Hull on 30 April, he thought: 'The heart of a general

[27] Berle Papers, box 54, folder: Aviation International 1942–43, Pogue to Berle, 2 Mar. 1943 and Berle to Stettinius, 7 Jan. 1943; D. J. Mrozek, 'The Truman Administration and the Enlistment of the Aviation Industry in Postwar Defence'. *Business History Review*, 48 (1974), 73–94.

[28] FDR OF 5288, Berle to Roosevelt, 12 Mar. 1943.

[29] Berle Papers, box 54, folder: Aviation International 1942–43, R. G. H. Jr. to Berle, 15 June 1943.

navigation agreement would have to rest on an agreement between the United States and the British Commonwealth of Nations.' But unlike Pogue, he favoured multilateral international agreement for the commercial as well as the technical side of aviation. In the spring of 1943 the differences between Berle and Pogue were not very obvious, but that changed as the months passed. Berle did not want to adopt such a combative stance as Pogue, not because he loved the British more than Pogue did, but because he feared them more: 'If we start a policy of exclusion, the British can exclude quite as well as we can.' Berle described to Hull the resentment which talk of the 'American Century' had aroused abroad and how it was affecting aviation matters. Countries were becoming fearful of postwar American dominance, including of aviation. In an attempt to overcome such problems, Berle's Committee advocated 'a generalised settlement of the problem of air navigation rights on an equitable basis'. It was largely because of these considerations that the United States did not allow the matter of their overseas bases to intrude directly into talks on civil aviation, and in any case, US advocacy of international rights to transit and technical stop diminished the need to seek those kinds of rights unilaterally. (The United States continued to acquire overseas military bases, but in the main this was kept separate from civil aviation.) The United States was also wary of denying foreigners the right to purchase US aeroplanes, for fear that this would backfire and increase foreign tendencies to become overly defensive regarding the overseas expansion of US aviation.[30]

On 19 June Pogue's Committee completed a series of further considerations and reached near unanimous agreement on a tentative list of heads of policy. Air sovereignty was to be upheld; there were to be the widest possible rights of transit, technical stop, and commercial entry, subject to the reservations of cabotage and the establishment of some no-go security areas; minimum rates were to be agreed; negotiations were to be conducted exclusively by governments; an international body was to have similar authority to the Paris Convention; and finally both the subcommittee and the full Committee recommended that PAA should lose its favoured-instrument status.[31]

[30] Ibid., Berle to Hull, 30 Apr., 1943.
[31] Ibid., Berle memo 'Main Heads of Policy', 19 June 1943.

Despite these promising developments, Berle was still unhappy and worried by the possibility of Britain pursuing an exclusionist policy. On 9 July he wrote to Hull referring to elements within the British government who favoured such a policy and explaining that, although they were a minority and had been temporarily held in check by the Halifax Agreement, he still felt that America should take an initiative with a view to starting talks on post-war aviation, and that therefore the President should be apprised of the situation. He felt that there were also domestic reasons for moving more energetically on aviation policy. In particular, PAA was trying to ingratiate itself with BOAC, in order to try to carve up the international market, and at the same time the US aircraft-manufacturers were forming a lobby which looked as if it would have the backing of the Luce Press. Berle felt that could further fuel foreign suspicion of American post-war commercial intentions. In the face of this overall picture, Berle promoted the idea of a multilateral approach, as a means of both solving international aviation problems and promoting America's best interests. He did not think that bilateral talks with the British would of themselves be 'too helpful' and he thought that four-power talks drawing in the Soviets and the Chinese would be impractical. He thus concluded that talks which drew in a number of countries and led eventually to a United Nations conference seemed 'to be the likeliest way of going at it'.[32]

In August there were important developments in civil aviation. Between 10 and 25 August Roosevelt and Churchill held council at Quebec. They were joined there on the 20 August by Hull, who had been briefed by Berle in a paper which expressed concern over America's state of unpreparedness and deep-seated suspicion of British policy. It stressed that the prospect of talks with Britain should be sustained because 'a policy of "grab"' would benefit her more than the United States. It advised that if the British proposed a cartel arrangement at Quebec involving BOAC and PAA, this should be countered and rejected by arguments concerning US security interests. And if the awkward question of the sale of US aircraft to Britain were raised, especially in connection with the Lyttleton Agree-

[32] Ibid., box 55, folder: Aviation June–July 1943, Berle to Hull, 9 July 1943.

ment, Hull should say this would be sympathetically considered, but add that Britain had already received over four hundred transport aircraft which could be converted for civilian use. Actually, as Berle well knew, those planes were recallable at will by the United States at the war's end under Lend-Lease legislation. Finally, although the Americans wanted to keep the prospect for talks open, they were not in a position to conduct them immediately, and therefore Hull should counter any such suggestion from the British by saying that the administration needed to consult with Congress first.[33]

Churchill and Roosevelt did talk about post-war aviation at Quebec, but the difficulties and dangers envisaged by Berle did not arise in any serious way. What did become clear to Roosevelt was the urgent need to develop American aviation policy, not least of all in order to allay possible foreign suspicions about American monopolistic intentions.

While Roosevelt's thinking clearly favoured a post-war regime that would require multilateral agreement from an international conference, Berle's Committee on International Aviation, building upon the recommendations made by the subcommittee in June, produced conflicting views in a report of 26 August. Elements of American self-interest were expressed that could really only be pursued at the expense of multilateral actions, which were also contemplated. In the main, the report followed the lines of policy laid out in June, but it gave more emphasis to internationalism by advocating universal rights of transit and technical stop and proposing that airports be operated by an international body. Simultaneously, it called for bilateral attempts to get commercial rights of entry to bases constructed by the United States overseas and also expressed grave concern about America's deteriorating bargaining-position. There was clearly a dilemma arising about how to pursue American commercial interests. Should it be done by bilateral or multilateral agreements? Or by both? If the latter, then might not pursuit of bilateral prejudice the chances of international agreement? One thing that emerged clearly from this was that members of the Committee were particularly concerned to reach a satisfactory

[33] Ibid., folder: Aviation Aug.–Dec. 1943, Berle to Hull, memo 'Quebec Trip: Aviation', 18 Aug. 1943.

accord with the British. 'Without British co-operation, we could be denied access to many of the most important centres and would find it difficult to construct any around-the-world air service under the American flag.'[34]

The need to extract commercial rights from the British disposed men like Pogue strongly to favour bilateral talks. Pogue did not want an international agreement to establish multilateral commercial rights, particularly in the light of the report, and he commented: 'We are beginning to lose our lead in transport airlines, organization, and experience without securing any countervailing increase in the availability of air rights.' Time was running out, or at least so it seemed; international agreement would be a long-drawn-out business, and in the meantime America's position would continue to deteriorate. Furthermore, Pogue feared that an international conference which resulted in a multilateral exchange of commercial rights would benefit the imperial powers, which could operate freely within their colonial territories without opening them to the United States. To Pogue, the best way of gaining access to Britain and her Commonwealth and Empire was through bilateral negotiations in which America's bargaining-strengths could be most effectively brought into play.

At Berle's request, P. T. David, the Secretary of Pogue's subcommittee, was asked to do further work on a number of issues which had arisen from the report of the full Committee. The papers did little to resolve the difficult question of commercial rights, but they again pin-pointed US bargaining-weaknesses regarding overseas landing-rights, suggesting that the United States would gain little if transit and technical stop were negotiated for in isolation. America needed to use leverage from other aspects of civil aviation, where she was strong, to gain what she needed. Alternatively, there was the possibility, which had gained currency in Washington, of calling for international agreement to extend rights of technical stop and transit to all parties to an agreement. This option looked even more attractive, as doubts were now being expressed about the pos-

[34] Hopkins Papers, box 336, folder: book 9 Air Conference, Postwar Aviation (31 pp.), 'International Civil Aviation', revised and adopted by IDCIA, 26 Aug. 1943, 31 Aug. 1943.

sibility of successfully calling for aviation rights in relation to bases that America had built abroad, though it was still thought that they could play a part in talks with the British government. The other key-factor involved in America's bargaining-strength was the sale of planes, and as a memorandum of 2 September noted, this would be 'entirely unobjectionable, assuming agreement has been reached on commercial air rights'. The Americans had no intention of allowing Britain to acquire equipment with which to compete with the United States until a satisfactory agreement had been reached on commercial rights. And this was the case with the more internationalist-minded, as well as with Pogue and the US military establishment.[35]

Pogue, clearly concerned by developments, wrote to Harry Hopkins on 22 September and put him in the picture. He also made recommendations on 'Two Overriding Issues': that PAA's monopoly had to be broken and a competitive system take over; and that as a minimum in the international field the United States had to get landing-and commercial rights from Britain and her territories and Dominions. Just over a month later, with Roosevelt now active in aviation matters, Pogue sent another memorandum to Hopkins, drawing attention to item 2.

> The privilege of our . . . operators to discharge and take on traffic abroad and of foreign operators to do the same here, should be arranged for between, or with the approval of the government concerned from time to time. We should base our own decision in each case upon the desirability of the route from our national point of view and not upon any automatic formula which might result in starting unjustifiable operations.[36]

The American service departments shared Pogue's preference for a discriminating form of bilateral reciprocity, but that kind of policy had received a setback on 1 October, when Roosevelt, in a press conference, made his first public statement on post-war

[35] Ibid., memo by P. T. David, 'Rights to Engage in Air Commerce' and 'Rights of Transit and Technical Stop', both 1 Sept. and memo 'Allocation of Transport Planes', 2 Sept. 1943.

[36] Hopkins Papers, box 336, folder: book 9 Air Conference, Postwar Aviation, Pogue to Hopkins, 'Recommendations on Two Overriding Issues in the International Aviation Field', 22 Sept. 1943; ibid., folder: Air Conference 1, Pogue to Hopkins, 22 Sept. 1943; and Pogue to Hopkins, 28 Oct. 1943 enclosing memo 'President's Policy Relative to Postwar Aviation'.

aviation. He referred to talks that he had had with Churchill and made some remarks about the general character of post-war civil aviation. As reported by the *New York Times*, the President seemed to be using the term 'free air' as analogous to 'freedom of the seas'. Roosevelt was not particularly specific, but the tone was more internationalist than that used even by Berle.

On 20 October Roosevelt wrote to Stettinius, now Under-Secretary of State, saying that he wished to discuss civil aviation with him and Hull 'before our policies are too extensively developed'. He regarded aviation as 'a matter of very great importance' and he wanted to be sure that 'we have a meeting of minds before any steps are initiated which might give other nations an improper notion as to what course this government is going to pursue'.[37] Like Berle, he was clearly concerned to reassure foreign governments that an 'American Century' approach would not be adopted by the United States. The President scheduled a meeting for early November in order to inform key people of his views on aviation policy. In preparation for that, on 10 November Hopkins sent a précis of a report from the War Department which, on the key issues of the means by which to obtain transit, technical-stop, and commercial rights, spoke in terms of reciprocity, not of an international agreement. Hopkins's summary did not actually specifically deal with obtaining commercial rights, though like Pogue and the service departments he was sceptical about the benefit of a multilateral agreement so far as American commercial interests were concerned. Roosevelt thought differently, and he made that abundantly clear during the meeting, which was attended by Robert Lovett, the Assistant Secretary of War for Air; Pogue, Stettinius; Berle; and Hopkins.[38]

'Reading from a memorandum which he said he had himself prepared', the President 'indicated the policy he wanted followed.' Much of what Roosevelt said reflected the consensus on many issues which had emerged from the IDCIA. For example, PAA's monopoly was to be ended (though interestingly this

[37] *New York Times*, 2 Oct. 1943; Hopkins Papers, box 336, folder: book 9 Air Conference, Postwar Aviation, Roosevelt to Stettinius, 20 Oct. 1943.

[38] Ibid., Lovett to Hopkins, 3 Nov. 1943 enclosing War Department memo on 'Postwar Civil Aviation', and Hopkins to Roosevelt, 10 Nov. 1943 enclosing a summary of it.

was only mentioned after Stettinius had left the meeting), Germany and Japan were to be denied aviation industries, subsidies were to be regarded as a necessary expedient on routes only for as long as they remained unprofitable, each state should run its own airlines, and the United States should seek continued use of overseas bases she had constructed. On the question of procedure, Roosevelt wanted talks with the British to lead to a UN conference. But it was on the key question of gaining aviation rights from other countries that Roosevelt's position was most important, because he came down firmly and unambiguously on the side of multilateral agreement for commercial rights.

> As to air and landing rights, the President said that he wanted a very free interchange. That is, he wanted arrangements by which planes of one country could enter any other country for the purpose of discharging traffic of foreign origin and accepting foreign bound traffic.[39]

Within days, Pogue wrote to Hopkins saying that he had been a little confused during the meeting by what Roosevelt had said but that he wanted to make it clear that neither he nor his subcommittee favoured the automatic granting of rights to pick up and put down passengers, as suggested by the President.[40] Nevertheless, US policy developed in just that direction.

ANGLO-AMERICAN TALKS AND STALEMATE AT CHICAGO

Undeterred by the delay on the American side, Beaverbrook suggested in Cabinet on 27 October 1943 that he and Leathers should go to the United States for talks. He wanted to achieve a more favourable deal for British aviation in the Atlantic than that negotiated before the war, and secure British interests in the Mediterranean and Africa by making major concessions to the Americans in Latin America. The idea of regional arrangements was once again coming to the fore, and in fact it was pursued

[39] 800.796/495 memo of conversation by Berle, 11 Nov. 1943; C. Solberg, *Conquest of the Skies: A History of Commercial Aviation* (Little, Brown, and Co., Boston, 1979), 286–7.

[40] Hopkins Papers, box 336, folder: Air Conference 1, Pogue to Hopkins, 21 Nov. 1943.

independently with Trippe by BOAC, but neither company was now influential enough to impose such arrangements upon their respective governments, and nothing materialized.[41]

Beaverbrook's trip to the United States did not take place either, at least not until July 1944. Instead, Americans came to London. Despite some conciliatory remarks by Beaverbrook in the Lords on 19 January, Berle still thought that there would 'be quite a battle' between Britain and the United States. On 3 February he told Hull:

> It is plain that the British, if talks are not forthcoming pretty soon, will proceed on the theory that we are going to play a lone hand. Included in their plans are the organization of a European air bloc by BOAC; the setting up of a Portuguese holding company to cover Mediterranean and African routes and the purchase of local South American lines by British steamship companies.
>
> I suggest the President name his negotiating group immediately.[42]

As a result of this, Berle and Edward Warner of the CAB were authorized to go discreetly to London. They went via Canada, where they had brief talks about aviation and experienced few difficulties regarding technical matters, but major ones on commercial topics. In London the story was similar. Some things were agreed without great difficulty. Both sides wanted to uphold national air-sovereignty and define cabotage in such a way that the United States could keep control over Hawaii and other possessions in the Pacific and Caribbean, and Britain over her colonial possessions, but it was agreed that cabotage should not extend to self-governing Dominions. Over technical matters, the Americans agreed to international controls, which was seen as an important advance by the British. However, over bases and commercial controls, things were more difficult.

Berle sought a system of unrestricted competition, wanted to tie transit rights to commercial arrangements, and suggested that the United States be granted access to bases that they had financed in a way which Beaverbrook later told the Cabinet would have deprived the British of control over those on British territory. British counter-arguments forced a postponement of

[41] CAB 65/36, 146(43)3, 27 Oct. 1943; Berle, *Rapids*, 487–8, 23 June 1944.

[42] Ibid., 484–5, 2 Feb. 1944; Berle Papers, box 55, folder: Aviation 1944, Berle to Hull, 3 Feb. 1944, and extract from Beaverbrook's 19 Jan. speech in the Lords.

the matter of bases until an international conference could be called, and Beaverbrook successfully directed the discussion of commercial rights to draft proposals by Canada, but deadlock soon ensued.

The British wanted a system which would match traffic with transport capacity, arrange equitable participation for states, and control subsidies. The Americans agreed with the first aim, thought the third was acceptable in principle but would be difficult to achieve in practice, and thought that the second aim involved an undesirable level of control.

> . . . the United States felt that the wings of its aviation might be clipped if it agreed to the economic control proposed by the British. This gave rise to British statements that the United States was as backward in its conception of international organisations as the British were in commercial aviation.[43]

The British wanted a powerful international body that would control the industry; the Americans wanted it to be purely advisory and consultative. The British wanted to establish quotas which would determine the frequency of a country's services on the basis of the origin of traffic, irrespective of its nationality, which was interpreted by Berle to mean that there would be a fifty-fifty division of traffic between Britain and the United States on the Atlantic route. This was not acceptable to him.

> So far as the United States was concerned this would . . . subject twenty-five years of American development of international aviation, which had been invented, pioneered, developed, and defended by the United States, to the unrestricted rule of an . . . undetermined international body, upon unstated standards.[44]

At issue was the fact that before the war 80 per cent of all inter-oceanic civil aviation had been American. Berle did not imagine that the United States would be able to maintain that percentage after the war, but on the other hand he was not willing to see it dramatically pared down by an international organization. The simple fact was that British and American policies on the commercial side of aviation were totally at odds with each other.

[43] 841.796/6–0345. 'Summary of Developments', 3 June 1945.

[44] Berle Papers, box 63, folder: London Air Conversations, 'Report on Air Conversations', 19 Apr. 1944 (dates are given incorrectly in the report as 10–13 Apr.).

However, while Beaverbrook would have been prepared to countenance impasse with the United States, Churchill at this point was not. The Prime Minister had talks with Berle which reassured the American that an acceptable agreement was possible, and he also pressed Beaverbrook to compromise. As a result, differences were papered over by accepting an ambiguous report, drawn up by Balfour at the time of the Empire discussions on aviation the previous October, as a basis for future talks, on the understanding that it be treated flexibly in the give and take of negotiations.

The American report of the talks commented on this compromise: 'within the wording of the Balfour document, an international body could be set up and might be assigned functions similar to those which corresponded to the present views of the Government of the United States'. And furthermore it went on to add that: 'Especial note was made of the fact that the Balfour report did not, as did the Canadian document, assign by its terms power to the international body.'

More concrete agreement was reached about a suggestion from Berle that the Halifax Agreement be reaffirmed. The matter of acquiring foreign routes was still worrying the Americans, especially as the British seemed to be making progress, whilst at the same time using their influence to block the advancement of US airlines. The trump card that the Americans always held in relation to such matters was their control over the supply of suitable aircraft, but in London Beaverbrook managed to extract a commitment from Berle that the United States would make modern transports available to the British.

On 7 April a joint statement was issued. It stated that sufficient agreement had been reached, particularly on technical matters, to enable them to look to an international conference, though before then, the Soviets would have to be consulted.

British reaction to the talks was good, on the whole. The Cabinet was a little concerned about making the Balfour Report the basis of future talks, because, as the Chancellor of the Exchequer, Sir John Anderson, and Sinclair pointed out, it was subject to differing interpretations. But in the end Anderson 'expressed himself as entirely satisfied with [Beaverbrook's] explanation, on the understanding that we should interpret the provision of the Balfour Report as covering the international regulation of rates and frequencies, and that our representatives would attend the conference on this basis'. According to the American report of the talks, this was precisely what the British were not to do if agreement were to be possible. The April talks, far from solving problems, had only fudged the line of disagreement by an ambiguous compromise which created problems for the future.[45]

In the United States the response to the talks was complicated by American perceptions of the way British policy seemed to be developing. Throughout the spring and summer Berle was troubled by a series of incidents that indicated that the British were continuing to improve their position, often at the expense of America's, for operating post-war aviation. They included: an agreement between Air Chief Marshal Tedder and General Eisenhower which enabled Britain to use spare capacity on BOAC flights for commercial purposes; moves by BOAC and PAA to establish cartel-type arrangements; British political influence being used in Portugal, the Middle East, and Africa to obstruct the advancement of US civil aviation; and Anglo-Soviet talks for landing-rights in which the British had used Lend-Lease planes as part of the quid pro quo involved.

Berle, angered by these developments and no doubt regretting his 'commitment' to Beaverbrook about making US planes available to Britain, wrote to Lovett in May pointing out that the British intended to assign C-54 transports (the military version of the DC-4) for operation in BOAC. Lovett's reply was most gratifying: 'I believe I can assure you that the army is in no position to release any C-54 or Constellation aircraft to any United Nations in 1944, and it is doubtful if any will be available in the first six months of 1945.'[46]

[45] Ibid., box 63, folder: London Air Conversations, 'Report on Air Conversations', 19 Apr. 1944 (dates are given incorrectly in the report as 10–13 April); ibid., box 55, folder: Aviation 1944, Berle to Roosevelt, 19 May 1944; Beaverbrook Papers D/238, CAT mins., 6 Apr. 1944. The British were surprised at what Berle appeared to accept, but on 21 Apr. he made clear that it did not include international regulation; ibid., mins. by Masefield, 20 Apr., and Berle to Beaverbrook 21 Apr., CAB 65/42, 46(44), 7 Apr. 1944; Berle, *Rapids*, editorial comment 486, 497, 9 Oct. 1944.

[46] 841.796/612, /613 and /6–0345, R. G. H. Jr. to Berle, 18 Apr. 1944, Lovett to Berle, 24 May 1944, and 'Summary of Developments', 3 June 1945 respectively; Beaverbrook Papers D/289, Berle to Beaverbrook, 23 Aug. 1944; Berle, *Rapids*, 487–8, 23 June 1944 and 489–90, memo 30 June 1944.

Berle and other Americans were worried by British actions which seemed to be at odds both with Churchill's professed desire for an amicable accommodation with the United States and even with those of the charming, though more contentious, Beaverbrook. Suspicious of British policy, Hull decided it was better not to have a firm commitment to supply planes to Britain. The commitment made by Berle in April turned out not to have been a commitment after all. In May 'Hull formally assured the Senate that Mr Berle during his recent discussions with Lord Beaverbrook had made no commitments. The discussions were purely exploratory.'[47]

It was not only about supplying Britain with aircraft that Berle and other Americans began to have second thoughts. Organizational problems in the State Department caused by Welles's resignation, reluctance to move forward without the Soviet Union (they were engaged in talks in 1944), a continuing political shift towards business conservatism, Congressional discussion of post-war civil aviation, divergent views within government about the best way to proceed, and the forthcoming presidential election all contributed to an air of uncertainty and prolonged the development of US aviation policy. Was it really wise to proceed quickly to an international conference? Should a series of bilaterally negotiated reciprocal agreements be resorted to instead? In particular, the position of the Congress complicated things, because on 20 March 1944 Senator McCarran introduced the All American Flag Line Bill, which was an attempt to keep PAA's monopoly in practice while dispensing with it in theory. These developments all added to the complexity of America's evolving aviation policy, but the administration was reluctant to delay, any more than was unavoidable, further developments at the international level.

The British were certainly keen to move matters along, and in July Beaverbrook and Richard Law, Minister of State at the Foreign Office, went to the United States to discuss aviation. It is clear from his own account that Berle was somewhat bedazzled by Beaverbrook. But Berle would not commit himself to what the British wanted, despite their intimations that they would moderate their demands after making an initial play for a

[47] 841.796/637, Winant to Hull, 31 May 1944.

strong international authority at a conference. Berle was now concerned not so much with an early conference as with preventing the British from strengthening their position in the meantime—possibly by the use of discriminatory and exclusive agreements. This was why he had raised the Halifax Agreement in April, given that, on one interpretation, it came to an end once Britain and America engaged in aviation talks. He now pressed again for further agreement, and as a result at the end of August the British Embassy in Washington and the State Department began the process of exchanging draft notes to extend the Halifax Agreement. He also suggested that the two countries should begin to 'move out' on to foreign routes in an orderly way. Beaverbrook initially appears to have agreed to this suggestion, but later either changed his mind or was overruled by Cabinet colleagues.[48]

Once back in London, Beaverbrook suggested to Berle that, instead of beginning a move out, the United States should call a conference immediately, and if political difficulties prevented it from doing so (the presidential election was in November), he would understand, and Britain would do the honours instead by calling a conference in London. Neither side really trusted the other. The British were unhappy about a co-ordinated move out, because they wanted an international authority to allocate routes and determine commercial rights. Ironically, important figures in the United States were also unhappy about a co-ordinated move out, because they thought that they would lose out to the British if such a procedure were followed.[49]

On 1 September the British Cabinet considered civil aviation at length. Back in June Beaverbrook had proposed a more powerful set-up for it. In particular, it needed to be liberated from being constantly overshadowed by the RAF and military considerations, but Churchill decided that institutionally things should remain as they were until the end of the war, when civil

[48] 841.796/7–1944, memo of conversation, Wing Commander Dahl and Morgan, sent to Berle, 19 July 1944; Berle, *Rapids*, 491–95, memos 21 and 29–30 July 1944 respectively; Beaverbrook Papers D/289, Halifax to Foreign Office, 13 Aug. 1944, Foreign Office to Washington, 16 Aug. 1944; Taylor, *Beaverbrook*, 556–7.

[49] Beaverbrook Papers D/289, Masefield Notes on American Attitude 18 Aug. 1944 and Masefield memo 23 Aug. 1944; Berle Papers, box 55, folder: Aviation—1944, Beaverbrook to Berle, 29 Aug. 1944.

aviation would then be moved from the Air Ministry to the Ministry of Transport. In the meantime, however, in order to enhance its status, there would be an Under-Secretary of State at the Air Ministry whose sole brief would be civil aviation. The Cabinet also decided that because of civil aviation's great importance, something rather drastic would have to be done about acquiring suitable aircraft. It therefore agreed that resources would have to be shifted from war production to meet this need. This was a very sensitive and potentially controversial matter, as the British were at this time in the throes of arguing with the Americans for large amounts of Lend-Lease for after Germany's defeat. In order to disguise the switch from military to civilian production, it was decided that the new planes should be described as transports, not as civil airliners. Both institutional reorganization and production of civil aircraft were significant matters, but it was Beaverbrook's contribution to the meeting that was of the most immediate importance.

Beaverbrook told the Cabinet that Berle had abandoned the idea of an international conference and instead had proposed an orderly 'move-out' by Britain and America. Beaverbrook appears to have been unduly certain about Berle's position. The 'move out' procedure was described by Berle as only an interim measure, until a conference could be called. Berle may have been evasive about when a conference could take place, but there appears to be no evidence that he had abandoned the idea. However, it was unlikely that the Americans would agree to an immediate conference and it seems that, knowing that, Beaverbrook tried to set things up for a break with them on aviation policy. If they would not hold a conference on British terms, with the prospect of a strong international authority emerging from it, then Britain needed to pursue her own self-interest in a different way. Beaverbrook told the Cabinet that he had simply offered to call a conference in London and that he did not think that the Americans would be agreeable to that. He did not say that he had offered to do this only if the Americans were unable to call a conference. Could this have been because if he had told them that, it would not have been entirely compatible with his claim that Berle had given up on the idea of a conference altogether? Whatever the case was, Beaverbrook, after saying that the Americans were unlikely to attend a conference, stated that: 'Unless we took drastic action we should be left behind. He saw no alternative now to our going forward with development of airlines on our own, working in agreement with the United States so far as we could and making every effort to build up our own aircraft manufacturing industry.'

Amery agreed with this, as did Sinclair, though the latter also favoured pursuing an international agreement for technical matters. Bevin, however, was troubled by this turn of events. He remarked that internationalism was important for his party and suggested that they should seek to discover whether Berle's view (as reported by Beaverbrook) was the decided view of the US administration. The Cabinet accepted Bevin's point, and it was decided that Churchill should write to Roosevelt to elucidate matters. In fact, advice was already being given and decisions taken in the United States which would have surprised, and indeed later did surprise, the Cabinet, especially after what Beaverbrook had said.[50]

On 25 August Berle called together those involved in US aviation policy in order to try to finalize things. He commented in his diary: 'We can either try to shoot the whole idea with an international conference; or try to make interim arrangements. Either will be difficult.' Pogue was unhappy with the meeting and wrote to Hopkins expressing his frustration with present policy. In particular, regarding the orderly 'move out' he said: 'I don't think the British will agree to proceeding in any such manner because of the possibility of buttoning things up themselves behind the curtain if they can get us to wait.' He continued:

> I am convinced . . . that the American public would be horrified at the idea of our marking time because the British wanted us to or of even agreeing to keeping them informed of everything we are doing in the international air field. That just sounds very inept to me politically.
>
> I strongly urge you to stay firmly in this air picture. Rapid progress is absolutely indispensable now; our bargaining position deteriorates day by day.[51]

It was at this stage in developments that Berle received Beaverbrook's letter calling for an immediate conference. Two

[50] CAB 65/43, 114(44)1,2,3, and 4, 1 Sept. 1944.

[51] Berle, *Rapids*, 496, 25 Aug. 1944; Hopkins Papers, box 335, folder: Air Conference 2, Pogue to Hopkins 26 Aug 1944.

days later, on 31 August, he submitted a memorandum to Hull which he said he hoped would be accepted as IDCIA's recommendations on policy. The memorandum was essentially a summary of what had transpired so far, but it is of particular interest on three counts. Firstly, it disclosed the continuing conflict in the United States between a policy of bilateral negotiation for commercial rights, which, up to then, had been the public position adopted by the United States, and Roosevelt's preference 'to open designated ports freely to all comers in return for like rights elsewhere'. This was a policy which Berle himself inclined to: he thought it 'would probably be healthier'. And over the following weeks variations of this, with the backing of Roosevelt, finally became the stated policy of the United States.

Secondly, the recommendation that Berle made, and his reasons for doing so, are also significant. Berle explained that British policy was to try to get countries to refrain from acquiring landing-rights until an international conference were convened which would then, through the exercise of authority conferred upon it, allocate routes and landing-rights in what the British described as an equitable way. The United States had always opposed this and in July suggested an orderly 'move out'. Beaverbrook having now rejected that and proposed an immediate conference, Berle thought that there were two alternatives:

(1) To proceed to call an international air conference at once;
(2) To inform the British courteously that we have to act, and go ahead on our own. We should probably get the air rights, since I do not think many countries are in a position to tell us that we are to be excluded. But it will precipitate at once a competitive air race between Britain and the United States on a violent scale, which, of course, we should like to avoid.

Of the alternatives, it seems to me that the calling of a prompt international conference is preferable. This is in line with our steady intention.[52]

Furthermore, as Berle had indicated earlier in the paper, if an air battle with Britain did occur, she would have the upper hand in Europe, the Middle East, and Africa, and in the whole Empire

[52] Berle Papers, box 55, folder: Aviation 1944, Berle to Hull, 31 Aug. 1944.

except Canada. So Berle preferred an international conference, but, and this is the third point of interest, he also wanted to pursue bilateral agreements at the conference, in order to gain immediate access to the world's air commerce, though eventually such agreements would be superseded by international ones.

Pogue, and the Secretary of Commerce, Jesse Jones—a rough-hewn and pugnacious Texan—under whose suzerainty the CAB officially operated, both disagreed with Berle. On 6 September Jones forwarded a memorandum by Pogue to Roosevelt, and the general sentiments it expressed were: opposition both to any delay involving an international conference before advancing American aviation interests and to British ideas for a strong international authority which would assign routes and determine commercial rights. Regarding the latter, they feared that imperial powers would enjoy an advantage because of their automatic ability to service empire routes without having to obtain rights from the international body. As an alternative, Pogue wanted to negotiate with Britain directly and immediately, in order to secure aviation rights from her, her Empire, and her Dominions which would meet the specifications for US international routes laid down by the CAB on 14 June 1944. Pogue and Jones wanted to extract full co-operation from the British and proposed that Roosevelt should contact Churchill, with a view to getting him to convert the opposition in Britain to support for bilateralism. Unfortunately for them, Roosevelt was more internationalist even than Berle, and although there was an intention to engage in bilateral talks at an international conference, such talks were not to be a substitute for multilateral agreement. Consequently, on 9 September Berle wrote to Beaverbrook that the President had agreed to convene a conference in the United States on or around 1 November. The scene was almost set for Chicago.[53]

Between August and November there were two important developments which affected the British position at Chicago. Firstly, Beaverbrook relinquished his aviation brief, somewhat disillusioned because he had hoped to bring matters to a speedy

[53] Ibid., Berle to Beaverbrook, 9 Sept. 1944; FDR MR, box 162, folder: 5 sect. A4-2-Air Routes, Jones to Roosevelt, enclosing memo by Pogue, 7 Sept. 1944.

and satisfactory conclusion. He was replaced by Lord Swinton, who took up the new post in the Air Ministry reserved for civil aviation and in effect became its first Minister. He had been in the Air Ministry before the war, but the Cadman Report had made his tenure difficult and he had been replaced by Kingsley Wood. Swinton was a hard-working and able man, but also a protectionist, whose views were even more at odds with Berle's than Beaverbrook's. Secondly, in October the British government published a White Paper on aviation the crux of which reaffirmed the principles the British had followed in the April 1944 talks. There was to be national air-sovereignty and four freedoms—or privileges as the British preferred to call them: of transit; of technical stop; the right to pick up cargo and passengers from the country of origin and disembark them at a foreign stop; and the right to pick up passengers and cargo from a foreign destination and carry them to the aircraft's country of origin. However, these rights were to be subject to controls by an international authority. Regarding fifth-freedom rights, the paper observed that: 'The right to pick up and set down traffic to and from destinations which are not in the country of origin of the aircraft [and the right to engage in the cabotage of another country] would be a matter for negotiation.'[54]

Swinton wanted an international authority to allocate quotas and control frequencies in relation to the traffic generated by a country; this was in preference to the American idea of competition from a point determined by initial levels of carriage, which, as Swinton wryly observed, would give them a 'flying start'. The Americans had the planes to compete, other countries did not. If the Americans rejected international control, then Britain could proceed to form a convention itself, but Swinton was against this, preferring instead to embark upon a series of bilateral negotiations in which Britain and the Dominions would act as one. He observed: 'Bi-lateral negotiations over services and landing rights will afford the one opportunity of securing the reciprocal facilities which we and the dominions want from

[54] Berle, *Rapids*, 497, memo 9 Oct. 1944; Cmd. 6561, Oct. 1944. 'International Air Transport'; for Chicago Conference, as well as primary sources I have drawn on: Berle, *Rapids*; Viscount Swinton, *I Remember* (Hutchinson, London, 1946); Miller, 'Air Diplomacy'; H. Stannard, 'Civil Aviation: A Historical Survey', *International Affairs*, 21 (1945), 497–511; 'After Chicago: Imperial Interests in Civil Aviation', *Round Table*, 138 (1945), 130–6.

the United States, e.g. facilities on US airfields in the Pacific.' Swinton wanted to achieve rights of transit and technical stop, but he wanted to link them to a comprehensive agreement because of bargaining-considerations: the British were in a strong position regarding transit and technical stop but weak elsewhere; the American position was exactly the reverse of this, but it had led them to the same tactic of linking weak to strong bargaining-positions in April 1944.[55]

Swinton flew to Chicago via Montreal in order to talk with Dominion representatives beforehand. The atmosphere was cordial but an agreed British and Dominion view did not emerge. The Canadians, in the spring of 1944, had published a plan for post-war civil aviation which held the ground between the British and US positions. The Canadians continued to push that plan not only because they believed in it but also to try to avoid a serious rift between Britain and the United States, with both of whom it was important to keep on good terms. The New Zealand and Australian delegations, in contrast, favoured a truly international organization to operate routes. Given these and American views, Swinton arrived in Chicago knowing that things would be tough: he was not disappointed.

He took the slightly unusual, but understandable, measure, given his short time as Civil Aviation Minister, of requesting that a committee be set up in London to advise him. This was duly done and it brought Beaverbrook back on to the scene as its chairman. This committee as a whole, and in particular Beaverbrook and Cripps, both of whom were anti-American, played a major part in determining British policy. There are conflicting views as to just how well the British set-up for the Chicago Conference worked, but given their vulnerability to American pressure, one could say that a surprisingly effective rearguard action to defend British aviation interests was conducted.[56]

On 27 October Roosevelt appointed Berle to lead the US delegation and to chair the Chicago Conference. The Conference began on an inauspicious note in November, with Berle and Swinton taking an immediate dislike to each other and such

[55] CAB 66/56, WP(44)592 and 593, Swinton memos 25 Oct. 1944.

[56] CAB 65/44, 148(44)3, 8 Nov. 1944; for conflicting views, see J. A. Cross, *Lord Swinton* (OUP, Oxford, 1982), Miller, *Diplomacy*, and Berle, *Rapids*.

sentiments being strengthened as the Conference progressed. Over lunch on 1 November Swinton said that he was not prepared to discuss routes, but only the principles of an international convention to control aviation in an equitable way. Berle responded that this 'came down to a request by Britain to us to assign part of American traffic to support British aviation, and I thought it was as impossible now as when it was broached last spring'.[57]

This early exchange reinforced Berle's conviction about the wisdom of negotiating bilateral agreements which would create a fall-back position if the conference did not achieve its multilateral objective. Bilateral agreements would also bring pressure to bear on the British government with the prospect of US planes by-passing its territory.

Despite the unpromising start, the Conference made progress. On the second day it was clear for all to see that Britain and its Dominions were not united on policy and that many countries besides the United States had serious reservations about the British proposals. Swinton began to give ground. He conceded that any convention would have consultative powers only in its early days, soon began to refer to the October White Paper as only a view expressed by the British government, and in the light of other countries making progress on routes with the United States, he declared that he was prepared to do likewise. On 6 November Berle believed that: 'The major issues have been met and cracked.'[58]

There was little problem with the first two freedoms, though Swinton did not want to grant them in isolation from a satisfactory general agreement—if he did, then Britain would lose one of her most powerful bargaining-chips. It was in relation to commercial rights that difficulties arose in acute form. Britain's demand for an equitable distribution of frequencies by an international authority and America's for a free competitive system appeared irreconcilable. Then both sides made concessions on the basis of provisions taken from the Canadian plan—though the British delegation did so contrary to the wishes of the Cabinet. Nevertheless, this permitted a significant breakthrough: America

[57] Berle, *Rapids*, 498–9, 1 Nov. 1944.
[58] Ibid., 500–1, 6 Nov. 1944.

agreed to an equal division of traffic quotas with Britain, on the understanding that if an operator consistently flew at 65 per cent capacity, then he could increase his frequency of flights. This was known as 'the escalator'. That appeared to resolve the difficulties over third and fourth freedoms, but problems with the fifth remained. The Americans felt that if they were prevented from picking up intermediate traffic on long routes, and particularly on their much-hoped-for around-the-world route, they would not be commercially viable. The following example illustrates this predicament. Under third-freedom rights, on a New York–London–Paris route PAA could only take on passengers in New York, and under fourth-freedom rights only in Paris for the return flight. What the Americans wanted was intermediate or fifth-freedom rights to pick traffic up in London on both outward and inward flights. This was opposed by the British, but on 17 November a compromise seemed to be in sight. The British were prepared to accept the fifth-freedom on the condition that it be restricted by higher fares than those charged by local operators. The British believed that this would protect their gateway to Europe and the Empire from being dominated by US carriers. For a time it looked as if the Americans had agreed to this, but on 18 November it transpired that this was not so.

They then said that they had intended all along that there should be a fifth-freedom escalator. To the British this meant that there would be no effective restrictions on the number of American planes on any routes. For example, on a New York–London–Paris route, if there were twice the number of passengers offering for the London–Paris leg of the route, then the fifth-freedom escalator would justify doubling the frequency on the whole route, not just between London and Paris. Under no circumstances could the British allow such an untrammelled right. The result was the deadlock of the Conference and the introduction of heavy political artillery.[59]

Roosevelt opened correspondence on aviation matters with Churchill on 21 November. His letter, drafted by Hopkins (and

[59] Ibid., 501–5, 18 and 26 Nov. 1944; Beaverbrook Papers D/247, Special Air Committee Minutes, especially 9 and 30 Nov. and 1 Dec. 1944; ibid., Dominions Office to S. Rhodesia explaining controls on 5th freedom had to include right to withdraw and price differential for local operators.

amended by the State Department) explained that the President did not want the Conference to fail and made it clear that it was down to the British to change their stance. Referring to concessions made to Swinton regarding controls he said:

> This is as far as I can go. In addition [to the controls agreed], your people are now asking limitations on the number of planes between points regardless of the traffic offering. This seems to me a form of strangulation. It has been a cardinal point in [US] policy throughout that the ultimate judge should be the passenger and the shipper. The limitations now proposed would, I fear, place a dead hand on the use of the great air trade routes.[60]

In London the response to this was prepared by Beaverbrook's committee. It was temperate but absolutely firm in its refusal to give ground on the proposed fifth-freedom escalator. The British government had made great concessions already. It had agreed to open its bases all round the world to foreign airlines and was prepared to accept fifth-freedom rights provided local traffic was protected by a price differential. But the new American proposals, wrote Churchill, 'we could not accept, since they demand a share of the local traffic between two neighbouring countries by the aircraft of a third country far beyond that which the granting of the right to take up traffic on through service would warrant'. He suggested that if the British understanding of the 17 November proposals could not now be accepted, then they should seek to formalize agreement reached on technical matters and postpone the disputed issues to a later date.[61] This letter was not well received in Washington, where suspicions were aroused that the British, unable to achieve the controls that they wanted, were now seeking to delay the inception of international aviation until they had modern planes.

In fact, lack of competitive airliners was just one of many British worries about the transition to peacetime economic activity. Transitional problems had been discussed two months earlier at the Second Quebec Conference, at which Roosevelt and his Treasury Secretary, Henry Morgenthau, contrary to the

[60] CAB 66/56, WP(44)680, memo by Cripps, 22 Nov. 1944; Kimball, *Correspondence*, iii, 402–3, Roosevelt to Churchill, 21 Nov. 1944.

[61] Ibid., 404–5, Churchill to Roosevelt, 22 Nov. 1944; CAB 65/44, 153(44)2, 22 Nov. 1944.

wishes of the rest of the American Cabinet, had made generous and helpful arrangements regarding the supply of Lend-Lease to Britain for after the defeat of Germany. They had done so partly because they wished to get Churchill's agreement to Morgenthau's extremely harsh plan for pacifying post-war Germany, and partly because of a desperate plea for help by Churchill. However, once back in Washington, they were put under immense pressure from various departments to renege on the Lend-Lease commitments. Some believed that Roosevelt had exceeded the authority granted to him under the Lend-Lease legislation, others that it was unwise to afford Britain the possibility of greater economic independence before being sure that she would co-operate with the United States. Hull, in particular, opposed pledging large amounts of supplies, unless the British gave an unequivocal commitment to help craft a liberal post-war world-economy. As a result of all this (and the abandonment of Morgenthau's plan because of public and Cabinet pressures), the United States was already retreating from its Quebec commitments and was considering the possibility of using the carrot of other forms of aid and the stick of offering not to diminish Lend-Lease supplies further as means for moving the recalcitrant British to accept US policies.[62]

On 23 November Navy Secretary James Forrestal, referring to Lend-Lease and aviation policy, told Hopkins that he did not 'see that we would be doing anything more than acting in the national interest if we used the one negotiation to facilitate the progress of the other'. Hopkins and the State Department agreed: in a letter drafted for Roosevelt to send to Churchill, they ignored all the points raised in his letter of 22 November in favour of exerting outright pressure.

> We are doing our best to meet your Lend-Lease needs. [Three days earlier the President had decided that in the Washington talks to implement the 'Quebec Agreement' on Lend-Lease no formal commitments whatsoever should be given to the British.] We will face Congress on that subject in a few weeks and it will not be in a generous mood if it and the people feel that the United Kingdom has not agreed to a generally beneficial agreement.[63]

[62] Dobson, *Wartime Aid*, or Dobson, *Economic Special Relationship*, 65–74.

[63] W. Millis (ed.), *The Forrestal Diaries* (Viking, New York, 1951), 19, 23 Nov. 1944; Kimball, *Correspondence*, iii, 407–8, Roosevelt to Churchill, 24 Nov. 1944.

This letter was delivered to Churchill personally by Winant, so that he could add his own persuasiveness to that of the President. But these communications from the Americans angered the British: one of Churchill's personal secretaries described the letter as 'pure blackmail'. The aviation hoop was only one of many that the British were asked to jump through in order to be eligible for Lend-Lease and other forms of aid, but at this point the British would not comply.[64]

While the temperature of the dialogue between the leaders rose, the situation in Chicago continued to deteriorate. The Americans suspected that the British intended to compensate for the lack of fifth-freedom rights by using political influence to negotiate bilaterally for intermediate traffic in order to make BOAC's long-haul routes commercially viable. This was offensive not only to Americans, but to other countries as well. On 27 November the reception given to further British proposals made it clear to the Americans that many believed them to be overly restrictive. Encouraged by this, Berle urged acceptance on the following day of a simple plan: acceptance of the five freedoms, along with a purely advisory international authority. But he had overplayed his hand. The conferees were just as unhappy about such a free-for-all as they were about Britain's controlled system. Berle observed: 'the result was a session not very satisfactory from our point of view'. In the light of this continuing deadlock and Swinton's refusal to accept Canadian attempts at compromise, Berle began to think that there was nothing left to do but accept a British suggestion that decision on the issues in dispute be postponed and handed over to an interim aviation-council which the Conference intended to establish. Churchill's reply to Roosevelt's letter of 24 November reinforced that view.[65]

Churchill reiterated the fact that Britain had opened her bases to world aviation and added that this was despite being disadvantaged because of the Lyttleton Agreement. He commented that he did not think that these things had been given adequate weight. Britain could not accept America's version of fifth-

[64] M. Gilbert, *Churchill*, vii, 1074, quoting from Colville Diary, 25 Nov. 1944.
[65] Berle, *Rapids*, 507–8, 2 Dec. 1944.

freedom rights and so he was again proposing moving forward on the technical agreements that had been reached and postponing other matters to a later date: 'Such adjournments for a short time, if asked for by an intimately allied power like us, ought not to be denied, nor ought we to be confronted with such very serious contingencies as are set out in your message.' Even if such penalties were imposed, the Prime Minister said, he could not recommend the present US proposals to Parliament. He hoped that the American sense of justice would prevail.[66]

Although moves to bring the Conference to an end were now under way, LaGuardia of the American delegation had reserved the right to speak at the plenary session on 1 December, which provided one last, if rather unconventional, means of making progress on the five freedoms. Furthermore, the White House had certainly not given up the ghost. Admiral Leahy was busily drafting a letter which was more of an answer to the Prime Minister's of 22 November than that of 24 November had been. On 30 November Roosevelt sent it to London. After the economic threats of the 24 November, Roosevelt now switched his tactics and tried to reassure Churchill that the United States had no intention of monopolizing the world's aviation. He acknowledged Britain's wartime difficulties but insisted that the country should move forward and held out the prospect of American planes being made available to Britain on the same terms as to US airlines. He reassured the Prime Minister of America's intention to uphold justice and promote fair play, and suggested that they could come to an agreement on the basis of Canadian compromise-proposals if they both made some further concessions.[67]

On 1 December Churchill replied saying that, following consideration of the President's letter, there had been some movement in the Cabinet, both on the idea of protecting fifth-freedom traffic by a price differential and towards Canadian compromise-

[66] Kimball, *Correspondence*, iii, 418–21, Churchill to Roosevelt, 27 and 28 Nov. 1944.

[67] Ibid., 424–5, Roosevelt to Churchill, 30 Nov. 1944; W. D. Leahy, *I Was There*, (Victor Gollancz, London, 1950), 329; Leahy Papers, Diary, 29 Nov. 1944; LaGuardia was Mayor of New York and a leading Democrat.

proposals (Winant commented later that this was less than the Americans wanted). However, on hearing from Swinton that the Conference had agreed both on technical matters and on referring unfinished business to what became the Provisional International Civil Aviation Organization (PICAO), the Cabinet had decided not to put forward further proposals. Churchill explained that it was difficult for London to keep track of events in Chicago and that it would be easier to sort things out once Swinton had returned. Thereafter he would submit further proposals to the PICAO which he hoped would be agreeable to the United States. American officials in London blamed Beaverbrook for the obstinacy with which the British stuck to their guns, but in fact others had strong feelings about resisting American demands as well, notably Cripps, and Churchill himself, despite his strong desire to keep on good terms with the United States.[68]

At the plenary session on 1 December, LaGuardia made an impassioned plea for some progress to be made on the five freedoms, and it was taken up by the Dutch. In the end, Swinton, unwilling to be regarded as an obstructor of international aviation and with his abiding conviction about the importance of transit and technical stop for imperial communications, agreed to the proposal that the first two freedoms should be separated from the other three in order to get multilateral acceptance of them. Britain would have preferred to tie those to an agreement on commercial rights, but that had not been possible.

The Americans still tried to get the five freedoms accepted and so two separate documents were drawn up: one embodied the first two, the other all five, and it was left to each nation to decide freely which one they wished to sign. After hearing of these further movements at Chicago, which had been prompted by LaGuardia's speech at the plenary session, Roosevelt wrote again to Churchill, saying that the Conference felt as he did and that agreement should be reached. But Churchill would not be moved. He wrote to Swinton advising him to use 'damping

[68] Kimball, *Correspondence*, iii, 427, Churchill to Roosevelt, 1 Dec. 1944; Berle Papers, box 59, folder: International Civil Aviation Conference, Achilles memo 2 Dec. 1944; FDR MR, box 32, folder: Air Conference (i) Chicago Air Conference, Winant to Hull, 1 Dec. 1944.

down and dilatory processes' until London could get a reaction to a strong letter in which he had told Roosevelt.

> It is our desire, as it is yours, to reconcile the greatest possible freedom of air commerce with a broad justice to all nations, large and small.
>
> It is your desire, as it is ours, that the free play of enterprise should not degenerate into an exploitation of national advantages which would in the end be found mutually intolerable.

Churchill was not satisfied that they had found a solution acceptable to Parliament or public opinion. Thus the matter should be adjourned to a future date, when new and constructive proposals could be made. And that, so far as civil aviation at Chicago was concerned, was that. Roosevelt made no reply.[69]

In his report on the Chicago Conference, Berle grandiosely claimed: 'The International Conference on Civil Aviation has advanced civil air flying by at least twenty years.' In fact, it had fallen far short of American hopes. It established the PICAO, charged with responsibility for technical matters, and produced widespread agreement on the acceptance of a multilateral agreement to extend rights of transit and technical stop to all signatories. Agreement on the first two freedoms was a significant step forward and it certainly chipped away an important part of the British government's bargaining-strength. But on commercial matters, there was a complete stalemate. The only arrangements for commercial air-services between Britain and the United States were those negotiated in the 1930s for two services a week. It seemed that any progress on that state of affairs would have to be made on the basis of hard bilateral negotiation of the kind which had been conducted in the inter-war period and which, as the British October White Paper had observed, had 'introduced extraneous considerations' and had given rise to 'jealousies and mistrust'. Those things were likely to happen again, but now Britain was in a much weaker position. She still had no modern civil airliners, her economic difficulties made her extremely vulnerable to American pressures, and the Americans, in addition to their wartime experience,

[69] Berle, *Rapids*, 507–10, 2 and 6 Dec. 1944; CAB 66/56, WP(44)698, Churchill to Swinton, 5 Dec. 1944; Kimball, *Correspondence*, iii, 428 and 442–3, Roosevelt to Churchill 2 Dec. 1944 and Churchill to Roosevelt 6 Dec. 1944.

international stature, and possession of aircraft, now had wide-reaching rights of transit and technical stop. What they lacked was commensurate commercial rights, regarding which the British still had a powerful hand to play.[70]

[70] Berle Papers, box 59, folder: ICAC 1944, 'Summary' of Chicago Conference, 6 Dec. 1944; Cmd. 6561, Oct. 1944.

6
The Bermuda Truce and a Model for International Aviation

NOTWITHSTANDING national prejudices, economic competition, and political conflict between liberalism and imperialism, Britain and the United States developed a unique relationship in the Second World War, which Churchill justifiably described as 'special'. For two sovereign states there was an unprecedented level of military and intelligence co-operation. There were warm partnerships between Churchill and Roosevelt and many others, which often developed, with the help of a common language, into lasting friendships. These provided an informal dimension to the links which bound Britain and the United States to many common policies in the post-war period. As GIs flooded into the country, the influence of American popular culture, which had begun with the advent of the Hollywood film, went deeper than ever, establishing a pattern that Britain was unable to counter until the 1960s. However, well before then, the two peoples began to intermix more, firstly because of GI war-brides going to the United States, and then through business, educational exchanges, and tourism, all of which helped to nurture the Special Relationship at perhaps its most endearing level. Also, there was economic co-operation: for example, the United States provided Britain with over twenty-seven billion dollars' worth of Lend-Lease assistance, upon which depended a crucial margin of her war effort and, in 1941, possibly her very survival. These arrangements were advantageous, but in return the United States wanted economic co-operation from Britain, which caused difficulties.

Furthermore, although the relationship was special, it was not consistently or uniformly so. When Labour gained power in 1945 its socialism was disliked in Washington and there was little rapport between President Truman and Prime Minister Attlee. The Americans reneged on agreements both to give Britain generous Lend-Lease assistance to help with the difficult readjustment to peacetime production, and on its pledge to cooperate in nuclear weaponry. There were differences over how to deal with the Soviets. And the United States was suspicious of Britain's imperial intentions and feared that she would not keep her pledge of economic co-operation and would instead continue to discriminate against the United States through use of the Sterling Area and imperial tariff preferences. Relations were particularly stormy from 1945 until the end of 1946, after which the threat of Communism began to override causes of friction.[1]

These developments had implications for aviation, which in itself acquired unusual significance as the two countries moved towards the Bermuda Conference and a long-lasting agreement.

FROM CHICAGO TO BERMUDA: 1944–1946

Prior to the Chicago Conference many had hoped for a concurrent meeting of airline operators, but it was vetoed by the United States. However, there was one immediately afterwards, and it revived the old International Air Traffic Association (keeping the same acronym), under the slightly different name of International Air Transport Association (IATA). The meeting, attended by representatives of thirty-four airlines, called a conference for the following April in Havana, which then drew up the articles of association. Its aims were 'to promote safe, regular and economical air transport'. In practice, its most important achievements were the conduct of traffic conferences, which set international fares subject to government approval, and the development of the IATA ticket. So far as Anglo-American civil-aviation relations were concerned, IATA did not seem to be of great immediate significance, because the United States had set its face publicly against fare-setting. In fact, the United States was not hostile to such practices, providing they were conducted responsibly. Consequently, when it accepted a degree of fare control at Bermuda, IATA then became important in the Anglo-American aviation relationship.

[1] Alan P. Dobson, *The Politics of the Anglo-American Economic Special Relationship* (Wheatsheaf, Sussex and St. Martins, Brighton and New York, 1988); N. Longmate, *GIs: The Americans in Britain 1942–45* (Scribner's, New York, 1975); and D. Dimbleby and D. Reynolds, *An Ocean Apart* (Hodder & Stoughton, London, 1988).

But before there was any talk of concessions, both British and American aviation policy became more nationalistic and aggressively competitive as each country strove for maximum bargaining-strength. In Britain's case this involved some visible developments in policy, for example co-operation with Commonwealth countries, but also more covert moves. Economic dependence on the Americans meant that the British had to be careful not to antagonize them, or provide the American press with publicity that could be used to arouse adverse public opinion. Consequently, opposition to US attempts to get fifth-freedom rights was surreptitious and officially denied.

Beginning in Montreal and continuing in London, Swinton succeeded in pulling the Dominions together to form the Commonwealth Air Transport Council for co-ordinating aviation policy. Swinton had always believed in the importance of a united Commonwealth position irrespective of the outcome of Chicago, but now such a position was more important than ever. There were agreements on quotas and revenue-sharing with companies such as South African Airways and Qantas, but his more ambitious plans foundered on the rocks of nationalism. Britain, New Zealand, and Australia did form the British Commonwealth Pacific Airline (BCPA), but Canada refused to join and it had an unsettled life and was dissolved in 1954.

Swinton's proposals for Britain's post-war carriers had even less success. He wanted to make British airlines competitive by arranging a mixture of public corporations and private enterprise, but his plan ran into trouble with Labour. In the meantime, the British did their best both to persuade other countries not to grant fifth-freedom rights to the United States and to delay the revival of civil aviation in general until they had better equipment. But the Americans, fully aware of this and determined not to be denied their destiny, began to outmanœuvre the British and force them to a bilateral agreement which would yield what they had been denied at Chicago.[2]

[2] Swinton, *I Remember* (Hutchinson, London, 1946), 252–62; J. A. Cross, *Lord Swinton* (OUP, Oxford, 1982), 251–5; Beaverbrook Papers D/247, Gen. 47/13th, 18 Dec. 1944, Lord Swinton's Report to Beaverbrook's Special Air Committee; 841.796/3–2245, Winant to Secretary of State, /4–3045 and 711.4127/8–2746, both Satterthwaite to Secretary of State; CAB 128/5, 11(46)8, 4 Feb. 1946, Bevin's comments on 5th freedom; R. Y. Chuang, *The International Air Transport*

At the end of 1944 a number of new factors, and old ones with renewed importance, came into play and affected US policy. Roosevelt's re-election in November brought some changes of personnel, including the removal of Berle, who was persuaded to become Ambassador to Brazil. William Clayton, a strong-willed Texan and supporter of free trade entered the State Department as Assistant Secretary for Economic Affairs, and he assumed responsibility for aviation. Simultaneously with personnel changes there was a noticeable shift in American policy.

Even while the Chicago Conference was in progress, criticism had been expressed about the policy adopted by Berle and Roosevelt. PAA lobbyists, Pogue and other members of the CAB, along with the War Department all opposed, for one reason or another, aspects of liberal internationalism, and in particular the proposal for the multilateral exchange of routes. After the Conference, opposition continued, championed by Brewster in the Senate and by members of the CAB and the War Department within the administration. The latter in particular had thought long and hard about the wider role of aviation.

There had always been a military perspective on civil aviation, but from 1943 onwards it gained in importance in the United States. In 1943 Roosevelt asked a retired naval friend, Admiral R. E. Byrd, to investigate certain islands in the Pacific and assess America's future peacetime strategic and commercial interest in them. The report, forwarded to Roosevelt in April 1944, was accompanied by a letter from Byrd which said in part:

> . . . it is of the utmost importance [originally read: to our national preservation] that the United States know as soon as possible exactly what air routes, islands, landing fields, strategic areas, etc. are essential for the combined purposes of commerce and political and military

Association (A. W. Sijthoff, Leiden, 1972), 26–7. IATA was the successor to the International Air Traffic Association established at The Hague in Aug. 1919 by G. H. Thomas, owner of Aircraft Transport and Travel. Its purpose was to co-ordinate timetables, standardize insurance, and help members settle their accounts. It was one of the few aviation organizations that established trans-atlantic ties before the Second World War: in 1939 it was about to elect Trippe as its first American chairman, but war forced the Association's operations into limbo. Its successor—the International Air Transport Association—was different in that it was more political, both because its members were now mainly state as opposed to private airlines and because it had a significant role to play in setting air fares.

strategy, and to know also by careful planning how to get what we need and how to neutralize key islands we cannot get or afford to maintain.[3]

Later, a high-level review of the report indicated the reasons why civil aviation might be important to the military. Civil aviation could be: essential for the development of some strategic routes; a good basis for rearmament; an important supplement to the armed forces; a help with intelligence work; and finally, its commercial bases overseas could be used to deny facilities to others. These arguments resulted in an American strategic position regarding air power comparable to the Royal Navy's old 'two-navy standard', i.e. that it should be strong enough to defeat any other two navies combined. The United States had to have a dominant position in the air, and just as the merchant navy had been important in Britain's overall naval strategy, so was civil aviation in US air-strategy. The report commented further on, 'however tough or merciless foreign competition may be; this nation can not allow its . . . airlines to go bankrupt'. There were limits to what the United States would concede to the free market. The military perspective reinforced commercial and political reasons for achieving a framework within which American airlines could flourish. Consequently, the United States vigorously pursued routes and rights for her operators. There were renewed efforts to get bilateral agreements, and inevitably a greater degree of nationalism tended to spice such negotiations.[4]

The most important route was the Atlantic, where suspicion already existed between Britain and the United States because Newfoundland—the key transatlantic staging post—had been specifically excluded from the first- and second-freedom agreements Britain had made at Chicago. The British explained that

[3] FDR MR, box 162, folder: 5 sect. A4-2 Air Routes, Byrd to Dear Franklin, 14 Apr. 1944.

[4] Ibid., box 162, folder: 5 sect. A4-2 Air Routes, Byrd to Dear Franklin, 14 Apr. 1944, and ibid., box 207, Senior Members' Review of Byrd Report; D. J. Mrozek, 'The Truman Administration and the Enlistment of the Aviation Industry in Postwar Defence', *Business History Review*, 48 (1974), 73–94; interestingly, Admiral W. Brown noted on 27 Aug. 1943 that Roosevelt intended to open all US bases in the Pacific to foreign commercial airlines, FDR MR, box 162, memo for file. That is a good indicator of Roosevelt's liberal intent regarding the future of civil aviation.

the exception was because of Newfoundland political sensibilities and the need for consultations with its Commission of Government, but the United States remained suspicious that this was a self-serving ploy to strengthen the British bargaining-position: it was not, but there had been plenty of bona fide grounds for suspecting British motives in the past.

Well before Chicago, the Americans had been worried by British attempts to get a strong international regulatory body for aviation, or alternatively, as Pogue had put it, 'sew things up behind the curtain'. The former strategy was now at best a forlorn hope, but a version of the latter was still possible. It involved: delaying the restart of normal civilian services, which would have exposed the inadequacy of British equipment; continuing as long as possible to use BOAC for civilian carriage under the Eisenhower–Tedder agreement, which allowed BOAC to fill spare capacity with civilian passengers near western war-zones; and using persuasion (including at times Lend-Lease material as a quid pro quo) to gain commercial air-rights and to influence countries to deny them to the United States. The development of British civil-aviation interests in Portugal prompted some Americans to think about using Lend-Lease as a means of restraining the British, and at the Chicago Conference Roosevelt did use it to try to wring concessions from them. He was unsuccessful, but Clayton soon instigated enquiries about British use of Lend-Lease in aviation and renewed considerations about how it might be manipulated to exert pressure on them.[5]

The need to counteract British moves in civil aviation continued to grow in importance in American minds. There was considerable frustration over the fact that US Air Transport Command, unlike BOAC, was not allowed to accept civilian carriage. At Chicago worries mounted about US airlines being excluded from lucrative routes by Britain, and this increased American determination to press ahead immediately with as many bilateral agreements as possible. This in itself brought

[5] Beaverbrook Papers, D/247, Swinton's report, 18 Dec. 1944; B. B. Berle and T. B. Jacobs, *Navigating the Rapids 1918–71: From the Papers of A. A. Berle* (Harcourt Brace Jovanovich, New York, 1973), 489–90, Berle memo 30 June 1944; 841.796/6–0345, State Department Summary of [British] Developments and /4–1445 and /6–945, Clayton to Winant and his reply; 841.79653/10–1844, Hayes to Secretary of State.

pressure to bear on the British, but also, in the longer term, they had to cope with an American decision to take up the economic stick, waved over the Chicago negotiations to no avail, and blandish it in an ever more threatening manner.

The first line of attack on Britain came through Eire. It was not the first bilateral to be consummated by the United States, but it was the most significant and politically delicate. By the end of January the United States was about to sign a fifth-freedom agreement with Eire. When Churchill discovered this, he was furious. He was not privy to the account of policy given by Acting Secretary of State Grew in a letter of 29 January to the US delegation in Dublin, but, given the American position at Chicago and their known ambitions, it did not take clairvoyance to work out what the Americans were doing. Grew wrote:

> For your secret information and not for communication to anyone, we agree that our long range traffic interests are tied up much closer with Britain than with Eire. However, aftermath of Chicago conference makes it uncertain whether Britain will grant us rights to operate unlimited air services to London within near future. Apart from temporary wartime permits, our present transatlantic arrangements provide for only two schedules per week to Ireland and Britain. We therefore believe it desirable to implement without delay our arrangements made at Chicago . . . through bilateral agreements giving us as many gateways to Europe as possible and with no limitations on frequencies.[6]

Just as entry rights into France in 1939 had prompted the British government to end its obstruction of PAA flying into Britain, so it was now hoped that a similar threat of bypassing Britain would persuade it to negotiate a liberal bilateral with the United States.

Churchill was angry on three counts: Eire had consorted with the enemy throughout the war, and Britain believed that allied relations with her should therefore be cool (in the same way as Britain had cooled her relations at America's insistence with Fascist Argentina, upon whom she depended for much of her meat supply); the Americans had not informed London of what they were doing; and a bilateral between the United States and Eire would weaken Britain's bargaining-position. Churchill appealed personally to Roosevelt, saying: 'I cannot feel sure that

[6] 811.79641D/1–2945, Grew to US Legation, Dublin.

this affair has been brought to your notice . . . '. And that, 'The War Cabinet have very strong feelings on this . . . and we all earnestly hope as good friends that you will consider the matter personally yourself.'

Roosevelt made no reply. The State Department delayed signing the agreement until 3 February but advised the President that, 'British objections might possibly have ulterior motives and that further delay might expose us to Irish charges of bad faith and a domestic storm over British intervention in an Irish American matter.' Roosevelt did not oppose agreement and the bilateral was completed on 3 February without any further communication with the British.

On 6 March Churchill angrily wrote to Roosevelt that he believed that the bilateral had been completed despite being contrary to the views of both Secretary of State Stettinius and the President. Because of that, and for reasons to do with political relations with Eire, he wanted Roosevelt 'to take the necessary steps to have the agreement annulled'. On 15 March Roosevelt disabused Churchill of his mistaken beliefs. He agreed with him about Eire's reprehensible role during the war but explained that he did not oppose the agreement and added: 'There can of course be no question of annulling the agreement. I am sorry but there it is.' The President then went on to the attack and placed responsibility for current difficulties squarely on the British.

> You will recall how earnestly I endeavoured to secure your co-operation on the future of aviation during the Chicago conference. These bilateral . . . agreements were made necessary by the failure of that conference . . . I think it only fair to tell you that aviation circles in this country are becoming increasingly suspicious that certain elements in England intend to try to block the development of international flying . . . until the British aviation industry is further developed.[7]

The Eire episode was painful confirmation of what Swinton had said to Beaverbrook's committee on 18 December after returning from North America: 'We must now face the fact that

[7] FDR MR, box 32, folder: Air Conference, Grew to Roosevelt, 30 Jan. 1945; Churchill to Roosevelt 27 Jan. and 6 Mar. and Roosevelt's reply drafted by State Department, 15 Mar. 1945, in W. F. Kimball (ed.), *Churchill and Roosevelt: The Complete Correspondence* (3 vols.; Princeton University Press, New Jersey, 1984), iii, 519–20, 566–7.

the U.S. would be going out to make [bilateral] arrangements and that the United States would use Air Transport Command as a cover for establishing services which could be transferred at short notice to a civilian base. We must do the same.'[8]

The British hoped to counter American moves by trying to expand their own route-system, but they had little success. They wanted to make agreements in line with policy pursued at Chicago, which had been given formal structure in 'standard clauses'. As Masefield explained in late December 1944:

> These clauses contain the British principles of basic division of traffic, the 'traffic embarked' principle and the allocation of capacity in relation to an agreed load factor. They also contain provision for a limited amount of Fifth Freedom traffic and agreement for standard fares and arbitration on matters under dispute.[9]

Unfortunately, the British, unlike the Americans, had little economic inducement to offer foreign countries, nor did they have equipment with which to exploit fully any agreements reached. Their policy therefore became defensive: it was directed at cultivating Commonwealth solidarity and obstructing US attempts to get fifth-freedom rights. In March Swinton carried forward his plans for Commonwealth co-operation at a conference in South Africa and on his way back remarked in Cairo that British airlines would only buy British aircraft—a policy that was given formal status in the British Air Transport White Paper of that same month. Swinton's policy and his publicly expressed sentiments caused concern in the United States, but Swinton, 'had found the Americans very active in Egypt, trying to capture the aircraft market and acquire a share in Egyptian

[8] Beaverbrook Papers, D/247, Swinton's Report, 18 Dec. 1944.

[9] Ibid., D/281, Masefield, 'Comments on European Air Transport', 20 Dec. 1944. In recent correspondence and in a draft article which he kindly sent to me, Dr Marc Dierikx of the Katholieke Universiteit Nijmegen has somewhat amplified the part played by BOAC in British policy-making. In particular, BOAC wanted more freedom to negotiate and more allowance to be made for fifth-freedom rights in bilateral agreements than the Ministry of Aviation wanted to concede. However, BOAC's position undoubtedly influenced the government in its gradual shift in policy so that it became more receptive to demands for fifth-freedom rights at Bermuda in 1946. Unfortunately, Dierikx's paper, 'Shaping World Aviation: Anglo-American Civil Aviation Relations, 1944–46', is still only in an unpublished form.

airlines'. To his mind he was being no more aggressive than the Americans.[10]

British policy as laid out in the White Paper reflected Swinton's views on protection and free enterprise. The resulting scheme was for regulated competition—a half-way house between the nationalized industry preferred by Labour and a more competitive one as favoured by men like Beaverbrook who had criticized plans similar to Swinton's in the past as 'monopoly corporations'. The single chosen instrument was replaced by three, respectively serving: the domestic and European market (British European Airways—BEA); South America; the Commonwealth and the rest of the world. Free enterprise, primarily in the form of shipping and railway companies, was to have a significant role in British South American Airways (BSAA) and BOAC. There was to be co-operation with the Commonwealth, as small an element of subsidy as possible, and a policy of 'buy British'—dictated by a shortage of dollars with which to buy American aircraft as much as by anything else.[11]

American reaction to the White Paper, and to British policy in 1945, was mixed. Ambassador Winant welcomed the White Paper and thought that it brought Britain and the United States as close as they were likely to get and that it would facilitate a bilateral agreement between them. At the same time, however, he was disturbed by British moves to establish regional companies and cabotage areas aimed at excluding the United States. He suggested that the Halifax Agreement of 1942, which had been superseded by Chicago, should be revived by taking things up at the highest level. His Civil Aviation Attaché, Satterthwaite, took a more jaundiced view of things: 'As far as aviation is concerned . . . the British Government seems to be embarking on an extreme nationalistic and protectionist policy . . .'. He thought that Swinton would exclude the United States as far as possible from the Empire and Europe and promote British aircraft sales overseas by discriminating against US manufacturers through the regulation of the dollar supply to Sterling

[10] Beaverbrook Papers, D/370 Masefield, 19 Apr. 1945 comments on WP(45) 21B, South African Air Transport Conference Mar. 1945: 841.796/4–3045, Satterthwaite to Secretary of State.

[11] Ibid., D/298, Lord Privy Seal memo 'Organisation of Civil Airlines', 1944; Cmd. 6605, 13 Mar. 1945, 'British Air Transport'.

Area countries and by giving such countries technical aviation assistance.[12]

However, the British were vulnerable to American pressure and had to answer charges brought against them with regard to civilian use of BOAC and opposing fifth-freedom rights. Sir William Hildred, Director-General of Civil Aviation, argued that BOAC only used spare capacity to carry civilians engaged in matters of national interest. But Satterthwaite sarcastically commented, 'Sir William's statement . . . is a very careful analysis of the way in which British Overseas Airways Corporation legally operates.' The other British response also failed to satisfy the Americans. Considering the complaint about blocking fifth-freedom rights, Masefield caustically observed: 'What they really mean is that we are blocking their efforts to gain unrestricted Fifth Freedom traffic into and out of such countries as Greece, Egypt, Iraq and so forth. This is true.' Nevertheless, on 12 June the Foreign Office still felt able to send a message to Washington saying that the British government had 'no intention of opposing United States Government or any other Government in the acquisition of landing rights for civil aircraft in any country'. This was almost true, but it avoided the point, namely fifth-freedom rights. Not surprisingly, given their experience of British opposition in the field, the Americans were not reassured by these statements.[13]

During the summer of 1945 the tempo of development in civil aviation increased. On 1 June PAA finally lost its peacetime monopoly on foreign routes when the CAB awarded TWA and American Export Lines (it became American Overseas Airways (AOA) in November 1945, after amalgamating with American) routes across the Atlantic. The decision prompted Clayton to give more urgency to the negotiation of bilateral aviation-agreements. Among others, the Americans sought one with the French to bring pressure to bear on Britain, but in July Pogue complained to Acting Secretary of State Grew of continuing British opposition to America's pursuit of fifth-freedom rights,

[12] 841.796/3–1445 and /3–2245 Winant to Secretary of State, and /4–3045, Satterthwaite to Secretary of State.

[13] Ibid., /6–1245, Satterthwaite to Secretary of State; Beaverbrook Papers, D/370, comments on WP(45)21B; ibid., D/289, W-/24/802, Foreign Office to Washington, 12 June 1945.

and he suggested a more energetic policy—for example, withholding C-54 transports (which the War Department was then releasing to PAA, TWA, and AOA) from France until she granted the United States the rights she wanted. Grew, however, was reluctant to use such crude tactics, for fear of jeopardizing broader economic issues. But it was not long before both the realization of just how strong America's bargaining-position was and the danger of economic controls from the newly elected Labour government overcame American reluctance to use economic persuasion in specific areas.[14]

On 12 April 1945 Roosevelt died of a massive brain-haemorrhage and was succeeded by Harry Truman. Just over three months later, on 26 July, the Labour Party formed a new government in Britain, after defeating the Conservatives in the general election. Both changes were significant for civil aviation. The Truman Administration was more conservative in a number of ways than its predecessor, and that, combined with an increasingly conservative Congress, put the liberal internationalists on the defensive and gave more emphasis to a narrow view of American national interest in civil aviation. With a Labour government in Britain and the more conservative Truman Administration in Washington, the two countries diverged politically at a sensitive time. The Americans became more worried than ever that Britain might renege on commitments to economic liberalism, to which socialist policies of economic control seemed directly opposed. And as they became more fearful of what Britain might do, so the inclination to use economic leverage on her increased. Both past and future American generosity were to be linked with Britain's adoption of economic policies acceptable to the United States.

Although the respective changes in government made Anglo-American relations more difficult, initially the response of the Americans to the changed order in London was not unfavourable regarding aviation. Even Satterthwaite, though worried by Labour's nationalization policy, thought that the departure of Swinton and the rise in importance of Hildred were to be

[14] Clayton Papers, Reading File, July 1945, Clayton to Pogue, 4 July 1945; 811.79641/4–1945, Satterthwaite to Secretary of State; ibid., /7–545, Clayton to Morgan and attached memos; 800.796/7–1645, Pogue to Secretary of State and Grew's reply, 1 Aug. 1945.

welcomed. In fact, what little change was made by the Labour government to the international civil-aviation policy of its predecessor moved it closer to that of the United States. The new Minister for Civil Aviation, Lord Winster, relied heavily upon Hildred, who was both more liberal than Swinton and convinced of the need to reach agreement with the United States. Also, in its White Paper on aviation, published in December 1945 the Labour government moved decisively away from full internationalization because of its impracticality. Only in the sphere of the organization of the industry itself were there radical changes. On the insistence of Sir Stafford Cripps, the President of the Board of Trade, and Hugh Dalton, Chancellor of the Exchequer, there was a 'complete nationalization of Civil Aviation'. There were to be three companies, as under Swinton's proposals, but they were to be nationalized and under the supervision of the Ministry of Civil Aviation. The railway and shipping companies were out, and government capitalization, procurement of aircraft, and funding of R. & D. was in. In short, government was to have a much higher profile in aviation. There was an element of unjustifiable partisan criticism from the Conservatives, but nationalization did create long-term difficulties for British airlines.[15]

Naturally enough, aviation developments between Britain and the United States were delayed because of the changes of government, but in late August there were exploratory talks in London between Stokeley Morgan, Chief of the State Department Aviation Division, and Hildred. There had been no discussion about aviation at the Potsdam Conference when Attlee and his Foreign Secretary, Ernest Bevin, had taken over from Churchill and Eden, except for a mention of the need for bilateral talks. Now the Americans were eager to carry things forward. They thought that they had an opportunity to get the agreement they wanted, because of past favours such as Lend-Lease, British hopes for future help, and various wartime

[15] 841.796/7–3045, Satterthwaite to Secretary of State; Cmd. 6712, 20 Dec. 1945, 'British Air Services';—this was a distinct move away from policy expressed in the Labour Party publication *Wings for Peace*, 1944; S. Wheatcroft, *Air Transport Policy* (Michael Joseph, London, 1964), chs. 1–2; K. Hayward, *Government and British Civil Aerospace* (Manchester University Press, Manchester, 1983), chs. 1, 2, 6, 7; Hugh Dalton, *High Tide and After: Memoirs 1945–60* (Frederick Muller, London, 1962), 61.

commitments Britain had made to co-operate with the United States. In the past the British had tried to avoid some of the more free-market American demands, but now all that was to end. The United States was paying the piper and would now insist on calling the tune.

On Friday 24 August and on the following Monday, Stokeley Morgan and Satterthwaite talked with a small British group led by Hildred. The first meeting was also attended by Clayton, who was in London exploring an agenda for broader economic talks with the British government. Much was said, but in effect it boiled down to the problem that had proved so intractable in Chicago: the British would not give unfettered fifth-freedom rights to the United States. Clayton forthrightly declared that. 'the U.S.A. was not in favour of artificial restrictions which would impede the natural development of air transport'. On the Monday there was a very frank exchange of views. Morgan at one point claimed that Britain was proposing to establish a European gateway which would create an area of European cabotage. The British ridiculed this, saying that 60 per cent of the traffic from the United States would be destined for onward carriage to Europe. Interestingly, one of the other main difficulties at Chicago—the fixing of fares—was dealt with in a lower key. The Americans spoke well of IATA, which was envisaged by many as playing a leading role in this sphere, but they were still less inclined to fare-fixing than the British and had to bear in mind the strong opposition to it of PAA.[16]

The talks were necessarily inconclusive, because the Attlee Government still had to decide what it intended to do, but the Americans were pleased with Hildred and thought, despite the obvious differences, that there was hope for achieving a mutually acceptable bilateral agreement.

In Washington, Clayton met with Trippe and representatives of other airlines on 7 September to inform them about the recent talks with the British. C. R. Smith of American took the most belligerent line, demanding complete freedom of frequencies and untrammelled fifth-freedom rights, even if it meant a temporary halt in air services between the two countries. Trippe

[16] 811.79641/8–2145, Byrnes to Morgan; 841.796/9–445, Satterthwaite to Secretary of State enclosing memos of conversation, Morgan, Hildred, *et al.*, 24 and 27 Aug. 1945.

thought that that was shortsighted, because Britain could service the United States far better from Canada than the United States could service Europe from Eire, and so he favoured maintaining services to Britain even without fifth-freedom rights. Of course, PAA had more to lose than the others, namely her commercial rights for two landings a week in Britain. In the end, all agreed that there should be no compromise with the British except as a very final resort and 'Several present inquired if the forthcoming British discussions on economic and financial matters might not offer an excellent opportunity for us to achieve our desires.'[17]

In the past, particularly at the Second Quebec Conference in 1944, it seemed to many in the State Department that the British had taken advantage of poor co-ordination in the US administration in order to get economic help without having to make hard-and-fast commitments to co-operate in building a liberal world-economy. Now, any further help would only be given if Britain were to make her economic policies, including aviation, compatible with America's overall economic plan. Consequently, three days after the meeting with airline representatives, Morgan, in conversation with Peter Masefield, who was now the Civil Air Attaché in Washington, explained that the Americans saw civil aviation as part of an overall economic understanding to be sought with the British. Masefield was taken aback at this, but there was little he could do. They went on to talk about a number of matters, and both were well disposed towards further discussions taking place, even though Masefield was left in little doubt about the vigour with which the Americans would pursue their goal. For example, when they came to the problem of the lack of suitable British aircraft, Morgan said that American aircraft could be made available, but he added that, 'the allocation of surplus equipment to the British would in my opinion have to be contingent upon our working out a satisfactory air transport agreement'.[18]

This confronted the British with the prospect of a determined effort by the Americans to break the deadlock of Chicago, and if they did not come to an accommodation, then modern American planes would not be available for them, and desperately needed

[17] Clayton Papers, Office Files, folder: Aviation, meeting 7 Sept. 1945 with airline officials.

[18] 711.4127/9–1045, memo conversation between Morgan and Masefield.

economic help from the United States, to be discussed in Washington during November and December, would be jeopardized. That economic help was of overwhelming importance to Britain, which needed between three and five billion dollars to help with its expected post-war balance-of-payments deficit; also, Britain needed American generosity to wind up Lend-Lease without substantial payments being demanded. Given Britain's overall vulnerability to economic pressure, it was not surprising that the Americans wanted to use financial talks as the context within which to discuss civil aviation with the British government.

The British and Americans exchanged drafts of their current ideas on aviation, and Masefield assured Morgan that as soon as an impending debate in Parliament on civil aviation was out of the way, the British government would begin discussions with the United States. On 13 October the American Secretary of State, James Byrnes, observed with regret that little seemed to have changed since Chicago, but he added:

> The air transport problems faced by the two Governments form an integral part of their overall trade and economic problems. It is therefore urgently requested that the proper British authorities come to the United States for the purpose of negotiating a mutually satisfactory . . . agreement before the conclusion of the present Washington discussions.[19]

Talks were imminent, but then at the end of October PAA precipitated a crisis which shifted attention to the negotiation of a provisional agreement on air services.

During 1944–5 the government-led assault on the single favoured-instrument status of PAA came to a head. Trippe counter-attacked with the All American Flag Line Bill, which was sponsored and forcefully promoted by Senator Brewster. The Bill continued to be placed before Congress until 1947, but then Howard Hughes, in hearings about alleged wartime misconduct of his corporation before the War Investigating Committee, ridiculed and humiliated its Chairman, who was no other than Senator Brewster. After that, Brewster's career as a political force was extinguished, and with it went the last hope

[19] 711.4127/10–145, memo conversation between Morgan and Masefield; ibid., /10–1345, Byrnes to Winster.

for the already fading fortunes of the All American Flag Line. 1947 was a bad year for Trippe, because he also failed to get domestic US routes, not only to enhance his route system but also to retaliate against the domestic airlines that were now moving out onto 'his' foreign routes. PAA had to wait a long time before the CAB allowed it to enter the domestic market. The third ploy that Trippe tried in order to maintain dominance of overseas routes was fare-cutting. And here again he met with failure, at least in the short term.

The immediate problem facing PAA was that three American airlines had been authorized to fly the Atlantic. Although they had been assigned to different regions, Trippe still felt that they were a challenge and that there was scope for competitive fare-cuts to test their mettle. PAA announced a unilateral decision to reduce its one-way transatlantic fare by $100.

The British were furious. This was a prime example of the kind of cutthroat competition they had warned the United States about and which they had proposed to prevent through regulation. Swinton had found it difficult to understand why his plan had failed to curry more favour with the Americans when it was so similar to the regulatory CAB system; the fact was that they had hoped for the best of both worlds. They wanted to avoid harmful competition between American companies in the domestic sphere, and on international routes they wanted the competitive advantages of American airlines to be used, in the sense of being pitted not against each other, but against foreign operators. And it was they who were to be disrupted and possibly ploughed under. Now the picture changed. PAA was challenging other American operators, as well as foreign ones, and stirring up trouble for US civil aviation in general.

On 20 October the US Embassy reported to Washington about a meeting with British Foreign Office and Aviation Ministry officials, who had complained bitterly about the proposed PAA fare, claiming that it was uncommercial and intended to wipe out all competitors on the Atlantic route. They proposed a joint revocation of the 1937 exchange of notes between the United States and Britain concerning transatlantic services and the imposition of an interim agreement for five flights a week for PAA and three for AOA. The Embassy added: 'It would also provide agreement on rates (repeat agreement on rates).'

The British used the crisis caused by PAA to demonstrate to the Americans both the danger of unregulated competition and their determination to oppose it. They threatened to restrict PAA to the provisions of the 1937 agreement unless the old fare was maintained. This jeopardized the prospects for the bilateral agreement and threatened to create political problems in Washington by slowing down the return of demobbed GIs.[20]

In mid-November the British presented the State Department with formal proposals for an interim agreement, but these contained provisions for fixing rates, controlling frequency, and dividing up traffic. Furthermore, fifth-freedom rights were specifically excluded. Clayton rejected the proposals. He could not get other departments in Washington to agree to them; he thought they were unnecessary, given the imminence of bilateral talks, and in any case: 'Suggested Interim Agreement includes principles which this Government is still thoroughly against.'

Although the Americans rejected the proposals, PAA had landed them in an awkward position and they were unable to ignore comments made by Hildred, whom they had come to respect:

> British position with respect to third, fourth and fifth freedoms and the 'trappings' of the [world] order in the air was a lost one but [he] was equally emphatic that the British Govt. would never permit Panam or any other carrier to fly into England with unlimited frequencies and with unilateral power to set its rates without approval of either IATA or the govt.[21]

Hildred went on to say that if the United States condoned what PAA was trying to do, then American airlines would find the world an increasingly difficult place to fly in, and that until it made its position on rates clear, he thought it would be useless, and indeed harmful, to proceed to the discussion of a bilateral.

In the end, the Americans compromised. They would not accept the British principles, but they recognized that 'our carriers cannot, in the absence of an inter-governmental agree-

[20] R. Daley, *An American Saga: Juan Trippe and His Pan American Empire* (Random House, New York, 1980), 373ff.; C. Solberg, *Conquest of the Skies: A History of Commercial Aviation* (Little, Brown, and Co., Boston, 1979), 299; 811.79641/10–2045, Gallman to Secretary of State, /11–2545, memo by Morgan.

[21] 711.4127/11–2445, Winant to Secretary of State.

ment, operate into the U.K. except under such conditions as the British Government may prescribe, and we are prepared to have our carriers accept those conditions'.[22] For the interim, there thus had to be regulation of frequencies (daily services for PAA and AOA) and a fare acceptable to either the British government or IATA. On 30 November PAA, under threat of being restricted to two flights a week and seeing the possibility of its competitors taking up the slack, reluctantly backed down and agreed to maintain the $375 fare.

The whole episode was instructive with regard to what was to happen at the Bermuda Conference. Hildred, who was a major force in the British delegation and of whom it was widely known that he favoured an agreement with the United States, had made two things clear. Firstly, Britain would fight tooth and nail for fare regulation. He had explained to the Americans on more than one occasion that he was not opposed in principle to the fare of $275, providing it could be demonstrated that it was a commercial rate—the possibility of which he doubted—and providing it was introduced in a proper manner. He wanted all rates to be subject to government approval, preferably after being processed through IATA, and the Americans increasingly inclined to agree with that. Secondly, Hildred had indicated that he believed that American views on third, fourth, and fifth freedoms would probably prevail and that Britain's hopes for a strong international regulatory body had virtually expired. Such realism meant that Britain and the United States were closing the gap that had yawned so wide at Chicago.

While the PAA fare-dispute was going on, there were developments in planning-talks for a permanent bilateral. On 10 November Attlee arrived in Washington for his first meeting with Truman since the Potsdam Conference. The main item on the agenda was the future of the atom bomb, but two days before the talks Ambassador Halifax had informed Byrnes that Attlee would discuss civil aviation 'outside the financial and

[22] 711.4127/11–945, Winant to Secretary of State, /11–1345, *aide-mémoire* from Halifax with text of interim agreement and Clayton's response, /11–2445, Winant to Secretary of State, /11–2745, Halifax to Secretary of State; 811.79641/ 11–2545, memo by Morgan, /11–2645, memo of conversation between Trippe and Morgan, /11–2745, Halifax to Clayton, /11–3045, memo for files regarding talks with Vice-President Bixby of PAA.

trade discussions, [and] the question of making early arrangements for the holding of formal discussions about civil aviation'. In the end, the British succeeded in keeping some apparent distance between the Conference at Bermuda, which they agreed to in early January 1946, and the financial and economic talks in Washington conducted during November and early December 1945. But it was more appearance than reality. Although the Washington talks were over, Congress still had to ratify the US Loan Agreement, which extended a credit of $3.75 billion to Britain. And it was the necessity for Congressional approval, hanging like the sword of Damocles over the prostrate body of the British economy, that was used to help convince Britain that it had to make aviation concessions to the United States.[23]

It was not only that American policy-makers such as Clayton thought that it was in US interests to persuade the British government to their point of view about an aviation regime, they also genuinely feared both Congressional and public reaction if Britain did not come round. So the Americans took a hard line at Bermuda, not only because it was in their civil-aviation interests construed in the broadest sense, but also, as Clayton explained to Byrnes in early November:

> . . . the time of the conference is of greatest importance; first; because . . . opposition on the Hill. to the overall British agreements, if an aviation agreement is lacking, will unquestionably be very strong and, secondly, the position of the State Department in recommending to Congress the approval of the overall agreements without an aviation agreement, or the expectation of the almost immediate conclusion of one, may well appear to Congress and the public very weak.[24]

THE BERMUDA AGREEMENT 1946

The British went to Bermuda hoping that discussions could be kept to preliminaries for a full-scale ministerial conference to be held later: they soon discovered instead that for various compelling reasons they would have to comply with American wishes and conclude an agreement then and there. It took some weeks, but finally the Americans got most of what they wanted.

[23] 711.4127/11–845, Halifax to Secretary of State; Cmd. 6708, 6 Dec. 1945, 'Financial Agreement Between the US and the UK'.

[24] Ibid., Clayton to Secretary of State.

They moved towards the British position on two issues: the control of fares and a grievance procedure. But the first was hardly a concession. It was described later by the head of the American delegation, G. P. Baker, Director of Transport and Communications Policy in the State Department, as the 'ace in the hole'. The Americans knew how important control on fares was regarded by the British and so this was the 'concession' they made, but in fact by the time of Bermuda the United States itself wanted fare controls as well. The other matter, the grievance procedure, which was supposed to be a safeguard against the abuse of fifth-freedom rights and capacity levels—could only be invoked *ex post facto*. In reality things depended upon the self-control of American airlines, and therefore the provisions were little more than window-dressing to mollify the British.[25] Why then did the British concede at Bermuda so much of what they would not at Chicago?

The British had no aircraft. At least, they had no modern competitive ones and it was now peacetime and impossible to obstruct the development of civil aviation as they had done in the closing months of the war. Without suitable equipment the prospect of British air-services was unattractive to other countries, and if Britain resorted to protectionism, there was always the danger of being bypassed by the United States and other liberal aviation states like the Netherlands, with the result that Britain would find itself on the periphery rather than at the hub of aviation. The Brabazon Committee had successfully proposed a three-stage development of aircraft types—converted bombers, interim designs developed from bombers, and new Brabazon types—but only the first two kinds were available in early 1946, and of these, neither was successful. The Americans had been made aware of this weakness as early as June 1945, when a leading British aviation figure had told them that in his opinion it would be five years before Britain had a fully competitive type. The obvious way of filling the gap was with American planes, but that was a difficult choice for a number of reasons. Britain was prostrate economically and air travel was seen as a luxury. It would be difficult to buy American, because there was a

[25] HST, G. P. Baker oral history interview, 22–3; Cmd, 6747, Feb. 1946, 'US, UK Civil Air Services Agreement, Bermuda'.

shortage of dollars and because it would be difficult to justify politically when British aviation-industry workers were being laid off. There were also nationalistic and long-term manufacturing considerations which militated against buying American planes. But, in any case, the option was not available until Britain made an acceptable deal with the United States on the operation of commercial aviation.[26]

Swinton's hopes of relying on the strength of a united Commonwealth position and of keeping US civil aviation out of Europe had not materialized to the extent that Britain could maintain its Chicago position. Canada was the weak link in the Commonwealth. It would not participate in the BCPA and wanted a more competitive system in the Atlantic than did Britain. The European situation was even weaker. The Americans had again outmanœuvred the British. Using modern aircraft and economic pressure as inducements, the United States had concluded liberal bilaterals with Holland, Sweden, Eire, and Iceland. The tide was turning and both the British and the Americans knew that Britain would either have to swim with it or be flown over. Here was a powerful pressure on the British government to reach an accommodation.[27]

Since the departure of Swinton, and indeed Beaverbrook, the British position regarding civil-aviation relations with the United States had mellowed, though there were still some in the Ministry of Civil Aviation and some Cabinet Ministers, such as Cripps, who bitterly opposed concessions to the Americans right up to the signing of the Bermuda Agreement. Nevertheless, the key figure in the aviation relationship with the United States in the early months of the Labour government was Sir William Hildred. He made it clear during the PAA fare-controversy that there were some things that he would not compromise on, but he believed an acceptable overall deal could eventually be struck with the United States. Hildred was a realist and recognized the strength of the American position. Also, like many in the Cabinet, he knew that good relations with the United States were vitally important. Bevin had already made it clear that the

[26] Hayward, *British Aerospace*, ch. 1; 841.796/6–2245, Satterthwaite to Secretary of State, /6–0345 Summary of British Developments.

[27] 711.4127/8–2746, Satterthwaite to Secretary of State reviewing past US policy.

relationship with the United States was to be one of the main-stays of his foreign policy.[28]

Finally, there was Britain's economic vulnerability. G. P. Baker later recalled: 'I remember that the loan was very much at the back of everybody's mind.' Indeed it was. When the Cabinet came to decide whether or not to accept the Bermuda proposals, consideration of the effect rejection would have on the fortunes of the Loan Agreement in the US Congress was very prominent.[29]

At the opening session of the Bermuda Conference the Americans were forthright in their demands 'for full freedom of the world's skyways and the right to land commercial planes on military bases leased from the British for 99 years'. The bases referred to were in the Caribbean and Newfoundland, and had been traded for destroyers and munitions in the dark days of late 1940. The British initially resisted these demands, but within a few days Baker reported to Clayton:

> Conference progressing exactly along lines expected and discussed with Acheson before leaving. British appear to be willing to give up any control on third and fourth freedom traffic in return for satisfactory rate control arrangements.[30]

In addition, Baker was optimistic about the possibility of progress on the fifth freedom and also informed Clayton that a draft agreement had been drawn up on the military bases which it was hoped could be signed at the same time as the aviation bilateral. On 23 January the Americans made formal proposals which in effect were to provide the basis for eventual agreement. They offered to accept IATA rate-controls, subject to CAB approval, in return for 'there being no control of frequencies and if possible no restriction on Fifth Freedom although it is understood something may have to be worked out on that'. Hildred received this with obvious interest, but Sir Henry Self, the Permanent Secretary at the Ministry of Civil Aviation, and leader of the British delegation was less keen and clearly hoped for more concessions from the Americans.[31]

[28] A. Bullock, *Ernest Bevin: Foreign Secretary* (OUP, Oxford, 1985).

[29] HST, G. P. Baker oral history interview, 22–3.

[30] 841.796/1–1146, London to State Department, /1–1445, Winant to Acheson, /1–1946, Baker to Clayton.

[31] Ibid., /1–2346, Baker to Clayton.

There was a difference of opinion between Hildred and Self; at one point the former described the latter as mad and said that he was sure that an agreement could be reached on the basis of American proposals which Self wanted to reject. Nevertheless, drafting was difficult and the resulting proposals caused much concern in London.[32]

The British were being asked to give way completely on frequencies and capacity and more or less accept the US position on the fifth freedom. As Baker explained to Clayton:

> We believe that on frequency control they [the regulatory clauses] now offer no succour to the British concept since it has been made abundantly clear that we do not concede that any regulation is necessary to accomplish a close relationship between services offered and public demand. The Fifth Freedom traffic principles set forth are broad enough to allow an operator to operate satisfactorily and we believe would be violated only if an operator were to go in for really local services, something which the operators have denied they have any desire to do.[33]

The only positive gain by Britain was on fare control, but, as Baker smugly observed, all the US delegation believed that rate controls were desirable and so the overall arrangements proposed constituted 'a real victory'.

Winster's assessment of the proposals for the Cabinet was similar, except that he emphasized the disadvantages to Britain if she were to make so many concessions. BOAC would have to cope with American competition when it was in no position to do so. The US government in fact had no power to regulate fares or frequencies of its airlines and any abuse of the weak regulations in the proposals could only be dealt with *ex post facto*. In many ways, Britain would be placing herself at the mercy of American competition, with only expressions of good intent and hopes of American good faith to ameliorate the effects of that competition. As ever, there were reassurances from the Americans that modern US aircraft would be available for purchase by Britain, but her economic position would severely limit the numbers, even when opposition to such purchases from men like Cripps could be overcome.

[32] HST, G. P. Baker oral history interview.
[33] 841.796/1–2746, Baker to Clayton.

After the warnings, Winster put his finger on the decisive influences that were to affect the Cabinet. He said,

> if the Cabinet felt that the signing of the agreement was of vital importance from the point of view of our general relations with the United States and the consideration of the loan agreement by Congress, he was willing that our Delegation should be authorized to sign.

The Cabinet was divided. Dalton and Bevin reluctantly thought that they should sign because they were unlikely to get better terms. Dalton thought that it would help with the Loan, and Bevin did not think that they could maintain a civil-aviation policy independently of the United States, because of delays in producing suitable British aircraft. Cripps opposed the agreement because of the fifth-freedom rights, and there was widespread concern about this. On 22 January Winster had tried to limit possible damage from US fifth-freedom business by proposing that there should be no change of gauge for US airlines. In other words, that passengers from American airlines should not be carried forward from London in smaller planes which would thus compete with local carriers. The Americans had rejected this. There was also concern about US requests that the British government use its influence with Newfoundland and Canada to try to get them to grant commercial rights to the United States for bases constructed through Lend-Lease, and that British planes using the bases should buy fuel and spares only from the US military.[34]

The problems were referred to the Civil Aviation Committee, chaired by Viscount Addison, the Dominions Secretary, and as a result there were renewed efforts both to gain assurances that a permit to change gauge would not be abused and to reject the two unacceptable American proposals concerning bases.

The Americans allayed British worries about change of gauge by accepting their proposals, with minor redrafting, and they dropped both objectionable demands concerning the bases. On 11 February the Cabinet agreed to sign the extant Bermuda proposals and also the agreement on bases, after further consideration and subject to a later binding contract.[35]

[34] CAB 128/5, 11(46)8, 4 Feb. 1946 considering memos CP37(46) and CP39(46) by Winster and Dalton respectively.

[35] CAB 128/5, 13(46)7, 7 Feb. 1946, 14(46)6, 11 Feb. 1946; 841.796/2–1046, Baker to Secretary of State, /2–1246, Winant to Secretary of State, 'Summary of

The Bermuda Agreement had been struck. It reciprocally exchanged the five freedoms unfettered by specific regulation, though paragraph 6 stipulated the general principle that meeting the traffic requirements between the two countries was the primary objective in determining capacity. Fifth-freedom traffic was notionally controlled in the same way and by restrictions on the use of change of gauge such that it could not be a pretext for taking traffic at the expense of local operators. Unfortunately for the spirit of regulation, any departures from these guidelines could only be dealt with *ex post facto*, but the Americans did concede that if irresolvable differences were to arise, they would accept some form of arbitration in the form of advisory reports from the International Civil Aviation Organization (ICAO). Nevertheless, it was clear that British airlines were going to be subject to strong competition. On the other hand, there was the consolation that fares were to be controlled. The United States, while avoiding firm regulation, had agreed to use IATA if Congress would permit, and they kept to their pledge, with intermittent crises, until the 1970s. Also, the sale of five Constellation aircraft to Britain in February demonstrated that American good faith could be relied upon. Britain now at least had some equipment with which to compete on the North Atlantic route. And finally, Britain could denounce the Bermuda Agreement with twelve months notice. There is no denying that the United States won more concessions than she gave, but, on the whole, Bermuda turned out to be a satisfactory arrangement.[36]

BERMUDA AS A MODEL AGREEMENT

A basic pattern was established at Bermuda which lasted for thirty years. It provided a model that the Americans and the

Bermuda'; FO 371/54514, Report of Committee 2, Bermuda Conference 11 Feb. 1946; Foreign Office files relating to Bermuda are FO 371/54493–54516. Initially, the United States tried to link Bases Agreement with the air-services bilateral, but as difficulties intensified they retreated from that position; 841.796/2–146, Byrnes to Baker. For other accounts of Bermuda, see C. Jonsson, *International Aviation and the Politics of Regime Change* (Frances Pinter, London, 1987), chs. 2 and 6; B. Gidwitz, *The Politics of International Air Transport* (Heath, Boston, 1980), 50–52; J. C. Cooper, 'Some Historic Phases of British International Civil Aviation Policy', *International Affairs*, 23, ii (1947), 200.

[36] Cmd 6749, 1946.

British, with varying degrees of enthusiasm, soon recommended to the rest of the world. However, the early days of the Bermuda bilateral were troubled ones and its future appeared insecure. At the heart of the problem was Britain's inability to compete because of its lack of modern planes.

Americans wanted to sell planes to Britain in order to make BOAC more competitive and prevent a move away from the Bermuda principles to protectionism. In 1946 Britain bought five Constellations and six Boeing Stratocruisers, but it was done with great reluctance and no more were purchased until 1948, even though it was clear that BOAC was still uncompetitive.[37]

The Foreign Office wanted American planes for the sake of good international communications, and the airlines wanted them so that they could compete and be profitable. But the British government gave priority to British plane-manufacturers over the interests of the airlines. There were sound reasons for supporting British plane-makers (who were themselves force-fully lobbying in attempts to keep their market). If large orders went to the United States, jobs and desperately needed dollars would be lost. British prestige would suffer, and the prospects of Britain retaining independence in the field of military planes would be damaged by a general weakening of its manufacturing-base. Once there was a policy of buying American, it might be difficult to wean the airlines and bring them back to British products. And the British had, justifiably, great hopes for the future with the lead that they had established in jet engines and the imaginative decision of the wartime Brabazon Committee to call for jet-engined airliners. Finally, there was Cripps. First as President of the Board of Trade and then as Chancellor of the Exchequer, he did more than anyone else to oppose buying American aircraft. He opposed it on the grounds of finance and of the future of British aircraft-manufacturing, and because he disliked the idea of dependence on Americans.[38]

[37] Hansard, 13 Feb. 1946, vol. 419, cols. 120–1; CAB 128/6, 77(46)3, 7 Aug. 1946, considering CP(46)317, first report from Committee on Civil Aircraft Requirements; 841.796/9–346, Satterthwaite to Secretary of State; FO 371/54514, Addison to Attlee, 26 Aug. 1946.

[38] 841.796/5–1247, Douglas to Secretary of State; ibid., /5–747, Satterthwaite to Secretary of State; Hayward, *British Aerospace*, 13–15; 841.796102/3–2448 and /2–448, Gallman to Cripps.

By 1947, despite the determination not to, pressure to buy American planes was becoming irresistible. BOAC desperately needed modern equipment and British manufacturers were unable to supply it. There were serious problems with the Tudor long-range aircraft programme, the shorter-range Vickers Viking was grounded with de-icing problems for the early months of 1947, and BEA refused to accept delivery of the Bristol Wayfarer until its power was increased. The sorry state of British aircraft was such that even PAA and AOA now wanted BOAC to be re-equipped with modern American planes. Both the companies and the State Department were concerned that the British might denounce Bermuda and adopt protectionism because of their uncompetitiveness. There was also a further reason why the Americans wanted to sell planes to the British: the jet engine.

Talks had developed about the possibility of selling more Constellations to Britain, but fitted with British jet-engines. The Americans thought that this would give them valuable information about jets and help them to reduce Britain's technological lead in this area. The matter of whether or not to buy the Constellations came before Cabinet on 17 April. There was conflict between Lord Nathan, Minister of Civil Aviation since October 1946, who wanted to buy Constellations, and J. Wilmot, Minister of Supply, who did not. The matter was referred to the Civil Aviation Committee, chaired by Viscount Addison, who was convinced of the need to nurture the British aircraft-industry. Five days later he announced to the Cabinet that in the interests of British manufacturers it had been decided to rely on British types. The Americans were dismayed. They rightly blamed Cripps as a major force behind the decision and believed it was short-sighted and would ultimately prove to be very costly in terms of BOAC's operating losses and the continuing development and production of poor planes. Furthermore, there was resentment at the lost opportunity to co-operate on jet engines and fears that uncompetiveness would now push the British into protectionism.[39]

[39] CAB 128/9, 37(47)2, 17 Apr. 1947, 38(47)7, 22 Apr. 1947; 841.796/4–2447 and /5–747, Satterthwaite to Secretary of State, /4–2547 Douglas to Secretary of State, /7–847, Satterthwaite to Ambassador *et al.*, and Bell to Merchant, 8 July 1947.

In fact, despite the dire conditions of their economy in general, the British continued to co-operate in economic matters with the Americans, including within the Bermuda framework. And American worries about jet engines were partly allayed by their purchase of manufacturing-rights for the Rolls Royce Nene and Derwent engines in 1947. But one problem that did not go away was Britain's lack of modern equipment.

Throughout 1947 worries about the poor performance and cost of British aircraft continued to increase. The great Brabazon 1, which never flew commercially and was abandoned in 1951, cost over £13 million: the Princess Flying Boat was another expensive failure. Operating losses were also becoming prohibitive: £8 million for BOAC in the year ending March 1947. On 23 August a Tudor 2 crashed and in December a report by the Ministers for Civil Aviation and Supply on the Tudor 1 was so damaging to the aviation industry, BOAC, and the government that the Cabinet decided to keep it under wraps until a way could be found to deflect the inevitable public criticism. While the government could keep that bad news from the public for a while, it was not possible to avert an immediate crisis in January 1948, when a BSAA Tudor 4 crashed with thirty-one on board on route from the Azores to Bermuda.

Up to then, BSAA had been praised for its energetic management and its profitability. But now it was discovered that profits had only come at the expense of cutting corners on safety: its aircraft had only a ten-minute fuel-margin for transatlantic flights. The crash in January was the beginning of the end for BSAA, which agreed to merge with BOAC in March 1949. It also caused the grounding of the Tudors and another major equipment-crisis for British airlines.[40]

At the end of April the Cabinet decided to buy more Constellations. However, they managed to avoid paying in dollars by getting them second-hand from Eire. But, as George Cribbett,

[40] Hayward, *British Aerospace*, 15–18; Hansard, vols. for 1946–7; CAB 128/10, 95(47)5, 15 Dec. 1947. Cabinet authorized publication of interim report on Tudor 1, Cmd. 7307, on 15 Jan. 1948 (CAB 128/12, 4(48)2) and finally full report, Cmd. 7478, on 15 July 1948 (CAB 128/13, 51(48)5); 841.796/1–3048 and /2–1348, letters Gallman to Secretary of State and to London. Fortunately, one of the passengers that BSAA managed to convey safely to South America and back was my father-in-law, John Zinn: he was not, however, too happy to hear about the slim safety-margin for fuel.

Deputy Secretary in the Ministry of Civil Aviation and a major force there, correctly observed, although the government was still managing to uphold its 'buy British' policy in theory, the new Constellations from Eire would further demonstrate the competitiveness of American planes and bring nearer the day when the government would have to abandon its purchasing policy.[41]

In July Cribbett's prediction was verified in part. The government decided it would have to buy more American-designed planes, but, much to US annoyance, it opted for Canadian-built DC-4Ms. These were not as good as Constellations and again political considerations and broad economic ones put forward by Cripps had prevented direct purchases from the United States. The Americans had used intense diplomatic pressure to get orders from Britain and had offered very generous terms. They were thus particularly incensed that the Minister of Civil Aviation, now Lord Pakenham, when announcing the decision to buy Canadian-built planes made no mention of their helpful offer.[42]

As Britain reluctantly turned outward to US aircraft in order to make her airlines competitive, it also turned inwards to examine what had gone wrong. In 1948 the Hanbury-Williams Report, prompted by the tragedy of the Tudor programme, recommended a degree of disengagement by the government, to allow the airlines to deal directly with the manufacturers and make their own specifications. Subsequent legislation in 1948 and 1949 gave effect to the recommendations, and then in 1951, with the return to government of the Conservatives, an even more commercial approach to the airlines was taken. However, Britain never produced a long-range aircraft that could compete with American models. There was great success for the medium-range Vickers Viscount turbo-prop, which did much for the fortunes of BEA in the 1950s, but the Comet 1, the first commercial jet-airliner, which raised such hopes when it first flew in July 1949, was a different story. Lord Swinton expressed the optimism of many when he claimed in the Lords that Britain

[41] CAB 128/12, 30(48)11, 29 Apr. 1948; 841.796/5–1448, Douglas to Secretary of State.

[42] CAB 128/13, 51(48)5, 15 July 1948; 841.796/6–2348 and /7–748, Satterthwaite to Secretary of State and /7–2148, Douglas to Secretary of State.

had collared the market for a generation, but, tragically, it was not to be. Metal fatigue caused crashes in 1954, Comets were grounded, and Britain's last hope of an independent challenge to American supremacy in long-range aircraft was ended.[43]

The story of Britain's lack of competitive planes had been foreseen in the war and efforts had been made to alleviate the symptoms of this deficiency by the development of interim types such as the Tudors. There was little else that Britain could do to try to meet the challenge from the United States, though perhaps matters could have been handled more efficiently: the interim types were disasters. However, fears that the United States would steal and keep the entire world civil-aviation market were not borne out. The United States kept its pledge to make American planes available to other countries. Also, the need for Western co-operation in order to meet the challenge of Communism placed limits upon the extent to which the United States could ride roughshod over the interests, civil aviation or otherwise, of her allies. Within eighteen months of the end of the Second World War, although there continued to be friction, there was a renewal of the Special Relationship, largely in response to developments in Eastern Europe. It never reached the heights of the war years, but, in certain areas during specific periods, a Special Relationship did re-emerge. One area where it was eventually to be in evidence was the field of civil aviation, though immediately after Bermuda an impartial observer might have doubted the likelihood of that.

The Bermuda Agreement did not end British antagonism towards unfettered fifth-freedom rights, nor did it stop the Americans seeking such rights from other countries, and thus friction continued between the two allies. Britain made agreements with countries in Europe and in South America which were more restrictive than the Bermuda bilateral. Furthermore, although the Foreign Office constantly kept in mind the general welfare of Anglo-American relations, it nevertheless advised Middle Eastern governments not to give Americans unqualified fifth-freedom rights, in the interests of their own airlines—many of which were, coincidentally, part-owned, advised, or run by Britain.

[43] Hayward, *British Aerospace*, 18–22.

It did not take Satterthwaite long to report back to Washington about these British misdemeanours. But if Britain was not adhering to the Bermuda principles in subsequent agreements, neither, it seemed, was the United States. In June Masefield told the State Department that he thought that Bermuda was supposed to be a model both were to follow but that the United States was still pursuing untrammelled fifth-freedom rights. This was true, but in one respect regarding the five freedoms, the United States had moved closer to Britain. In the summer of 1946 the United States formally adopted the policy favoured by Pogue, the War Department, and Congress and renounced the multilateral five-freedom International Air Transport Agreement formulated at Chicago on 7 December 1944. The United States now favoured bilateral agreements in the short term and, in the longer term, a multilateral agreement which would provide for the liberal operation of routes, for example with full fifth-freedom rights, but only after the routes had been *bilaterally* arranged. Having abandoned the five-freedom multilateral model, the Americans wanted to urge a liberal bilateral model upon others in the international civil-aviation system, and the Bermuda model was the most promising candidate. However, differences with Britain over fifth-freedom rights were undermining this goal, and by August 1946 the situation was serious enough to merit high-level attention.[44]

On 13 August Acting Secretary of State Acheson wrote to Lord Inverchapel, the British Ambassador: 'there appears to be a trend away from certain of the Bermuda principles, especially those which impose no arbitrary limitations on frequencies and capacity, and which grant the right to carry Fifth Freedom traffic without undue restrictions'. In particular, Acheson referred to British agreements with France and Argentina. The Embassy replied that Bermuda did not debar the kind of agreements struck with those countries and, in any case, it had been they who had insisted on the conditions to which Acheson objected. Despite this spirited answer, the British were reluctant to see

[44] 841.796/3–1346 and /3–2746, Satterthwaite to Secretary of State, /6–1446, Masefield to Norton, /9–446, Gallman to Secretary of State; FO 371/54514, Gallman to Bevin, 30 July 1946, and AN3509/5/45, mins. by Mason, 4 Apr. 1946; J. C. Campbell *et al.*, *Council on Foreign Relations: The United States in World Affairs 1947–48* (Harper, New York, 1948), 298–304.

Bermuda threatened or Anglo-American relations endangered. Support for Bermuda had grown in the Cabinet, and even Cribbett, a long-standing opponent of American aviation policies was coming round to support Bermuda, and indeed over the next few years worked hard in its defence. Furthermore, although the British were not as liberally inclined as the Americans, it was not in their interests to see the world go protectionist in civil aviation: that had never been the wish of the government as a whole. What they wanted was an accommodation with the Americans that would take the steam out of the latter's vigorous pursuit of untrammelled fifth-freedom rights.[45]

From 12 to 14 September, at the invitation of the British, there was an informal conference in London to review the situation. The US delegation was led by James Landis, Chairman of the CAB, and by Garrison Norton, an Assistant Secretary of State. British representatives included Winster, Sir Henry Self, who had taken over as Director of Civil Aviation when Hildred left to become first Director of IATA in April 1946, Cribbett, and Masefield.

The three days of talks were not easy ones. Landis, a New Deal Liberal, was particularly difficult to appease from a British point of view. At one point he said that he would find it difficult to reaffirm the Bermuda Agreement jointly with the British if the agreements negotiated with France, Argentina, and Greece were upheld. Nevertheless, a number of factors convinced the British and the Americans that they should reaffirm Bermuda and, what is more, pursue its principles in future agreements and promote it to the rest of the world as a model to follow.

Since Chicago, Britain and the United States had moved closer to each other on fares and on routes, which both now believed should be negotiated bilaterally. Also, the British realized that they could not get their way in terms of controls once the United States had liberal bilaterals with countries like Sweden and Holland, and without competitive British planes they could not sustain an aviation policy independently of the United States. For their part, the Americans still saw dangers in British obstructionism, and in her going protectionist, and thus wanted to save Bermuda. Finally, both countries had common interests

[45] 800.796/8–1246 and /8–2946, Acheson to Inverchapel and reply.

which they were reluctant to damage by destroying the *modus vivendi* created at Bermuda. On the opening day of the talks Norton said,

> there was a feeling in U.S.A. circles that the present position had serious implications, and that in civil aviation, as in other spheres, the U.S.A. and the U.K. should, as far as possible, stand together and present a united front.

In the end they did. They pledged themselves in a joint statement to negotiate future bilaterals in accordance with Bermuda. They specifically reiterated the guiding principles for fifth-freedom traffic and that there should be machinery 'to obviate unfair competition by unjustifiable increases of frequencies or capacity'. Both of these statements were desired by the British. And they also required, this time for American interests, 'the elimination of formulae for the predetermination of frequencies or capacity or of any arbitrary division of air traffic between countries and their national airline'—something which the Americans rightly suspected the British of aiming for in various agreements they had pursued in Europe and the Middle East. Bermuda was now to be recommended to the world as the model to follow; however, the American suggestion that it should be the basis of an international multilateral agreement was received with caution by Self and Cribbett, who preferred to seek as many bilaterals as possible on the Bermuda model first, and then try for a multilateral agreement. No firm decision on this was taken in London, but as problems arose again in 1947, and as the danger from British retrenchment threatened to develop into protectionism, the United States saw the adherence to a multilateral, not just of other states but of Britain as well, as the best way of sustaining a liberal international aviation system.[46]

Britain's position deteriorated in 1947. The equipment problem went from bad to worse, as did the political situation in Europe. The massive economic problems confronting Britain turned into a crisis, largely because of the requirement of the US Loan Agreement that sterling be made convertible. Both eco-

[46] 711.4127/10–1746, Record of Discussions of Civil Aviation, 12–14 Sept. 1946; FO 371/54515, Joint Statement, 23 Sept. 1946; HST PSF, box 225, folder: Central Intelligence Reports, 'Prospects for International Air Transport', 26 Mar. 1948.

nomic and political developments tended to push Britain and the United States closer together (even in the economic realm, for Britain had nowhere else to turn for help), increasing their interdependence. The crises also distracted British attention away from civil aviation and made it more difficult to care for her interests there.

While British airlines stumbled from one problem into another and cut back on their operations, PAA went from strength to strength. It had lost the first round in fare cuts in 1945, but had continued to press its case. By 1947 a number of modest reductions had been made, or were in the process of being made, and British opposition was ineffective. Perhaps more worrying was something which even the US Embassy in London thought was contrary to the Bermuda Agreement. PAA proposed, and its proposal was eventually accepted, that there should be a change of gauge in London which was not timetabled to link with incoming flights from the United States and which established, 'what looks suspiciously like a regional operation'.

Developments such as these, and Britain's ever-present equipment problem, made the United States keen to tie Britain into a multilateral aviation-agreement, in order to make it as difficult as possible for her to go protectionist. Cribbett, now a full convert to Bermuda, and the British government in general (despite some misgivings in the Air and Civil Aviation Ministries and the Foreign Office), also saw benefits in a multilateral agreement.[47]

At the first meeting of the ICAO at Montreal in early 1947 the Americans objected to proposals for a multilateral agreement put forward by its Council on the ground that they were too restrictive and unrealistic; instead, they tabled an alternative drawn up by the US Air Co-ordinating Committee (of which more later) and based on Bermuda. There was insufficient support, and matters were postponed to November, when a further attempt was to be made at a special conference of the ICAO in Geneva.

[47] 841.796/9–1747, Douglas to Secretary of State, /9–3047, Satterthwaite to Secretary of State, /5–247, Vass to Secretary of State, /3–2447, Douglas to Secretary of State; 811.79641/4–247, Douglas to Secretary of State; 841.79600/8–2647, Satterthwaite to Merchant; FO 371/70170, mins. by J. Murray, 5 Nov. 1948, /65484, Washington to Foreign Office, 26 Dec. 1946.

The position which the two countries advocated there was the same as they had agreed on in September 1946. They proposed that routes should be bilaterally negotiated and their operation governed by a liberal regime. As always, the main stumbling-bloc was fifth-freedom rights, which were to operate under the same principles as Bermuda. The British would have been happy to bring in tighter controls, but publicly they held firm with the Americans. However, their stance was to no avail. When it came to the vote, a bloc led by Mexico, fearing that the controls were inadequate, won the day by 13 to 9.[48]

The failure at Geneva was a set-back for American hopes of tying Britain inextricably into a liberal regime, but other developments in 1947 and early 1948 augured well for Anglo-American aviation co-operation. In early 1947 the British and Americans had secret talks to try to co-ordinate their aviation policies with regard to the Soviet Union. Just over a year later the importance of such a strategy was demonstrated when the Soviets imposed a road and rail blockade on routes to West Berlin. That prompted the British and Americans to mount the Berlin airlift. The airlift did much to help the fortunes of Britain's small independent airlines, but more importantly it demonstrated the need for allied, not just American, strength in the air. The cold war strengthened Anglo-American co-operation, but in addition, in February 1948 the two countries managed to put to rest some differences that had been rumbling on since Bermuda. These concerned the civil air rights the United States wanted for aerodromes it had built during the war on bases leased from Britain in the Caribbean and Newfoundland. The final accord gave both the United States and Britain the same, very limited, rights, though the latter's also included cabotage traffic.[49]

Despite these developments, which on the whole were encouraging for those who sought to nurture good civil-aviation relations between the United States and Britain, problems remained. In particular, the Americans continued to fear a return

[48] Ibid.; Campbell, *World Affairs*, 298–304; HST PSF, box 225, folder: Central Intelligence Reports, 20 May 1948.

[49] FO 371/65535, Freese-Pennefather memo, 'Proposed Aviation Talks with the Americans', 1 Feb. 1947 and Foreign Office to Washington, 28 Feb. 1947 and following, also Washington to Foreign Office, 13 June 1947; Cmd. 7389. 1948, 'Agreement on Military Airbases'.

to protectionism by Britain because of her inadequate equipment, and they were also troubled by what they perceived as a lack of British determination to secure Bermuda-type bilateral agreements with other countries. Once again it was Cribbett who had to sort things out.

In November 1948 he had a series of talks with the Americans in Washington. According to one report they gave, 'Sir George an unpleasant time.' If that were so, it was not intentional. Garrison Norton regarded the talks as 'highly important', and as Cribbett was acknowledged to be the main defender of Anglo-American international air-transport policy, he therefore thought it 'vital to the preservation of our present policies that Sir George be accorded every possible courtesy during his visit'.

The talks were difficult but amicable. The Americans were having difficulties themselves in getting the Bermuda principles accepted, for example by Peru, and this made them even more determined to try to persuade Britain not to set bad precedents by giving way to pressures for restrictive agreements. Cribbett managed to persuade them that Britain's difficulties with countries such as Egypt and India were as real as America's with Peru. He told them that Britain had no intention of departing from the Bermuda principles but that sometimes it might be unavoidable. Cribbett reported that in the end, 'We undertook to press negotiations to the extreme limit and not to make concessions lightly which would involve major departures from basic principles of Bermuda.'[50]

Bermuda thus became the firm cornerstone of the aviation relationship between the two countries. It never became a universal model: agreements to which the United States was not a party were much more restrictive than Bermuda, and many of Britain's agreements with European countries involved traffic-sharing and controls over frequencies and fifth-freedom traffic. Also, air communications between the members of the British Commonwealth were exempted from the Bermuda model. Nevertheless, in many ways Bermuda set a standard by which aviation relations could be judged. It governed the relations

[50] FO 371/70170, mins. by Murray, 5 Nov. 1948, Foreign Office mins. 13 Nov. 1948, mins. by Murray, 27 Nov. 1948, and Cribbett to Overton, 24 Nov. 1948; 811.79641/10–2348, Holmes to Secretary of State, /10–2648, memo by Norton, and /2–2149, memo of discussions between the United States and Britain.

between the United States and Britain for thirty years, and for much of that time there was little further challenge to its broad principles. However, problems arose from time to time over the bilateral negotiation of routes and the level at which fares should be set. It was in these two operational areas, rather than over matters of principle, that British and American diplomatic energy was spent in the decades following Bermuda.

7
Routes, Rates, and Rearrangements 1946–1973

FROM 1946 to 1973 the United States played the dominant role in world aviation, and the liberal model of Bermuda was the benchmark by which it judged the policies of other states. In 1970 America's airlines flew over 45 per cent of the world's passenger miles and its industry dominated the civil-aircraft market. Nevertheless, the United States did not always have its own way. Liberalism was a major influence on the world's aviation system, but Britain, while keeping to the Bermuda Agreement, made others which were much more restrictive. There were cases, notably that of Holland, where liberalism flourished more than in Britain, but the rest of the world, although pressed into Bermuda-type agreements with the United States, generally made arrangements involving more controls.

Despite British and American differences about competition, which put pressure on the Bermuda Agreement, it survived intact for thirty years. It weathered the Chandler rate-crisis of 1962–3, which, though comparable in some ways to that provoked by PAA's unilateral Atlantic fare-cut in late 1945, was the most serious controversy about fares during the lifetime of the Bermuda regime. It also survived a long dispute involving US demands for rights in Hong Kong and British designs for a through-route via the United States to Australia. An agreement was eventually struck in the spring of 1966 which involved the most extensive amendments that were ever made to the Bermuda bilateral. However, a few years later everything was thrown into turmoil by the oil crisis of 1973–4. In particular, the crisis revived concern about capacity and controls and prompted Britain to seek radical amendments to the Bermuda Agreement.

Before that, the tussle that went on between Britain and the United States within the framework of Bermuda 1 was influenced by international agreements and traditional diplomatic factors. It was also affected by the political arrangements which governed civil aviation and by the development of passenger aircraft, and these matters need to be considered before we look at the substantive difficulties that arose regarding routes and rates, in order that the position of both sides may be fully grasped.

POLITICS, PLANES, AND CIVIL AVIATION IN THE UNITED STATES AND BRITAIN 1946–1973

Until the 1980s it was easy for politics to take precedence over commercial considerations in British aviation because the main airlines were nationalized. The British government's post-war decision that airlines should buy British aircraft whenever possible, and the role of the Ministry of Supply in making aircraft specifications both illustrate how government interference caused commercial problems. The government's decision to support British manufacturers, and its specifications for planes resulted in a series of commercially disastrous aircraft, many of which had to be used by BOAC even though they were uneconomic. BOAC still had equipment problems in 1957, when the United States offered Britain a fair deal involving a much-sought-after Pacific route, but the fact that the company had no suitable planes to operate on it was one reason why it was rejected. In 1948 the Hanbury Williams Report had corrected some of the failings which afflicted civil aviation, but even when the more free-market Conservatives returned in 1951, they still obliged BOAC to continue both with uneconomic routes and with costly assistance to countries like Kuwait. These commercial handicaps, together with muddled management, compromised BOAC's chances of commercial success and over time financial difficulties quietly accumulated. Then, in 1960–1, the growth of the passenger market slumped—just after acquisition of new aircraft by airlines had already caused over-capacity—and BOAC's economic problems became impossible to ignore.

Apart from the nationalized airlines, there were a number of private companies, and in 1951 the Conservatives tried to help these by empowering the Air Transport Advisory Council (ATAC), established in 1946, to grant independent operators licences for routes which would not steal custom from BOAC and BEA. A number of them flourished by plying such routes and by developing the charter business, which was helped by contracts from the military. At the end of the 1950s the

Macmillan Government took this policy further in the Civil Aviation Licensing Act of 1960, which created the Air Traffic Licensing Board (ATLB). After that, it was possible to grant routes to private airlines even if they competed with BOAC and BEA. In 1961 Cunard Eagle provided a test case for the new dispensation by applying for a transatlantic route. One was awarded, but it was at a time when established carriers were in difficulties, and in response to representations from BOAC (operating at the time with a load factor under 50 per cent) the award was rescinded the following year, largely on the grounds that Cunard Eagle could only operate at the expense of BOAC, which was not in the public interest. For the time being, British dual designation and the increased competition it involved did not develop.[1]

Ironically, Conservatives, while trying to inject more of the free market into the airlines, felt obliged to renew direct support for aircraft manufacturing. At the start of the 1950s they had tried to shift responsibility for R. & D. on to the plane makers, but serious difficulties ensued. From 1956 onwards Britain had to order American planes in large numbers and efforts to rationalize British manufacturing through mergers had only limited success. The Comet and the Britannia turbo-prop both put great strain on British companies; the long-range, medium-sized VC-10 was expensive to operate and, as the world's airports were enlarged in order to cater for large jets, its main selling-strategy of being able to go where the large jets could not was negated. In 1959 the British government decided to relax its 'buy British' policy, but it was not until the mid-1960s that the need to do so was forced home. Matters came to a head after the Corbett Inquiry into BOAC's financial problems in 1963. In the shake-up that followed, Sir Giles Guthrie became head of the company,

[1] S. Wheatcroft, *Air Transport Policy* (Michael Joseph, London, 1964), ch. 2; K. Hayward, *Government and British Civil Aerospace* (Manchester University Press, Manchester, 1983), chs. 1–2; D. Corbett, *Politics and the Airlines* (George Allen & Unwin, London, 1965), 248–69; R. Baldwin, *Regulating the Airlines: Administrative Justice and Agency Discretion* (Clarendon, Oxford, 1985), chs. 2–3. The success of US aviation manufacturing continues in the 1990s: Boeing in 1989 and 1990 received orders worth $46.62 billion and $47.7 respectively. This section is primarily concerned with summarizing domestic developments, and I have relied heavily on the works cited above, along with the relevant Command Papers and the Annual Reports of BOAC for the 1950s and early 1960s.

with a pledge from the government that he could operate commercially. But within months there arose the vexed question of the sale of VC-10s which the company did not want to buy. The government, in order to reconcile its commitment to support the aircraft industry with its pledge to Guthrie, agreed to subsidize purchases of VC-10s by BOAC. The government was getting the worst of all worlds by funding the development of uncommercial planes and then subsidizing their use.

Faced with difficulties in the manufacturing sphere, the Conservatives had abolished the Ministry of Supply and the Ministry of Civil Aviation in 1959 and replaced them with the Ministry of Aviation. Private enterprise was again to be helped directly by government funds for R. & D., and more rationalization of British aeroplane-manufacturing was to be encouraged. But the VC-10 was Britain's last independent attempt to challenge the Americans in long-range passenger-jets. The jumbo was the next generation of plane and no country has produced competitors for the American Boeing-747s, DC-10s, and Lockheed Tristars.

By the 1960s the cost of developing new planes was becoming prohibitive for an economy like Britain's, but that did not deter the British government from trying to spearhead new technology—though realism prevailed to the extent that it realized that it needed to collaborate with a foreign partner. The British turned to the French and signed a treaty in November 1962 to develop the Concorde SST, in order to try to steal a lead on the Americans (though this was only after the United States had declined to enter a co-operative supersonic transport (SST) venture with them). It came under review by the Labour government of Harold Wilson in 1964–5, but emerged unscathed. Perhaps it were better it had not. The idea was to give the British aircraft-industry and the airlines new prestige and a competitive edge on their rivals, but, rather like the technological gamble involved with the Comet—though not as tragically—the project did not work out as planned. But for a while it looked as if there would be a contest between jumbos and SSTs. In the United States the prospect of a successful SST taking to the air over France and Britain caused concern mounting at times to panic.

Although Concorde went ahead, many other projects were abandoned and in the Plowden Report in 1965 rationalization was again recommended. It proceeded steadily until 1977, when the two remaining consortia, Hawker Siddeley Aviation and the British Aircraft Corporation, were joined and nationalized to form British Aerospace. The political structure overseeing aviation also underwent major changes. In 1966 the Ministry of Aviation was abolished and the Board of Trade took responsibility for civil aviation, and the Ministry of Technology for R. & D. That regime did not survive long. By the end of the decade there was unease about its effectiveness, especially as civil aviation had boomed after 1962 without a corresponding increase in the fortunes of British aviation. In 1960–1 PAA and TWA had flown totals of around five or six billion passenger miles, with TWA's mileage actually declining slightly in 1961; in 1969 PAA flew over seventeen billion and TWA over nineteen billion passenger miles. The industry was vibrant with confidence: the Boeing-747 made its maiden flight on 9 February 1969, and eleven months later it inaugurated the first wide-bodied jet service in the world between New York and London, under the colours of PAA. These developments, and unease about British civil aviation's performance, prompted the British government to new action.[2]

In 1969 the Edwards Report, commissioned by the Labour government, recommended radical changes. The report was critical of the ATLB and of ministerial interference in civil aviation, and its main thrust was for a more competitive system. It proposed the creation of a Civil Aviation Authority (CAA) with similar functions to the American CAB, and with a similar degree of independence from political interference. Furthermore, while the nationalized companies might remain—though more commercially managed—Edwards thought that they ought to have more competition by nurturing a 'second force' airline from the private sector and by introducing some dual designation. The whole tenor of the Report was somewhat at odds with Labour's previous policy. For example, in 1965 the then Aviation Minister, Roy Jenkins, had declared that it was not in BOAC's interests to have dual designation. Nevertheless, the

[2] Hayward, *British Aerospace*, chs. 1–3; Cmd. 5, 'The Financial problems of BOAC', 1963; Cmd. 2853, 'The Plowden Report', 1964; TWA and PAA passenger miles quoted from R. E. G. Davies, *Airlines of the United States Since 1914* (Putnam, London, 1982), App. 3.

government accepted the Edwards Report, but was unable to enact it before Labour's surprise defeat in the general election of 1970. It was left to the Heath Government to implement changes, which it did in 1971 with little alteration to extant proposals. The only exception was that it kept more discretionary power to intervene than the Edwards Report had thought desirable.

The Civil Aviation Act of 1971 created the CAA and placed ministerial responsibility for civil aviation in the Department of Trade and Industry. Over the following months the government used its influence to bolster the position of British Caledonian Airways (B.Cal.) through route swaps between it and BOAC, which created a third overseas regional chosen instrument (though in 1974 BOAC and BEA, in an attempt to improve their performance were merged to form British Airways (BA), thus once again reducing the chosen instruments to two). In addition to enlarging the independent route-system of B.Cal., the Conservatives also introduced dual designation: the company was awarded a fifteen-year licence to ply the Atlantic route.[3]

From 1946 to the early 1970s British civil aviation was subjected to a series of changes both in terms of the political structure overseeing it and in terms of general policy. Changes between Labour and Conservative normally heralded different emphases on market forces and on the degree of freedom to be allowed to the nationalized airlines to conduct their business, and in particular to decide their equipment needs. Political influence was easily exerted on the industry because of nationalization and it resulted in conflicting lines of responsibility between chairmen of the companies and their political overlords. Purchasing-policy, which was affected by political considerations and the failure of British plane-manufacturers to produce competitive planes (with the notable exception of the Viscount), adversely affected BOAC, and in particular burdened it with large proving-costs for the Comet and the Britannia—there were ten years between the latter's first flight and its entry into commercial service. Political considerations also required BOAC to maintain

[3] Cmd. 4018, 'The Edwards Report', 1969; Cmd. 4899, 'Civil Aviation Policy Guidance', 1972; Baldwin, *Regulating*, chs. 7–11; A. Sampson, *Empires of the Sky: The Politics, Contests and Cartels of World Airlines* (Hodder & Stoughton, London, 1984), ch. 11.

a number of subsidiaries and to provide services to foreign countries which further damaged its profit-making potential. All these things placed Britain at a disadvantage in its dealings with the United States during the lifetime of the Bermuda Agreement and resulted in generally defensive and cautious policies. US airlines also incurred burdens through political demands from their own government, but they were generally in better positions to shoulder them and were not subject to the same level of political interference; nor did they suffer to the same extent from changing political policies or a general lack of any clear direction in policy. Nevertheless, it should be noted that by the 1970s British civil aviation was coming to terms better with the competitive world in which it operated, and was still the second in importance after the United States in international aviation. The Conservatives had consistently tried to foster more competition and this was to bear fruit in the following two decades. Also, British Aerospace did not suffer from quite such delusions of grandeur as its predecessors and produced, in co-operation with European nations, some successful planes. But British success in civil aviation after 1970 must be ascribed largely to its abandonment of the 'buy British' policy and the acquisition of American jumbos, for it was by them that the future success of civil aviation was determined.

There were substantial changes in the United States during 1946–73 in the political structure that regulated aviation, but generally these changes had only an indirect influence upon foreign operations. Unlike in Britain, where there was a disruptive, changing mixture of both ministerial control and authority exercised by the ATAC, the ATLB, and the CAA, in the United States the CAB retained authority in conjunction with the President to award routes to airlines. However, there were other important political movements, culminating in the creation of the Department of Transport (DOT) in 1966.

After the war there continued to be concern about the direction of aviation policy, and so in 1946 Truman elevated the status of the Air Coordinating Committee (ACC), which had been set up the previous year. From its enhanced position it was to formulate integrated policies by drawing together the various departments with aviation interests. In its early years it performed a valuable role, and even in the 1950s, when it became deadlocked by conflicting views and lack of strong direction from above, it still acted as a source of ideas for reform.

In 1947 strategic considerations also had an impact on the development of civil aviation. Wartime concern with the military aspect of aviation was given renewed emphasis in the report of the President's Air Policy Commission, chaired by Thomas K. Finletter, later Secretary of the Air Force. Truman agreed with its proposals to build up air power and manufacturing-potential, and with the importance accorded civil aviation, which he hoped would not suffer as a result of being regarded as subordinate to the military. In fact, civil aviation did temporarily suffer from that, once the Korean War broke out. Resources were diverted from civilian to military projects, which slowed down development of both American civilian jets and the domestic infrastructure for the coming age of mass air-transport.[4]

In 1953, when Eisenhower came into office, there was mounting pressure for new initiatives. Organizationally, things were unsatisfactory. One result of the Finletter Report had been the appointment of an Under-Secretary of Transportation in the Commerce Department, which established a third tier of responsibility in the sphere of domestic aviation, between the Secretary of Commerce and the CAA. Consequently, government leadership for civil-aviation policy was less effective than it might otherwise have been. On 19 August 1953 Charles Cary, Executive Secretary of the ACC, sent a memorandum to Charles Willis, the President's Special Assistant on Aviation, which criticized the lack of direction in aviation policy. He emphasized its overwhelming economic and military importance and he suggested that the ACC should either be enabled to do a proper

[4] HST, Adams Papers, box 5, folder: CAB Coordinated Federal Program for Transportation; ibid., President's Air Policy Commission, July 1947–Jan. 1948, boxes 31 and 34, folder: Draft of letter Truman to Congress; S. I. Rochester, *Take-off at Mid-Century: Federal Aviation Policy in the Eisenhower Years 1953–61* (US Department of Transport, Federal Aviation Authority, Washington DC, 1976), 18–69. As in the comparable section on British policy, I have relied on secondary works, in particular Rochester's book and its sequel by R. J. Kent, *Safe, Separated and Soaring: A History of Civil Aviation 1961–72* (US Department of Transport, Federal Aviation Authority, Washington DC, 1980), which are vols. iii and iv in a series of five. Additional material is from various presidential libraries as indicated.

job or be abolished, and also that a general statement of policy should be drawn up for presidential approval.[5]

This was the beginning of a series of reappraisals. Firstly, as a direct result of Cary's initiative, there emerged the January 1954 Review of National Air Policy, recommending that subsidies be drastically reduced, that more emphasis be given to free enterprise (which was to be the creative force in civil aviation), and that there should be closer civil–military co-operation and more government direction. Despite a rather complacent tone in the report, momentum for more action grew because of concerns about safety and because of the need to develop both airports and, above all, an integrated and comprehensive system of air-traffic control.

In July 1954, as part of the review of national transport, which until then had concentrated on the development of an interstate highway-system, Eisenhower appointed William Barclay Harding to review air policy. Harding led the Aviation Facilities Study Group and as a direct result of his work, later carried forward successively by Edward Curtis, head of Aviation Facilities Planning, and Lieutenant General Elwood R. 'Pete' Quesada, the Federal Aviation Authority (FAA) was created in 1958, with independent and considerably expanded powers. (Shortly after that, the ACC was abolished on the recommendation of Quesada, the first Administrator of the FAA.) This process of elevating the importance of civil aviation continued in the 1960s, culminating in 1966 with the creation of an independent DOT headed by a previous CAB Chairman, Alan Boyd. The DOT played a more important role in the international side of aviation than either of its two predecessors, the CAA and the FAA. However, foreign matters remained largely in the hands of the CAB, the President, and the State Department until the CAB's demise in 1984, when those of its responsibilities which were not abolished outright were assumed by the DOT.[6]

[5] DDE CF CF, box 1, folder: ACC, Cary memo. 'The Development of a National Aviation Policy and the Functions of the ACC', to Willis, 19 Aug. 1953; ibid., folder: ACC (2) Eisenhower to Chairman of ACC, Murray, 23 Sept. 1953; Rochester, *Take-off*.

[6] DDE CF CF, box 2, 'Review of National Air Policy', 19 Jan. 1954; DDE CFEP 1954–61, box 2, folder: aviation (2), 11 Aug. 1960; *FRUS* 1952–4, 1 (i), 428–34,

Political attitudes about international aviation in the United States, particularly about competition, fluctuated somewhat as they did in Britain, but they did so in response more to market conditions and differences between departments and agencies than to political doctrines. In 1950 Truman required TWA and PAA to compete with each other directly on the Atlantic routes, but later in the decade and during the slump of the early 1960s that attitude mellowed. Nevertheless, the United States repeatedly reasserted its commitment to the liberal model of the Bermuda Agreement. It did not always live up to its own standards—for example, it withheld reciprocal rights from other countries if it was possible to get away with it—but on the whole its commitment to an internationally open and competitive regime remained solid. In particular, the US government, though not always all its airlines, became increasingly sceptical about the benefits of IATA. By the end of the 1960s it had become openly hostile to IATA fare-fixing, and gradually British governments also became marginally less supportive and began to place more importance upon bilateral arrangements and market forces, though this did not prevent serious difficulties over fares with the Americans in the early 1980s.[7]

Government in both Britain and the United States did their best to foster the interests of their respective airlines, but US policy was more consistent, commercially oriented, and competitive. It was less troubled by changes of political policy, and politicians and bureaucrats did not have the power to interfere directly in the management of the airlines. When government policy did affect the airlines, it tended to be constructive and helpful—even if, as in the case of developing an integrated system of air-traffic control for the United States, it was a slow and difficult affair. When US government policy appeared to

'Current Economic Developments', 11 May, 1954; Rochester, *Take-off*; Kent, *Soaring*.

[7] For differences between CAB and Commerce Dept., see Adams Papers, box 5, folder: CAB Coordinated Federal Program for Transportation, O'Connell to Steelman, 30 Jan. 1950; for protectionist tendency in Congress, see H. A. Wassenbergh, *Aspects of Air Law and Civil Air Policy in the Seventies* (Martinus Nijhoff, The Hague, 1970), 17–20; R. Y. Chuang, *The International Air Transport Association* (A. W. Sijthoff, Leiden, 1972), ch. 9. The Americans reasserted their commitment to Bermuda most notably in Sept. 1946, in Apr. 1963, in 1966, and 1970, and they were reluctant to modify it in 1976/77.

lose its way, the leadership of the airlines was usually strong and imaginative enough to carry forward their own interests anyway. In making these unfavourable comparisons with British experience, one must not forget that US airlines at the end of the war were bigger, better equipped, and, with the exception of PAA, had the advantage of exclusive access to the massive American market. They also had direct access to companies with R. & D. experience that facilitated the production of the new generation of post-war civil passenger-planes. And even in the one area where US government and airlines alike seemed confused and uncertain—the development of SST—things turned out favourably in the end.

On two occasions in the post-war period, aircraft developments in Britain threatened to give British airlines a competitive edge over American ones and thus affect the overall relationship of the two countries in the sphere of aviation. In both cases the immediate result in the United States was panic. But unfortunately for Britain, the first innovation—the introduction of the Comet—simply saddled her with a costly failure and stimulated the Americans to develop their own jets rapidly, and these subsequently dominated the market. The second innovation was Concorde, which greatly drained British and French manufacturing and financial resources and in pure commercial terms has been a gigantic failure. For their part, the Americans, more by good luck than good management, avoided the unpleasant consequences reaped by the British and the French.

The Americans came close to making the same mistake. In November 1962, when Concorde was given the signal to proceed, the CAB Chairman, Najeeb Halaby, wrote in panic to Kennedy that the United States was in danger of relinquishing its leadership in aviation. Failure to develop an American SST: would force the United States to spend three billion dollars to acquire European ones; would lose the United States four billion dollars in possible exports and 50,000 jobs; would make the United States dependent on Britain and France for a military version; and, horror of horrors, would 'conceivably, persuade the President of the United States to fly in a foreign aircraft'.[8]

[8] JFK POF, box 78, folder: FAA 1963, Halaby to Kennedy, 15 Nov. 1962; ibid., box 90, folder: Depts. and Agencies, Treasury 5/63, Treasury Secretary Dillon to Kennedy, 31 May 1963 urging him to authorize SST.

Thus began ten years of agonizing over whether or not to proceed with an American SST. Successive high-level reports from government committees declared themselves in favour, and prototype models were produced. But as the 1960s wore on, and Vietnam put American finances under strain, more caution about a full-scale development became evident. Doubts about the commercial profitability of SSTs had always existed, but they now became more telling. By the end of the decade the environmental effects had also assumed great importance. In 1970 President Nixon's newly appointed Council on Environmental Quality expressed dissent from its own government's policy on SST. Simultaneously with this division in government and with the expression of concern about the commercial prospects of the SST, matters were brought to a head in hearings before Senator Proxmire's Subcommittee on Economy in Government. The result was fatal for the SST, and finally, on 24 March 1971, the Senate, following the House, refused to vote further money for its development.[9]

American aviation enjoyed many advantages over its British counterpart during the life of the Bermuda 1 regime. American airlines were commercially managed; both the political framework and the help they received was generally better; they had superior equipment; and on the two occasions that they lagged behind Britain in the development of aircraft, the gods seemed to be with them and their fortunes prospered in the end. These advantages were often evident in specific problems that they had with their British counterparts over routes and fares, but, because civil aviation is not an island unto itself, the Americans, for wider reasons of State, did not always emerge triumphant.

ROUTES

Britain and the United States have had difficulties over routes ever since intercontinental flights began. Problems have arisen from their different circumstances and the different advantages and disadvantages these confer concerning aviation routes. The different perspectives on civil aviation which result from

[9] LBJ CF CF, boxes 4 and 39, folder: President's Advisory Committee on SST; Kent, *Soaring*, 101 ff.

this go a long way towards accounting for the difficulties that Britain and the United States have experienced in their aviation relations.

Because of the Empire, Britain inherited many overseas connections which have benefited its civil aviation, but its domestic base has never been sufficient to support anything but small airlines. The United States does not have the same number of historical connections overseas, but it looks on to the Pacific and the Atlantic, both of which it dominated in terms of transoceanic flight until the 1960s. Thereafter, other countries began to challenge US airlines, but only with American-made aircraft. America's main advantage has been, and still is, its vast domestic market, operations in which have often subsidized American overseas operations. But even when they have not, the size of the United States has given American airlines advantages over companies like BOAC, because TWA (but not PAA, at least not until 1979) could arrange its schedule in order to connect overseas flights with its internal flights, for onward carriage of passengers to their final US destination. The size of Britain meant that onward flights there were simply not necessary, or, if they were, destinations were equally accessible by rail. Furthermore, the United States had ample opportunity for collecting fifth-freedom traffic in London, but the option for the same kind of traffic in New York and other American entry-points for British airlines was, and is, extremely limited. American cabotage has never been opened to British airlines, and onward destinations like Mexico, South America, New Zealand, or Australia appeared commercially unviable in the 1950s and early 1960s—at least if the routes were operated independently by BOAC.

One might say that Britain's 'hinterland' was Europe, which the United States had rights to exploit, and that America's was its domestic market, which was out of bounds to British operators. This situation, and America's advantage in having large fleets of modern aircraft, meant that she dominated international civil aviation in the first two post-war decades. However, although the United States carried a massive proportion of the world's traffic, this percentage declined steadily over the years, and by the mid-1960s there was an unfavourable gap between the percentage of traffic generated by the United States

(66 per cent) and the percentage carried by its airlines on the Atlantic route (50 per cent), and that seemed unfair to some Americans. From this angle, America's position overall was not as dominant as it should have been, and that appeared to justify a vigorous defence and expansion of US airline-operations overseas.

What follows is not a comprehensive account of all the route problems which arose under Bermuda between Britain and the United States, but a story of conflict in one particular area which illustrates characteristic difficulties. Things were far from being all sweetness and light under the Bermuda model. A member of the Foreign Office wrote of the general character of civil-aviation diplomacy in the second half of the 1950s:

> Its hard-headedness and hard-heartedness seemed total. This was one area, one was told, in which one could not afford to oblige political friends or disoblige the not so friendly. It was pointed out with ruthless logic by the airlines, supported by the Ministry of Civil Aviation, that the only way to secure much needed commercial rights was to use to the full such bargaining power as we had.[10]

The Pacific was an area fraught with difficulties. The US position there was even more commanding than in the Atlantic, and, as already noted, the Americans in the 1930s and during the war were at pains to secure Pacific bases even at the expense of intense friction with Britain. The most celebrated case was that of Canton Island, where eventually dual, Anglo-American suzerainty was agreed upon. Nevertheless, there were still some things that the United States needed in the Pacific, especially after TWA and Northwestern Airlines (NWA) were granted routes there: in particular it wanted more access to Hong Kong. The Pacific was also important for the British, because it held the key to a round-the-world Commonwealth route.

Towards the end of 1946 there were talks between British and US officials to amend the Bermuda route-provisions. The changes were modest, but they included a new route for the British from New Zealand and Australia to Vancouver via Fiji, Canton Island, Honolulu, and San Francisco. In return, PAA

[10] Paul Gore-Booth, *With Great Truth and Respect* (Constable, London, 1974), 240–41; LBJ NSF Country File, box 208, 209, folder: memos vol. 6 7/65–9/65, memo of conversation between Rusk and Dean, 12 Aug. 1965.

received a parallel route. Notes were exchanged on 20 December 1946 and 27 January 1947, and paragraph 2 stated in part: 'In accordance with Article 2 of the Agreement, His Majesty's Government . . . propose to designate British Commonwealth Pacific Airways.' For a while the British, in conjunction with their Australian and New Zealand partners in BCPA, had access to the west coast of America. But when BCPA expired, Qantas successfully negotiated to take over the route, leaving BOAC without the means to fly in the South Pacific.[11]

In 1955, shortly after the demise of BCPA, the United States and Britain had a round of wide-ranging talks about routes. During these talks, the British enquired whether the 1947 Exchange of Notes could be interpreted to allow them to license a British carrier for the South Pacific. The Americans were surprised and hesitated, then replied negatively. For the time being, the British seemed to accept that judgement, but they soon began to press for a different interpretation. The Suez Crisis made all things difficult in 1956 and no progress was achieved that year. Then in 1957 the question of routes was raised again, and the Americans countered British demands for rights in the Pacific with requests for rights in Hong Kong and between London and Frankfurt.[12]

The problems involved in exchanging routes were discussed at Bermuda in March 1957 and taken up again by Satterthwaite of the State Department and Fitzgerald of the CAB in London between 18 and 27 June. Mr Wilson of the Ministry of Transport and Civil Aviation chaired the discussions and he had a very difficult situation to handle so far as British interests were concerned. Hovering in the background was a danger of momentum developing towards general protectionism, which was already being felt in civil aviation. The American negotiators urged Britain to an agreement, arguing that in the future things would be more difficult because of the growing political strength of American domestic airlines, which took an illiberal view of foreign traffic rights. The British in turn pointed to problems arising in Europe, but pronounced that they did not favour the

[11] Cmd. 7209, 'Exchange of Notes Amending Bermuda', 1947; Sampson, *Empires*, 88–9.

[12] LBJ NSF Country File, box 208, 209, folder: UK memos, vol. 7, 10/65–1/66, memo 'The Civil Air Dispute with Britain', 18 Oct. 1965.

idea bruited elsewhere of establishing European cabotage.[13]

While the British dissociated themselves from more extreme forms of protectionism, they were very much on the defensive. The same month that the talks took place, news came through that the Americans had granted Qantas an extension of its South Pacific route, enabling it to cross the United States via San Francisco and New York. On 11 December the CAB granted Qantas Pacific stops on its route and disclosed some of the reasons involved, which were highly political: Australia, geographically isolated, had important links with the United States, and these were particularly valuable during an unsettled period in the Far East. Interestingly, despite the greater commercial competition between Britain and the United States, the Americans also saw political reasons for an accommodation with the British government on an exchange of routes. Before the talks, US Ambassador Whitney called on Foreign Secretary Lloyd 'to urge the wider political importance of reaching agreement. The State Department spoke similarly to Her Majesty's Ambassador [Caccia], adding in particular that failure on [Britain's] part to agree to the route request for TWA might prevent the airline placing important order for Viscount aircraft.' The Americans wanted to ensure that decisions were taken at a high political level, but the equipment crisis that was then plaguing BOAC resulted in a wholly defensive response from the company, and its was the decisive say on the British position in the negotiations.[14]

The Ministry of Transport and Civil Aviation (MTCA) and the Foreign Office both favoured an agreement with the United States that would yield the South Pacific route to BOAC. The MTCA's response to the news of Qantas's success in getting the South Pacific route extended across America was that 'sooner or later the Australians will be wanting rights in London which . . . will necessitate BOAC running a parallel route London/San Francisco/Sydney'. It believed that BOAC would do well to get

[13] FO 371/127693, Foreign Office mins. 'Talks 18–27 June 1957 with Satterthwaite and Fitzgerald', 16 July 1957; DDE AWF, box 20, folder: Macmillan, Oct. 23–5, 1957 (2), memo of conversation between Dillon, Lloyd, *et al.*, 25 Oct. 1957.

[14] DDE CF CF, box 15, folder: CAB (17), 11 Dec. 1957, Docket 9019; FO 371/127693, mins. P. S. Falla, American Department, 18 July 1957.

that route now rather than wait and pay a far higher price later. The prime motive for BOAC duplicating Qantas's operation was to extend the general pooling and sharing of profits on parallel routes that already went on between the two companies. However, George Cribbett, Deputy Chairman of BOAC, had two lines of reasoning which opposed the deal with the United States.[15]

First of all, Cribbett did not want the Pacific route in 1957. BOAC did not have the planes to operate it. The company's equipment crisis was unlikely to be solved before 1960, and in any case he thought that the route would lose money initially and never make substantial profits. Secondly, no American concession to Britain could compensate for the gains to be had by the United States and the damage that would be inflicted on BOAC from allowing NWA into Hong Kong and from granting TWA rights between London and Frankfurt. At a meeting on the morning of 18 June, the British position was set, when representatives from the MTCA, the Foreign Office, and the Commonwealth Office all 'came to the reluctant conclusion that we could not ask ministers to overrule BOAC on this'. So, in effect, the talks were doomed to fail in substance right from their start.[16]

Although the talks ended on 27 June, matters were not allowed to rest there. And it was not only the Americans who were unhappy. A Foreign Office official, with some venom, observed that at a meeting on 26 June at the MTCA, Cribbett's attitude was very cavalier, and a month later Sir Paul Gore-Booth, also of the Foreign Office, lamented the MTCA's apparent inability to stand up to BOAC and thought that there would be adverse political repercussions once it became known that the British government had turned down the opportunity of getting the Pacific route. However, others in the Foreign Office did not think that anything further could be done. There appeared to be insufficient grounds for taking the matter to the Cabinet,

[15] FO 371/127692, Foreign Office mins. by D. A. H. Wright, 18 June 1957; by Jan. 1958 Qantas had the first round-the-world service that crossed the continental United States: PAA's equivalent service did not link the east and west coasts of the United States.

[16] Ibid.; FO 371/127693, mins. by Falla, 18 July 1957 and mins. by Gore-Booth, 29 July 1957.

especially as little could be achieved for British interests until BOAC was more adequately equipped with aircraft. [17]

The Americans decided that the failure of the June talks should not prevent them from pursuing the issue. At the end of July, Mr Carter and Mr Tank of the US Embassy had talks with Gore-Booth and Philip Giles of the Foreign Office. They made two requests: that charter arrangements should be agreed involving Hong Kong Airlines and NWA; and that NWA should be allowed to take over a weekly service between Tokyo and Hong Kong from a Formosan airline. The charter arrangement was turned down because of opposition from BOAC, and the Americans accepted that, but when Giles said that he thought that the NWA route request would also fail, Carter became angry. Gore-Booth had explained the previous day that NWA was different from the Formosan airline because the new route for NWA would link up with its greater route-system, but Carter said that it was 'unrealistic', 'fantastic', to maintain that NWA's one entry a week into Hong Kong could be considered as a serious challenge to BOAC. Giles countered with the observation that any NWA operation should also be seen in the light of the considerable capacity which PAA already had in Hong Kong, and at that point the discussions ended.[18]

The increasingly aggressive line taken by the Americans was reciprocated to some extent by the MTCA, from where, on 2 August, C. P. Scott-Malden wrote to Giles that on one reading of the 1947 Exchange of Notes, 'it is quite arguable that we do after all possess the Pacific route between San Francisco and Australia/New Zealand which we have been trying so hard to obtain from the U.S. for the last two years'. He believed that in 1947 Britain had paid for general, not just BCPA, operating rights for the Pacific route. The Foreign Office was more timid. No response was made until 12 September, and then it expressed the view that, despite some ambiguity, legal opinion was that BCPA could be the only carrier for the route under the Exchange of Notes. The Foreign Office official went on to say: 'I should mention . . . that we would not wish to enter into dispute with the Americans . . . since we feel that to do so would

[17] FO 371/127692, Giles mins., 27 June 1957; FO 371/127693, mins. by Gore-Booth, 24 July 1957 and mins. by Wright, 22 July 1957.

[18] Ibid., mins. 30 and 31 July 1957 by Gore-Booth and Giles respectively.

greatly exacerbate our present relations . . . which as you know are already somewhat strained.'[19]

Indeed they were. On 22 July Caccia reported that Whitney was going to raise the matter of aviation routes with Prime Minister Macmillan. Instead, on 1 August, after dinner at 10 Downing Street, Whitney spoke to Foreign Secretary Lloyd and asked him to look urgently into NWA's route request. On the following day Lloyd informed the Ambassador that the British government could not allow NWA into Hong Kong, in particular because of PAA's existing operations there. Later in the year, during Macmillan's October visit to Washington, Douglas Dillon, Under-Secretary of State for Economic Affairs, again broached the subject with Lloyd, but to no immediate avail, and the affair submerged for a while. The British had been purely defensive, to the unease of some in the Foreign Office, but had avoided taking an aggressive line such as interpreting the 1947 Exchange of Notes to the effect that they already had Pacific operating rights. However, the next time round that was to change.[20]

In 1959, instead of exchanging routes with the British in order to get access to Hong Kong for NWA, the Americans tried to designate NWA as a second carrier after PAA, on the basis of existing route-provisions in the Bermuda Agreement. The ploy was complicated by the fact that the British were also seeking some dual designation. They wanted to add Cunard Eagle Airline to the Bahamas-to-Florida route. Assistant Secretary of State Thomas Mann argued that connecting the two route-requests was undesirable from an American point of view, but that this might have to be done in the end if there were no other way to get Britain to accept dual designation into Hong Kong. Another matter pending with the British was their request for a great circle route to Los Angeles, but as no American airline opposed this, Mann did not see any difficulties.[21]

[19] Ibid., Scott-Malden to Giles and his reply, 2 Aug. and 12 Sept. 1957.

[20] Ibid., Washington to Foreign Office, 22 July 1957; mins. of conversation 1 Aug. 1957 and Lloyd to Whitney 2 Aug. 1957; DDE AWF, box 20, folder: Macmillan Oct. 23–5 1957 (2), Wesley Jones to Dulles, 'Topics for Possible Conversation with Lloyd', 24 Oct. 1957 and memo of conversation Dillon, Lloyd, *et al.*, 25 Oct. 1957; DDE CF CF, Subject Series, box 74, folder: State Department Briefing Book, Oct. 1957 Macmillan Visit.

[21] DDE, McPhee Papers, box 2, folder: CAB International Air Routes US–UK Negotiations, Mann to McPhee, 17 Nov. 1959.

Talks progressed in 1960, even though the British now openly took a hard line on the South Pacific route, claiming that they had paid for it at the time of the 1947 Exchange of Notes. The Americans were equally adamant in denying that they had. Eventually an agreement was built up, but then it collapsed at the last minute. The Americans were willing to allow Britain to operate the great circle or Polar route across to the US west coast and connect up with a South Pacific route, but they found that this was not what the British wanted. CAB Chairman Gillilland wrote to Secretary of State Herter on 8 June:

> Board is opposed to the grant to the British of the option to establish the route to the South Pacific as a continuation of UK Route 1 (from London via New York to San Francisco). This would permit a U.K. carrier to provide a one-plane service from New York as well as San Francisco to the South Pacific, an additional market of major importance which, in the Board's view, is entirely unwarranted by the value of the rights to be received by the United States.[22]

In the light of this judgement, agreement was not possible.

The Americans were irritated by the British, and subsequently some were angered by the breaking of what they believed had been a gentlemen's understanding, reached with the British government at one point in the long saga of the Hong Kong route discussions, that NWA would be designated as a second US carrier. The British had then taken no action and NWA was left hovering, though still hoping that it might yet gain access to the British colony. In early 1961, when BOAC applied to expand its operations in the United States, one CAB member, Mr Bragdon, strongly opposed granting permission, in retaliation for British failure to comply with the designation of NWA as the second US carrier for the Hong Kong route, but he was outvoted. Interestingly, especially given all the difficulties that the two countries had recently had over routes, part of the reason for the decision to assent to BOAC's request was to try to nurture good relations between the two countries, 'which are the corner-stone of the world-wide operating practices of U.S. airlines'. The upholding of the Bermuda Agreement and concord with the British were still seen by the Americans as vital

[22] DDE, McPhee Papers, Gillilland to Secretary of State Herter, 8 June 1960; LBJ NSF Country File, box 208, 209, 'The Civil Air Dispute', 18 Oct. 1965.

components in sustaining their civil-aviation interests in the form of an international system that was as liberal as possible. This was publicly confirmed in April 1963, when, as a result of work by Dr Wilfred Owen's Committee to Formulate a National Transport Policy, the US government stated that it continued to support the Bermuda Agreement and a liberal international aviation-system.[23]

It was June 1964 before the unresolved route-problems were once again discussed, this time by Allen Ferguson, Economic Bureau Aviation Chief in the State Department, in staff-level talks in London. As a result, the British came to believe that the American position had softened somewhat, and in December, after further talks, they presented an *aide-mémoire* to the United States which proposed

For Britain
1. a through route London–New York–San Francisco–Australia
2. onward operating rights to the West Indies for the London–New York route
3. withdrawal of US objections that BOAC laid over too long in New York in order to garner more passengers for flights to Jamaica

For the United States
1. a Hong Kong route for NWA
2. a London–Cairo route for TWA
3. PAA to be able to serve Jamaica and Nassau on the same flight [24]

The Americans thought that this was thin gruel for their airlines and rather mischievously counter-proposed the same package in May 1965, except that the South Pacific and London–Cairo routes were deleted. It was now Britain's turn to be indignant. The British Ambassador, Patrick Dean, told Secretary of State Rusk that given the omission of the South Pacific route from the American proposals they felt that they were being 'led up the garden path', and he deplored the 'bad feelings which

[23] JFK CF, box 33, folder: CA 7/UK-US, Deputy Director BOB to Kennedy, 18 Feb. 1961, CAB Docket 11897; Wheatcroft, *Transport*, 63.

[24] LBJ NSF Country File, box 208, 209, 'The Civil Air Dispute with Britain', 18 Oct. 1965.

had developed'. In effect, the British charged the Americans with bad faith, as they claimed that Ferguson had indicated that the United States would agree to the proposals which the British had submitted in December. The Americans made no substantial response to this at the time (though Rusk tried to placate Dean). Instead, a CAB staff study of the whole system of civil-aviation relations between the United States and Britain was put in motion so that the entire business could be reviewed.

In August Dean made what was now a standard request to Mann that the Americans should review their interpretation of the 1947 Exchange of Notes, i.e. that they should concede that Britain had a right to designate BOAC to operate on the South Pacific route. He was informed that the United States would not take matters further until the CAB review was completed. The British, however, were now becoming impatient and saw the acquisition of new routes in the United States and the Pacific as of increasing importance. Rusk was rather puzzled by the British sense of urgency and at a meeting on 10 September asked Dean directly what was causing it, when a South Pacific route for BOAC would probably be unprofitable. Dean responded that the British were adamant about getting the route partly because they believed that they had already paid for it in 1947, and partly because they would be disadvantaged in negotiations with Qantas concerning pooling arrangements if they were unable to mount a parallel route to Qantas's in the South Pacific. In November Foreign Secretary Stewart raised the matter yet again with Rusk, but still no progress was made.[25]

The British position was awkward because, while they wanted new routes, their bargaining-position was weakened by the fact that BOAC was in difficulties. Its route system was unsatisfactory from a commercial point of view and the company's potential for profit-making had been compromised in a number of ways by political decisions. At the end of 1963 the British government had published a White Paper, 'The Financial Problems of the BOAC', which had assessed the company's losses at over £80 million and had indicated some of the uncommercial practices that had lead to this parlous state of affairs, but it had failed

[25] LBJ NSF Country File; LBJ, Harry McPherson Papers, box 9, folder: Office Files International Air, Read to Smith, 3 Mar. 1966.

to give any clear direction as to how the company should evolve in order to overcome its difficulties. BOAC and the British government still had no positive strategy for solving the company's problems by 1966, but were determined both to defend what commercial routes they had and to break into the Pacific via a route across the United States. At one meeting with Mann in August 1965 the British resorted to a devious ploy to bring pressure to bear on the United States and make up for BOAC's weak bargaining-position. Ambassador Dean lamented the poor state of BOAC's routes and said that the British government was considering a deal with the Soviets which would yield Aeroflot a London–Havana connection. The British knew that this would be unpalatable to the Americans and they undoubtedly hoped that the Americans would infer that if they were to be accommodating with regard to the South Pacific route, then Britain might be persuaded to withhold the London stop-over for Aeroflot.[26]

The Americans had no illusions as to the main purpose of the British manœuvres: 'What the Brits really want is another counter in their profit-sharing game with Qantas . . . . What they do *not* want is to pay for the South Pacific route with sizeable concessions to the U.S. particularly TWA access to Hong Kong.' The Americans were in a strong position once it was clear that Britain badly wanted the South Pacific route, but they had complications of their own.

> Our external objective is to collect as large a price as possible for the South Pacific route. Our internal problem is that both that concession and the ones we would hope to receive would be harmful to the same carrier—Pan Am. What we want most from the British now is double new access to Hong Kong—for Northwest from the East (*sic*), and for TWA from the West (*sic*). This would complete the second U.S.-flag around-the-world route and, of course, create competition for the first—Pan Am's. Connection of TWA European routes with London and Cairo would also hurt Pan Am, though not so directly.[27]

[26] LBJ NSF Country File, box 208, 209, 'The Civil Air Dispute with Britain', 18 Oct. 1965; ibid., folder: UK memos, vol. 7, 10/65–1/66, memo of conversation between Rusk and Dean, 10 Sept. 1965; Wheatcroft, *Transport*, 118–19.

[27] LBJ NSF Country File, box 208, 209, 'The Civil Air Dispute with Britain', 18 Oct. 1965.

In December 1965 the US reappraisal of the route situation was completed and an agenda for talks was sent to the British. Talks were renewed in Washington on 28 February and continued for two months. Delegations were headed by Robert Burns, Deputy Secretary of the Ministry of Aviation and by Frank Loy, a Deputy Assistant Secretary of State. Although they were relatively junior officials, high politics played a major role in the talks.

On 3 March Benjamin Read, Special Assistant to the Secretary of State, wrote to Bromley Smith, Executive Secretary of the National Security Council, advising that if the United States did not grant Britain the much-sought-after Pacific route, the talks would fail and there would be much bitterness in Britain. On 8 March he sent Smith another note emphasizing the importance of reaching an agreement; one of the 'must' conditions was entry for NWA into Hong Kong. Just over a week later, Harry McPherson, Special Counsel to the President, explained the situation to Lyndon Johnson. McPherson had studied the matter carefully and discussed it with Mann of the State Department, and he had concluded that giving Britain the South Pacific route would hurt PAA, but he observed that the government had done a good deal for PAA in the past and if the grant to the British was not made, then NWA would be damaged because it would not get the Hong Kong route. The tactic he suggested for proceeding was to say to the British that the United States might be willing to concede the Pacific route but that only the President could decide—then wait to see what they offered in return. The President accepted this recommendation and the United States proceeded accordingly.[28]

Since the breakdown of talks in 1960, the United States had increased its presence in the Far East because of Vietnam, and the Pacific was becoming a major civil-aviation market, not only because of the Vietnam War, but also because of the emergence of dynamic economies in Japan and round the Pacific rim. In short, there was now more need than ever to get access to Hong Kong, in order to build up the route network of US airlines in the region, and that in turn meant a greater willingness to make concessions to the British in order to achieve this priority. As

[28] McPherson Papers, box 9, folder: Office Files International Air, Read to Smith 3 March 1966 and box 27, Mcpherson to Johnson, 11 March 1966.

opposed to its position in 1960, the United States was now prepared to grant Britain an extension of the Bermuda Agreement Route 1—London to New York—on across the United States to San Francisco and on to Australia. A further reason for an accommodation was that the Americans thought that the granting to Britain of the Pacific route would be '"a crucial factor" in the U.K. decision on the Russian proposal [for transit rights for Aeroflot on its way to Cuba]'.[29]

For their part, the British now had the equipment to operate the route, which they had not had in 1957. They also saw the commercial potential of the Pacific market, wanted the route for political reasons to do with tying the Commonwealth together, and viewed it as important in connection with pooling agreements BOAC had with Qantas. By April the makings of an agreement were in sight.

Sometime after the agreement was signed on 27 May 1966, McPherson informed the President that all US agencies approved of it and that the State Department thought that it was as near to a fifty-fifty agreement as could be achieved. It provided for the most extensive revision of the Bermuda Agreement undertaken up to that time. Some unused routes were deleted and others expanded, but it was with regard to new routes that the agreement was most important. Reciprocal rights were granted for operations between London and Miami, to begin after 1 January 1970. There were new rights for both Britain and the United States in the Caribbean and the Far East which improved their respective route-networks, but the main achievement of the agreement was the resolution of the long-running controversy over Hong Kong and the South Pacific route. In exchange for a through route London–New York–San Francisco–Australia, Britain granted access to Hong Kong for NWA and TWA. Thus the omens for the future as the 1960s drew to a close looked promising. The Bermuda Agreement was still there and was still very much the model held up to the world by the United States.[30]

[29] LBJ NSF Country File, box 215, 216, folder: P.M. Wilson's Visit, Briefing Book 12/17/65, 11 Dec. 1965, 'Civil Aviation Questions'.

[30] Ibid., box 215, 216, folder: P.M. Wilson's Visit, Briefing Book 12/17/65, 11 Dec. 1965; ibid., box 208, 209, folder: UK memos, vol. 8, 1/66–7/66, 'Signing of Amendments to Air Services Agreement Between the United States and the United Kingdom', 1966, and Read to Rostow, 17 May 1966, and Bator to Johnson, 13 May 1966; LBJ GEN CO 305, box 75, folder: CO 305, 7/13/66–11/3/66,

FARES AND COMPETITION

Britain's demand for controlled fares was agreed to by the United States at Bermuda in 1946, and the IATA, with headquarters in Montreal and Geneva, provided the mechanism for operating the system. Fixing fares by what looked suspiciously like a cartel posed no problems for the British government, but it did for the US government because of its antitrust laws. However, the 1938 Civil Aeronautics Act exempted the CAB and airlines from prosecution for controlling domestic fares and it was now used to create similar immunity in the international sphere. In other words, if the CAB were to approve fares proposed by IATA, then they could be adopted by American airlines.[31] To some, US acquiescence in fare-fixing seemed to be a radical shift in US policy, but in fact the IDCIA had indicated in 1943 that it thought that some form of control was desirable. By the time of Bermuda, when the Americans formally committed themselves, the so-called concession to the British turned out to be something the United States considered to be in its own interests as well.

But the fact that fare-fixing had been accepted did not mean that there ceased to be problems. Throughout the lifetime of Bermuda 1, the Americans tended to be generally in favour of lower fares than the British, and PAA in particular pressed for them aggressively in the early years. This was largely to do with trying to recapture its chosen-instrument status by either driving American competitors back to the domestic market or taking them over after they had been weakened by aggressive competition. The US government was not always happy with PAA's more extreme tactics on fares, but there were limits to the influence it could exert on a private company.

After the débâcle over Atlantic rates in late 1945, there was an IATA conference on rates early the following year in New York which agreed to bring down the $375 price of a one-way transatlantic ticket by 5 per cent. Compared with the 30 per cent proposed by PAA a few weeks earlier, this was modest and

McPherson to Johnson; Cmd. 3015, 'Exchange of Notes Amending Bermuda Agreement', 27 May 1966.

[31] See Chuang, *IATA*, and R. Pryke, *Competition Among International Airlines* (Gower, Aldershot, 1987).

tended to confirm PAA's beliefs that IATA would be a cartel to keep the less efficient in business. Be that as it may, according to American sources, Hildred, who was about to take up his post as Director-General of IATA, was also dissatisfied with the reduction and hoped that the fare would soon come down to around $300.

In fact, there was not a great deal of difference between the respective positions of the US and British governments. The British worried more about unilateral fare-reductions, and feared that premature action by PAA to implement IATA decisions on rates might disrupt things and recreate the chaos of late 1945, but in principle they were not opposed to modest reductions in fares. By 1948 BOAC wanted lower second- and third-class fares and expected an eventual 20 per cent reduction across the board. By now, one of the overriding considerations for the British government was the adverse British balance of payments. Tourism earnt Britain dollars and it was better to have tourists coming in large numbers, even if they had to travel on American airlines, than to see their numbers reduced because of high fares. Unfortunately, so far as BOAC was concerned, a lowering of fares would not result in a significant increase in its load factor, because problems with equipment meant that there was little spare capacity to be filled.

Despite the convergence of official attitudes on fares, PAA was a source of worry to both Britain and the United States. The British continued to suspect that Trippe's company was determined to torpedo IATA; the US government believed that PAA, while unhappy, had accepted it as a necessary evil. The truth lay with the latter rather than the former, but various developments, and company policy, resulted in PAA being a disruptive element in the international fare-system.[32]

The years following the war were not easy ones for American airlines. Since Roosevelt's cancellation of airmail contracts in 1934, subsidies had been subject to ever closer scrutiny, and in 1947 renewed pressure for their reduction and eventual elimination gathered force. On 1 August Assistant Secretary of State Norton, in his capacity as Chairman of the ACC, issued a

[32] 841.79603/3–1546 and 10–2546, both Satterthwaite to Secretary of State; 841.796/10–1948, Holmes to Secretary of State, and Lovett to US Embassy.

'Statement of Certain Policies', calling for more stringent conditions for granting subsidies, which 'should continue for required services only until the carriers are financially self-supporting'. Over the following years subsidies were separated from mail payments, and in 1952 and 1957 TWA and PAA respectively ceased receiving them directly. In contrast, by 1963 BOAC had accumulated a deficit of £77 million responsibility for which was assumed by the government. In the United States the reduction of subsidies exacerbated the precarious financial position of the airlines, which had to swim or sink as private companies.[33]

With subsidies disappearing, competition growing, and the market sluggish, PAA understandably felt obliged to adopt an aggressively competitive policy. Trippe saw lower fares as the solution to three problems. First, he reasoned that an increase in the number of passengers would bring about a growth in revenue, and he ordered planes in expectation that this would come about. Secondly, he reckoned that the competition would drive other American airlines off overseas routes and re-establish PAA's chosen-instrument status. And thirdly, he thought that by advocating cheaper fares and posing as the champion of the common man, he would enhance the public image of his company. In May 1950, in 'The Future of the Individual Under American Capitalism', Trippe, while suggesting that tourism could take over where Marshall Aid would leave off in 1952 by distributing US dollars overseas, also said: 'American tourists now leave abroad one billion dollars annually. This sum can be doubled if transatlantic fares are established at a level the average man can afford.'[34]

Trippe aimed to reduce fares by introducing tourist-class seats. He began to urge this upon IATA in 1948, but it was some time before he was successful. In the meantime, the low level of traffic growth and the high level of competition on the Atlantic began to bite, and by 1948 AOA had had enough and wanted to sell out. Trippe made them an offer and a deal was struck, but it was opposed by TWA and by the CAB.

[33] Solberg, *Conquest of the Skies: A History of Commercial Aviation* (Little, Brown, and Co., Boston, 1979), 346–7; FO 371/65484, 'Statement of Certain Policies' by Norton, 1 Aug. 1947; 399.72ICAO/3–2553, Smith to Bolster.

[34] Trippe Papers, box 2, folder L 70, 'The Future of the Individual Under American Capitalism'. 18 May 1950.

The final decision on the matter, however, was Truman's, and it came before him at the same time as the war in Korea broke out, which partly accounts for the muddle which followed. In early 1950, departments with an interest in the affair had been canvassed for their views. The Defense Department did not care one way or the other so long as the United States kept AOA's routes. Commerce favoured the merger, but all the others were against it, as was the pronouncement of the CAB on 1 June. In the first instance, a month later, the President agreed with the CAB. Then, as a result of various pressures from lobbyists, he changed his mind, but there was a sting in the tail for PAA. TWA lobbyists had been at work and, interestingly, TWA operated out of Kansas City, the next-door-neighbour to Truman's home town of Independence. The outcome was that the merger was approved by Truman, 'but with route adjustments in the case of the two remaining carriers so that they could compete with each other to London, Frankfurt . . . Paris and Rome'. Trippe had achieved the elimination of the third American carrier on the Atlantic route, but only at the price of more direct competition with TWA. Over the following years PAA overshadowed TWA, with its larger percentage of the transatlantic traffic and more successful policy on purchasing equipment. In fact, under the wayward direction of Howard Hughes, TWA was in serious difficulties by the 1960s, but after his departure things improved markedly.[35]

After PAA's successful take-over of AOA, lower fares became an even more urgent matter, for unless they could be introduced, PAA was heading for difficulties. It had increased its capacity on the Atlantic and was about to embark upon a gamble to increase it even more. Trippe had already tested the feasibility of a tourist fare between New York and Puerto Rico and it had been highly successful. He now decided to order a stretched version of the DC-6 for tourist flights across the Atlantic. To make these plans profitable, he had to have lower fares. For nearly four years PAA pressed for the introduction of a tourist rate. In the end,

[35] HST PSF, box 142, folder: Agencies and Airport Data, memo 22 Jan. 1950; Library of Congress, Landis Papers, box 133, the North Atlantic Route Case; 911.5200/7–2850, Douglas to Secretary of State; Solberg, *Conquest*, 305–8; R. Daley, *An American Saga: Juan Trippe and His Pan American Empire* (Random House, New York, 1980), 385–6.

faced with a steady decline in the rate of traffic growth on the Atlantic route, the European opponents of fare reductions eventually relented, accepting that something had to be done in order to increase demand. In 1952 IATA approved tourist fares and the market responded in 1953 by growing 17 per cent.[36] This and PAA's subsequent policy of moving over to jet aircraft resulted in its dominating the transatlantic route for the rest of the decade.

For much of the 1950s there was little the British could do to counter these developments, especially after the disaster of the Comet. British equipment was simply inferior, though for a short time, when it appeared that Britain might steal a march on the rest of the world with the Comet, the Americans took fright. They obstructed the use of the Comet by denying it an airworthiness certificate. Prime Minister Churchill protested, but to no apparent avail. When the American CAA finally did approve certificates for jets, it was too late for the now grounded Comet, but the Viscount made a commercial impact in the United States and that model, along with initial American fears about Britain having taken a major lead with the Comet, stimulated Americans to concentrate on developing civilian jets. Such work had been neglected because of military priorities introduced at the time of the outbreak of the Korean War, but when R. & D. on civilian jets was renewed in the United States, it was possible to take advantage of British experience without paying the costs incurred by the pioneering work on the Comet.[37]

Towards the end of the 1950s the stimulus to American development of civilian jets from Britain, ironically, resulted in US domination of the jet market, with planes such as the long-range Boeing-707 and the DC-8. These planes were bought in large numbers by PAA, which moved straight from piston-engine long-range aircraft to jets. In Britain, after the grounding of the Comet, BOAC relied heavily on the in-between turbo-prop type, of which the short-range Viscount was very successful for BEA but BOAC's long-range Britannia had problems. After delays, it was introduced in 1957, but became obsolescent two years later with the appearance of the new American long-

[36] Daley, *American Saga*, 347; Sampson, *Empires*, 73; Daley, *American Saga*, 400.

[37] FO 371/93148, memos. R. F. G. Sarell, 17 Feb. 1951 and C. Clarkson, 30 Mar. 1951; Rochester, *Take-off* 106 ff.

TABLE 4. *BOAC Share of Passenger Market between Britain and North America*

	Total	BOAC Total	BOAC %
1958–59	453,073	170,081	37.5
1959–60	558,995	222,837	39.9
1960–61	770,315	319,108	41.4
1961–62	802,134	334,893	41.8

range jets. A modified version of the Comet, the Comet 4, was flown in 1958 and nineteen were acquired by BOAC, but they were only medium-range and not as economical as the Boeing-707, of which by 1963 it had also bought nineteen. The obsolescence of the Britannia and the commercial imperative to buy long-range jets hit BOAC's finances badly, but its operations on the Atlantic had had some success in the late 1950s. Furthermore, introduction of the Britannia had helped to persuade the British that lower fares for the growing mass-market were desirable, and in 1958, largely as a result of British pressure, the tourist-class fare gave way to the economy fare.

The BOAC Annual Report of 1961–2 was interesting, for despite the company's difficulties, there were achievements to be proud of on the Atlantic route. (See Table 4.)

Between 1952 and 1961 the company's operating profit was £17m. but it had other burdens to carry apart from its own operations.

> It did not . . . make sufficient profits to meet the losses incurred by its subsidiary and associated companies, the exceptional costs of proving and introducing Britannia and Comet aircraft, or the abnormal depreciation that the shorter life of those aircraft now shows to have been necessary.[38]

So, despite considerable success in operating on the Atlantic, the company's finances were in a dreadful mess. And the prospects for the future did not look good. There was a slump in air travel at the opening of the 1960s and in 1962–3 BOAC's

[38] *BOAC Annual Report and Accounts* (HMSO, London, 1962), 57 and 25; A. P. Ellison and E. M. Stafford, *The Dynamics of the Civil Aviation Industry* (Saxon House, Hants, 1974), 9–21.

TABLE 5. *Rate of Return on Investment for Transatlantic Carriers*

	1956	1957	1958	1959	1960	1961	1962	1963	1964
PAA	9.6	9.2	3.8	6.8	6.5	4.3	5.6	11.8	11.7
TWA	0.4	2.9	−5.9	−8.6	15.8	−11.2	12.8	23.6	20.2

Source: *CAB Airline Statistics 1965*, pp. 309, 307.[39]

percentage of the Atlantic market dropped nearly 4.5 per cent. The previous year's report had struck a note of caution about further fare-cuts, estimating that a 20 per cent reduction in fares would need to generate an extra 100,000 passengers in order for the company to improve on the already inadequate revenue earned from existing fares. In short, both the company's own fortunes and the depressed state of the market tended to make BOAC and the British government defensive and cautious about further fare-reductions. Indeed, as the IATA rate conference met at Chandler, Arizona, there was a move to raise fares. In the US government, however, though not among the US airlines, there was stubborn resistance to this, which resulted in the most serious dispute about fares during the life of the Bermuda 1 regime.

The Chandler dispute was important not only because of the political level at which it was conducted, but also because it marked a departure from the consensus on fares that had existed throughout most of the 1950s between the CAB and the US airlines. In the early 1960s American airlines, like their British counterparts, were hit by recession, and for a time TWA was threatened by take-over from PAA. The two American giants had only recently gambled enormous sums of money to re-equip with jets. As William Patterson of United Airlines (UA) had put it in 1953, 'The price of the jet age is in the conversational stage, but even the conversation is staggering.' It was indeed, and the investment was only just beginning to show substantial returns in 1962–3. (See Table 5.)

In 1962–3 TWA was beginning to make profits after a lean period and was unwilling to jeopardize its recovery by reduc-

[39] Rochester, *Take-off*, 103; figs. from Chuang, *IATA*, 119.

ing fares, which was something even PAA was no longer enthusiastic about. From then on, there was periodic friction between the established American airlines and the US government over fare policy.

At Chandler, Arizona in September and October the IATA conference established new rates. On the Atlantic the economy fare for a return ticket went up $27 to $513. Both TWA and PAA voted for the increase. However, when the members of the CAB, and particularly its market-oriented Chairman, Alan Boyd, heard of this, they were dismayed. On 10 December they met with members of the main US airlines and asked them to justify the increase. By 12 February 1963 the CAB had received formal responses from PAA and Northwestern, but it found neither of them satisfactory, and so on 18 March it rejected the new rate.[40]

What followed was a crisis that was largely attributable to misassessment by the CAB of Britain's determination to stick by IATA procedures, even though it was generally well disposed to reducing fares when possible. The affair was also partly a result of the different emphasis that Britain and the United States respectively gave to the principle of competition, and in particular Boyd's belief that the present price-fixing by the IATA cartel was contrary to the public interest. The CAB's guide-lines for acceptable returns on capital for US airlines was 10 per cent, so as TWA was set to get over double that in 1963, the stance that Boyd and his colleagues took was understandable.

On 28 March the CAB instructed PAA and TWA to maintain their existing fares. At this point, urged on by BOAC, the British government took a strong stand and 'chose to play David to the American Goliath'. Discussions in Washington and London in April failed to resolve differences, and on 9 May the British amended TWA's operating certificate for London, requiring it to charge the Chandler rate. Two days later the Americans received an *aide-mémoire* from the British which indicated that Britain might withdraw landing-rights from US carriers if they did not charge the higher fare. In fact, what the British did was to collect the $27 difference from passengers and give it to PAA and TWA.

[40] JFK POF, folder: CAB 1961–63, Chairman Boyd to Kennedy, 22 May 1963; Chuang, *IATA*, 104–5 and 119–20; Wheatcroft, *Transport*, 72–8.

Matters had now reached crisis point and President Kennedy sent a brusque memorandum to Boyd asking for an explanation of how things had deteriorated so badly. Boyd gave him a frank appraisal, which blamed the secrecy of the Chandler conference for the unexpectedness of the fare increase, and criticized the British for professing to be in favour of lowering fares and then defending the Chandler rate so stubbornly and without due notice to the United States. He made it clear that he thought that the new rate had been introduced in a manner contrary to the normal procedures of the IATA (which should maintain existing rates if there were not unanimous agreement on new ones), and that the new rate was not in the public interest. Nevertheless, in the light of the crisis that had developed and because of concern in the State Department about the difficulties that had arisen, he told Kennedy that his plans included approving 'without delay any reasonable compromise to the immediate impasse that may result from an IATA conference to be convened in Montreal on Friday, May 24, 1963'.[41]

In effect the Americans were forced to retreat, though there was some compromise and later in July 1963, at a governmental meeting at Ottawa, it was agreed that CAB representatives could sit in as observers at IATA rate conferences. After Chandler the US government continued to be wary of its operations and as the years passed became less and less happy, as, indeed, did some US airlines, especially after the new competitive dispensation was inaugurated by the Carter Administration in 1977.

As the 1970s began, there seemed to be a convergence of US and British policies on civil aviation. The 1960s had been prosperous for the airlines, and massive new investment in jumbos had been undertaken. There was growing demand in Britain as well as in the United States for lower fares, and the latter was actively undermining IATA's fare-fixing role. The Conservative government of Edward Heath was keen to encourage private enterprise, and the 1971 Aviation Act was a definite move towards the United States in respect of increased competition and dual designation; but Britain tended to look to charter

[41] R. P. Stebbins *et al.*, *Council on Foreign Relations: The United States in World Affairs 1963* (Harper, New York, 1964); JFK POF, folder: CAB 1961–63, Kennedy to Boyd and his reply, 15 and 22 May 1963, and draft statement by Boyd, 24 April 1963.

companies and promotional fares with tickets such as the Advance Purchase Excursion to cut the cost of travel. The British no longer supported IATA as strongly as they had in the past, but they were still a long way from actively undermining it as the Americans were doing. Nevertheless, Britain felt more confident about being able to compete now that it had equipment equal to that of American airlines. And, in addition to the possibility of capturing a greater share of what seemed to be an ever burgeoning market, there were two important developments which seemed to demand a more competitive attitude. Firstly, there was the challenge from Third World airlines, many of which, in the early stage of their development, wanted to keep fares high by working through IATA, thus enabling them to compete with more efficient British and US airlines. Secondly, there was also the challenge from the charter companies. Since 1953 these companies had been notionally constrained by an affinity rule, i.e. they could only charter to groups with a genuine common interest. In fact, this had proved impossible to enforce (one notorious charter was that to the Left-handed Society) and was eventually abandoned. By 1970 the charter business was carrying about one-third of transatlantic passengers. Politically, it was impossible for Britain to put a stop to the charter business, and so here was another forceful element in the move towards greater competition. In 1972 the British government awarded a transatlantic schedule to one of the new pioneers of civil aviation, Freddie Laker, and the direction of policy looked clear and well set. But trouble in the Middle East soon changed all that, and as the civil-aviation market slumped, competition gave way to protectionism both in Britain and, to a lesser extent and for a shorter period of time, in the United States as well. However, although both countries turned to favour more controls and less competition, they did not do so to a uniform degree, and soon there were serious differences between them, culminating in the British denunciation of Bermuda 1 and negotiations for its replacement.

8
From Bermuda 1 to Bermuda 2 and Beyond

> All of us believe that the US must not lose, and if it has lost it better, by God, regain its position of undisputed world leadership in aviation.
>
> Alexander Butterfield, US Transport Secretary, quoted in E. Preston, *Troubled Passage*.

THE 1970s and 1980s were turbulent economically, and by no means least disrupted was civil aviation. Its whole international system was struck by economic and political shock-waves which refashioned its character by forcing both airlines and governments to rethink their policies.

The most disruptive change was the massive increase in oil prices after 1973, as a result of the Yom Kippur War and the actions of the OPEC cartel. The rise in fuel prices damaged the airlines both directly, by raising their costs, and indirectly, by exacerbating general economic problems that had developed during the 1960s. In the recession that followed, the number of people travelling by air fell, while costs continued to climb. But even worse, this was at a time when airline capacity had just been increased enormously, at astronomic cost. In 1965 Trippe made his final bequest to civil aviation before his retirement in 1968. He successfully negotiated specifications for the first jumbo with Boeing and ordered twenty-five of what became the 747s. Their total cost was about $550 million and in the early 1970s that entailed instalments of $10 million a month for PAA. Even before the 1973 crisis, traffic was not growing quickly enough to fill the capacity provided by jumbos, and in 1971 PAA made losses of $46 million: in 1974 these had risen to $81.7 million and by 1978 the decade's accumulated losses amounted to $320 million. Such figures provide dimension to the difficulties that confronted all airlines in the 1970s.[1]

[1] A. Sampson, *Empires of the Sky: The Politics, Contests and Cartels of World Airlines* (Hodder & Stoughton, London, 1984), 125; R. Daley, *An American Saga:*

The problem of over-capacity and the downward pressure that this exerted on fares was not solely to do with the introduction of jumbos. New airlines from the Third World provided a large amount of capacity, which was often not commercially but politically justified, in terms of status and prestige. Such airlines were unsettling for aviation because of their capacity and also because they were subsidized and thus able to offer cheap fares from time to time by lapsing from IATA regulations. While the Third World strove to gain a niche in international aviation, and in so doing contributed to its problems, Western charter airlines were attempting to achieve the same thing.

The growth of package holidays in Europe stimulated the growth of charter airlines in Britain during the 1960s, and companies such as B.Cal. and Laker Airways emerged as important actors in the international system. In the United States changes of law in 1962, and more significantly in 1966, facilitated the growth of charters there. By the early 1970s charters accounted for over one-quarter of the transatlantic market, largely because of attractive fares and the fact that rules intended to restrict their operations were difficult to enforce. For example, in 1973 the affinity rule was abandoned and replaced by advanced booking charters, but by then the impact of the charters had already been felt, with the downward pressure that they had exerted on fares. Scheduled airlines had been forced to respond with a series of discounted tickets—group inclusive tours, 1967; excursion tickets, 1970; and, the most well known of all, APEX, introduced in 1974. Of similar importance to the impact charter airlines had on fares was the capacity that they provided. So, just like Third World airlines, charters added to the problem both of over-capacity and of low fares, at a time when scheduled airlines were suffering enormous losses and when it was becoming increasingly difficult to control international aviation because of various political developments.[2]

The success that OPEC had in raising oil prices was somewhat

Juan Trippe and His Pan American Empire (Random House, New York, 1980), 446–7.

[2] H. A. Wassenbergh, *Aspects of Air Law and Civil Air Policy in the Seventies* (Martinus Nijhoff, The Hague, 1970), ch. 3; R. E. G. Davies, *Airlines of the United States Since 1914* (Putnam, London, 1982), 458, 465; R. Pryke, *Competition Among International Airlines* (Gower, Aldershot, 1987), chs. 1 and 2; R. Y. Chuang, *The International Air Transport Association* (A. W. Sijthoff, Leiden, 1972).

characteristic of the growing political impact Third World countries were having on the international system, and neither IATA nor the ICAO were immune from their influence. The United States in particular took umbrage at some of the political antics which became commonplace in the ICAO. Its role since 1944 had been low-key, being mainly concerned with safety and technical matters and providing a forum for discussion. Hopes that it might provide the institutional base for the government of a multilateral aviation-system were never fulfilled, but towards the end of the 1960s it was politicized by the developing countries, and voting began to follow political rather than aviation considerations. So much so that in 1971 Secor Browne, Chairman of the CAB, led the US delegation in a protest walk-out. IATA suffered from similar, though less prominent, political problems, but of more concern were the commercial practices of many of its newer members. Often, airlines of developing countries were not commercially viable and so they sought to maintain or impose high fares through IATA. At the same time some of them failed to keep to the rules and subsequently sold heavily discounted tickets. Partly because of this and partly because they were under pressure from the US government and public opinion, PAA, TWA, and other American airlines began to disengage from IATA fare-setting. This was not because they (at least PAA and TWA) were against controlling fares, but because IATA rules were not being upheld and its cartel operations were not easily defended in the United States. In contrast, the US government disliked IATA because of a more principled stand against fare-setting. Thus, by the 1970s the main actor was in the process of distancing itself from aviation's international organizations. At the very time that aviation needed regulation more than it had done since the 1930s, its international framework, never strong, was being weakened further.[3]

But this is only one aspect of the political developments which affected civil aviation in the 1970s. There was also the US policy of deregulation, which had a major impact upon its own and on international aviation, especially in Britain, where a modified form of deregulation was followed. American policy was very

[3] B. Gidwitz, *The Politics of International Air Transport* (Heath, Boston, 1980), 86.

much in tune with the revival of the free market in the aftermath of what appeared to be the failure of Keynesianism, particularly with regard to dealing with the problem of stagflation. The federal government had a model to imitate in California, where deregulation had enabled airlines like Pacific Southwestern to flourish and the Los Angeles–San Francisco route to become the busiest and cheapest in the world. The deregulation campaign was taken up by a Cornell economics professor, Alfred Kahn, who later became President Carter's CAB Chairman, and by a Californian academic, Michael Levine, who later acted as Kahn's Chief of Staff. In Britain the drive for more competition came partly from the industry itself, most notably in the form of Laker, and from the Heath and Thatcher Governments; but even in the Labour administrations of 1974–9, competition was not entirely shunned, as the policy of Edmund Dell, Trade Secretary from 1976 to 1978, demonstrated. He was responsible for denouncing Bermuda 1 and seeking more effective controls over various aspects of the industry, but he was also well disposed towards both Laker Airways and its designation as a second British carrier to compete on the New York–London route.[4]

These—the oil crisis; over-capacity because of jumbos; Third World airlines; and charters; the weakening of the already rather feeble organizations charged with overseeing international civil aviation; and the development of political doctrines which discounted the value of concerted international action and favoured the free play of the market—were the main factors which moulded the context within which Britain and the United States conducted aviation diplomacy and formulated their respective civil-aviation policies after 1970.

CONTROLS AND COMPETITION 1970–1977

Both the Heath and Nixon Governments announced intentions to promote more competition in civil aviation. Heath and his Trade and Industry Secretary, John Davies, pushed ahead with

[4] Interview with the Rt. Hon. Edmund Dell, Secretary of State for Trade 1976–8, conducted by the author, 8 Dec. 1989; Sampson, *Empires*, 135; Davies, *Airlines*, 675–8, 'Essay on Deregulation'.

legislative reform and with strengthening the position of B.Cal. as a second-force international carrier. Guide-lines for the new dispensation were given in the 1971 Civil Aviation Act and in the Policy Guidance White Paper of February 1972. One result was that B.Cal. was licensed for the London–New York–Los Angeles route, and in April 1973 began to operate on it, in parallel with BA. Also in 1972, the CAA licensed Laker to operate Skytrain from Stansted to New York for a ten-year period beginning in 1973. This was a significant victory for Laker in the battle to establish his company as a cheap scheduled carrier on the Atlantic, but he was now thwarted by the American CAB, which procrastinated, and prevented him from operating into New York. The prospect of competing with Laker's incredibly cheap walk-on, walk-off service worried the Americans. They advocated competition, but were not always willing to accept its consequences. For a while at least, Laker's Skytrain, which would eventually force fares down even further and add to the disorder that already existed in civil aviation, was kept off the Atlantic route.[5]

In Washington the Nixon Administration took a close look at civil aviation in 1970, and its instinct was to encourage more competition in accordance with the general principles of the Bermuda Model: as yet there was no great pressure for deregulation. In June 1970 Professor Paul Cherington, head of Nixon's task force on international aviation policy, put forward draft proposals which had much in common with the British Edwards Report of 1969. US commitment to Bermuda and to seek a multilateral agreement were reiterated, and emphasis was given to increasing competitiveness by encouraging US charter companies and by granting more multiple designation. It was hoped that these two strategies would enlarge America's percentage of world traffic.

One negative aspect of the report was unease with IATA fare-setting, and in fact fares became a serious problem as the civil-aviation boom of the 1960s gave way to the recession of the 1970s. Scheduled airlines' over-capacity, made worse by the

[5] Cmd. 4899, 'Civil Aviation Policy Guidance', Feb. 1972; R. Baldwin, *Regulating the Airlines: Administrative Justice and Agency Discretion* (Clarendon, Oxford, 1985), 111–14.

growth of charters and Third World airlines, resulted in keener competition for passengers, and in 1971 it threw the scheduled carriers and IATA rate conferences into turmoil. At Montreal in June, IATA members were unable to reach agreement. Subsequently, at Honolulu, they had more success, and off-peak returns from London to New York were reduced to their lowest ever up to that time. But most fares held steady, and even the introduction of APEX in 1974 failed to bring any immediate improvement. The situation for IATA members on the Atlantic remained grim and losses mounted alarmingly: in 1975–6 they flew 6.5 million empty seats across the Atlantic and lost $524 million. Both Britain and the United States had premised their arguments for more competition on the assumption that the market would continue to grow rapidly and that fuel would remain cheap, but already in 1971–2 it was clear that passenger growth was lagging behind growth in capacity. B.Cal., operating its new Atlantic route, struggled from the start, and then in October 1973 came the Yom Kippur War, an Arab oil-embargo, and subsequently action by OPEC to keep the price of oil high. The impact on aviation was traumatic. Almost within a year B.Cal. had to withdraw from its US route: it was not commercially viable. The idea of more competition, and in particular dual designation, now had to be reappraised.[6]

In Britain retrenchment to a less competitive position was facilitated by the fact that the Labour Party had returned to power in 1974 with Wilson's surprise victory over Heath. Faced with crisis in civil aviation because of falling revenue, a decline in the number of passengers, rising costs and over-capacity, the Labour government decided that it had to act. There was little in its political doctrine to inhibit it from reining in the already somewhat ineffective drive for more competition, and there were sound practical reasons for doing it. The precarious state of the British economy emphasized the need to avoid having to subsidize BA's losses and highlighted the desirability of BA increasing its overseas earnings to help with the ever-present

[6] Wassenbergh, *Civil Air Policy*, app. 1, text of 1970 'Statement on US International Aviation Policy'; Davies, *Airlines*, 577; *Flight International* (hereafter *Flight*), 25 Sept. 1976, 960–1; Cmd. 6400, 'Future Civil Aviation Policy', Feb. 1976.

balance-of-payments problem. In July 1975 Trade Secretary Peter Shore declared that dual designation was no longer British policy, and in February 1976 he amplified and developed his views about the future.

> . . . recent developments have weakened even further the case for double designation. There is now virtually no major long-haul route on which it would be possible to introduce a second British airline on terms which would leave any scope for the British share of total earnings from the route to be increased.[7]

Dual designation was out of favour and Shore also decided to withdraw Laker's licence for the Stansted-New York route. It was felt that Skytrain could only operate at the cost of some loss to BA's market, which was probably true, but of little consolation to Laker, who challenged Shore's decision in the courts. That challenge was to have important consequences for British aviation some months later, but for the time being the government sought to reduce capacity and avoid cutthroat competition, in order to make remaining operations commercially viable. It also wanted to nurture BA and B.Cal. as chosen instruments, but in separate regional compartments which would not allow them to compete with each other.

In the United States, airlines, including PAA and TWA, were also in severe difficulties, and just as the British retreated from competition, so did they—for a while. The CAB under Secor Browne and his successor, Robert Timm, was as yet still free from the hands of the ardent deregulators, and so it was possible to rationalize domestic and foreign routes involving airlines such as American, NWA, TWA, and PAA. Also, the latter two were allowed leeway to arrange capacity reductions with British airlines on the Atlantic route. For the time being, it looked as if Britain and America were responding in unison to the crisis that had hit the airlines. However, as over-capacity persisted and the challenge from Third World and charter airlines continued, the deregulation forces in the United States gained more influence over policy and advocated a more combative strategy to cope with the problems confronting the industry. Even before President Carter came into office in 1977 there had been a major change of attitude in the CAB with President Ford's appoint-

[7] Hansard, 29 July 1975, vol. 896, col. 1502; Cmd. 6400, Feb. 1976.

ment of John Robson, a deregulator, as Chairman. American policy was by no means set in a new mould, for there continued to be friction between the deregulators at the CAB and in the White House on the one hand, and the regulators in the DOT on the other, even during the heyday of deregulation in the late 1970s, when Kahn presided over the CAB; the State Department generally speaking adopted a position somewhere between the two factions. However, there was movement towards deregulation in 1976 and it coincided with a change of personnel in the British government. Harold Wilson resigned and was replaced by James Callaghan, but more importantly for civil aviation, Edmund Dell took over from Peter Shore as Secretary of State for Trade, and that resulted in a more confrontational approach to the United States in aviation at a time when the two seemed to be at the parting of the ways on policy.[8]

Dell had serious problems to deal with during 1976–8. Overshadowing all was Britain's economic weakness and her inability to balance her overseas account. These things put great pressure on the pound and eventually led Britain to appeal to the IMF for help. It was given, but at the price of deflation and cuts in government expenditure which greatly damaged both the unity of the Labour Party and its electoral fortunes. Clearly, such matters were vital and were dealt with at the highest political level. In contrast, as a specific issue, civil aviation was not brought before the Cabinet, but departmentally it was of the highest importance. It was also part and parcel of Britain's overall economic problem, and in that context it occasionally won the attention of the Prime Minister.[9]

On coming into office, Dell reviewed the operations of the Bermuda Agreement. He consulted his own officials, the CAA, and the airlines, and what he learnt he did not like. First of all, there was the general problem of over-capacity, the waste of fuel it involved and the financial losses it entailed. Secondly, competition from US airlines was becoming predatory and looked likely to get worse. During the summer of 1976 the American CAB considered applications from Delta and NWA to join PAA,

[8] Sampson, *Empires*, 139–49; *Flight*, 25 Sept. 1976, 'Bermuda Battle Lines', 960–1.

[9] Dell interview.

TWA, and National in operating the Atlantic routes and it recommended in their favour. Thirdly, although BA was the largest single operator on the Atlantic, with over 37 per cent of the traffic, its position was coming under more intensive attack from American airlines at a time when Dell wanted to increase Britain's overall percentage of the transatlantic market. And finally, the United States garnered more revenue than Britain on routes designated under the Bermuda Agreement. According to DOT calculations, the United States earned £350 million and Britain £120 million a year. Dell decided that the situation needed adjusting. He wanted a larger percentage of traffic and a more equitable division of spoils from the reciprocal exchange of routes, both of which would help Britain's balance of payments. Such changes would radically alter existing arrangements, and so, because of that and to force the Americans to negotiate without delay, Dell decided that he would exercise Britain's right under the Bermuda Agreement to denounce it with twelve months notice, in order that they could make a new start.[10]

Before doing so, he consulted with both the British Embassy in Washington and the Foreign Office. Neither of them were at all happy with his proposal. The Foreign Office 'said, more or less, we think this is most ill-advised, but it's your departmental business, if you want to do it, get on with it'. Dell was also cautioned by the US State and Transportation Departments and by the US Ambassador in London not to denounce the Bermuda Agreement because 'the last situation would be worse than the first' for Britain. Nevertheless, Dell remained resolute, and as the Foreign Office had not categorically opposed denunciation, there was no need for him to take matters before Cabinet, and therefore, on 22 June 1976, he formally denounced the Bermuda 1 Agreement.[11]

His denunciation came at a particularly sensitive time. Only weeks earlier, the United States had reluctantly contributed to a stand-by credit to support the failing pound. It had been initiated by Dr Jelle Ziljstra of BIS and the Dutch Central Bank, but the Americans insisted that the full amount would have to be repaid no later than 7 December or else Britain would have to go

[10] Dell interview; *Flight*, 3 July 1976, 4 and 25 Sept. 961.
[11] Dell interview.

to the IMF for further help. Edwin Yeo of the US Treasury went to London to explain these unprecedented conditions, which, understandably, were much resented by Britain. When the British government was subsequently unable to cope with the resources it had to hand, the only course of action left was to go to the IMF and accept what were known would be harsh terms imposed in a humiliating way—something which the United States had contrived to achieve all along (according to some with the connivance of British Treasury and Bank of England officials). In short, Anglo-American relations were already sour because of economic matters. Nevertheless, Dell maintains that no direct link was made at the time in the sense of the British saying that if the United States were going to play it tough in the economic sphere, then why should not the British do the same by denouncing the Bermuda Agreement. Indeed, he points to the fact that it was in British interests to keep on friendly terms with the Americans in the economic sphere. However, although no direct link was made, there is little doubt that if Anglo-American relations had been more cordial there would have been less chance of Dell taking the controversial, though courageous, course of action he took.[12]

The British had a number of specific aims in the negotiations that followed. The three main objectives were: a more even—ideally a fifty-fifty—division of traffic on the Atlantic between British and US carriers; more entry-points into the United States; single designation and a system of airline consultation to arrange capacity levels (which was to replace the ineffective Bermuda 1 procedure of *ex post facto* adjustments). In addition, they wanted to withdraw US fifth-freedom rights from London and Hong Kong. The Americans thought that the British government's approach to the problem of their aviation relationship was aggressive and particularly ill timed because of the imminent presidential election. For his part, Dell was prompted to action by a sense of urgency brought about by Britain's economic problems, but there was some force to the charge that he lacked sensitivity to American domestic political developments. So far

[12] Ibid.; interview with James Callaghan (then MP) conducted by the author, Feb. 1987; J. Callaghan, *Time and Chance* (Collins, London, 1987), ch. 14; *Sunday Times*, 14 May 1978, 'How the Hard Men Took Over Britain', by S. Fay and H. Young; '1976 IMF Crisis Symposium', *Contemporary Record*, 3, (1989), 39–45.

as the apparent aggressiveness of the British position was concerned, some demands were clearly made with a view to the hard bargaining which the British knew would ensue. Furthermore, that bargaining would be difficult not only because of American strength, but also because of British economic weakness and other complicating factors.

Dell's public position on single designation at the outset of the talks was that it should be universal, but he was under no illusion about the likelihood of that being accepted by the United States: 'to achieve single designation on [the] New York–London [route] would have been a miracle'. In addition to this realism, court decisions strengthened the possibilities for dual designation. Laker's challenge in the High Court was successful and was confirmed in the Appeal Court. The withdrawal of Laker's licence and Shore's attempt to abolish dual designation by ministerial fiat were both deemed to be unlawful. The matter was embarrassing for the government, but as Dell was prepared to concede a limited amount of dual designation, he was rather pleased by developments. Dell had been unhappy about Shore's withdrawal of Laker's Atlantic licence, and although he believed that the legal reasoning in the Appeal Court was unsound, he welcomed the decision that Shore had acted *ultra vires* because it gave him another card to play in his dealings with the Americans. If he had to agree to dual designation, he could now name Laker as Britain's second operator. Dell was keen to do that, and thus he opposed colleagues in Cabinet Committee who wanted to take the Laker case to the House of Lords for a final appeal, and he won the argument. In early 1977 it became known that the government would not appeal against the Laker decision in the Lords. Not only did Britain now have another option for designation, but the free-market symbolism of Laker strengthened Dell's hand and helped him to recapture some of the moral high-ground that was under attack from the Americans by their claim that Britain was opposed to competition. Dell could now use Laker to demonstrate that the British government was not against competition in principle, but only against its damaging forms; he could also tweak American consciences by reminding them of their long opposition to allowing Laker to compete on the Atlantic.

The Laker affair complicated, but in the end strengthened, the British position, and the same was true of Concorde. Concorde was another contributor to the friction which existed concerning transatlantic aviation. Various US authorities were against its operating into New York. The objections arose from environmental considerations—namely, noise—but the British rightly suspected that other, more nationalistic, motives were also involved. For a country that was critical of Britain for being too control-minded, the United States seemed particularly restrictive in matters that were likely to affect its interests adversely—for example, competition from Laker and from the supersonic attraction of Concorde. As the controversy over Bermuda 2 developed, the British government adopted the position that a new bilateral would have to be conditional upon a satisfactory settlement of the Concorde affair.[13]

Dell's denunciation of Bermuda generated an angry mood in the United States. The Americans were unhappy at being forced to abandon what they still considered to be a satisfactory agreement and negotiate a new one within a twelve-month period, especially when things would be complicated by a presidential election and possibly by a change of administration. Also, they thought that they had answers for British objections to Bermuda 1. It seemed odd to them that the British should contend that BA was being swamped by American airlines on the Atlantic route when BA had the largest percentage of the traffic and more than it had ever had. If Britain were so concerned about competition from multiple US airlines, why had it not tried to reply in kind instead of revoking Laker's licence? And why were the British unwilling to include charter operations in the proposed Bermuda 2 talks? (The simple answer to the latter point was that the British did not think that rules for scheduled services could be sorted out within a twelve-month period if charters were dealt with as well.[14]) The British idea that traffic should be

[13] Dell interview; E. Dell, 'Interdependence and the Judges: Civil Aviation and Antitrust' *International Affairs*, 61 (1985), 355–73; *Flight*, 21 May 1977, 'Concorde Could Block Bermuda 2'.

[14] Britain and the United States made an interim agreement for charter services between their two countries in April 1977 and commited themselves in Bermuda 2 to enter negotiations for a new agreement before Dec. 1977. However, the importance of charters declined in relative terms very rapidly under deregulation, as scheduled carriers offered lower fares and as more of them

equally shared was anathema to Americans, given their belief in competition, but the fact that the United States generated 60–70 per cent of the traffic on the Atlantic challenged the equity of the British proposal even on the premisses of their own arguments. The United States certainly saw no reason to concede automatically a higher percentage of the traffic to BA. With regard to capacity controls, British arguments were weakened in American minds both by the reductions that had already occurred because of market pressure and by an estimated increase of over 10 per cent in traffic volume during 1976. Finally, the United States countered British conservation arguments about the waste of fuel involved in flying empty seats by pointing to the extravagant use of fuel by Concorde, which they dubbed 'the flying kerosene tank'.[15]

Anglo-American talks began in London in September, but only after an inauspicious development which further prejudiced their character. In the late summer a row developed over the level of winter capacity appropriate for the routes from Miami and Chicago to London. Agreement proved elusive and in the end Britain took unilateral and, in American eyes, illegal action to regulate capacity. As a result, even before the Bermuda 2 talks began, US Commerce Secretary, Elliott Richardson, advised US airlines to draw up contingency plans in case there were a breakdown of air services between the United States and Britain. This did not augur well for what both sides had already acknowledged would be difficult negotiations.[16]

The victory of Jimmy Carter over Gerald Ford in November presented a further complication. Three rounds of talks were conducted by the Ford Administration, including business sessions in Washington starting on 18 October, and in London in December, but the latter was understandably in low key, as matters now needed to be taken up by whomsoever Carter appointed to the DOT and the CAB. The fourth session of talks, scheduled initially for January, was postponed to late February in order to allow the new US administration to find its feet.

entered the market. See interview with Senior Foreign Office official conducted by the author, 8 Dec. 1989.

[15] *Flight*, 21 May 1977, 31 July 1976 editorial, 25 Sept. 1961, and 27 Nov. 1976, 1514; Dell, 'Interdependence', 358.

[16] *Flight*, 24 August., 4 Sept., and 23 Oct. 1976.

During the first three meetings little was achieved other than a fuller understanding of each side's position. The Americans were unhappy about British proposals involving airlines fixing capacity, withdrawal of US fifth-freedom rights, equal division of Atlantic traffic, and single designation. There appeared to be some consensus on fares, in that neither side was happy with existing arrangements, but a satisfactory solution had not as yet emerged. Also, the United States appeared to be willing to make some concessions on capacity, but not necessarily of a kind that would mollify the British. The matter of more gateways for Britain remained unresolved. Perhaps the most worrying aspect of the talks, however, was the ill temper with which they were conducted. Both sides were aggressively pursuing their own interests, and a satisfactory accommodation seemed a long way away. In the face of deteriorating relations in the second round of talks, the Americans took the line that they should simply reaffirm Bermuda 1, but the British rejected that.

The Americans were worried that Britain might act as it had done regarding Miami and Chicago and impose unilateral regulations if an agreement were not reached. Trouble of that scope with Britain was deemed undesirable. The United States had a number of other aviation negotiations in the pipeline and was eager that its arrangements with Britain should continue to set a good precedent for others to follow. The stakes were not just bilateral relations with Britain; the impact that such relations would have on the international system had to be taken into account as well.

During the period from December to the end of February, when it was difficult to make progress at the formal level because of the change-over from Ford to Carter, the two sides nevertheless continued to develop their positions. The Skytrain decision was reaffirmed in late December by the Court of Appeal, and that allowed Dell to develop his hand in a way not entirely expected by the Americans, especially with regard to the matter of competition and dual designation. But even before that the British had taken pains to explain that they were not against competition in general, but only when it was destructive and wasteful. Such arguments were made by Ross Stainton of BA in Washington in early December and by Dell in February, when he addressed the London Chamber of Commerce.

We need capacity control to avoid waste. We need balanced routes, which give similar opportunity to both sides. We need competition as a guarantee to the consumer, and we need a better opportunity for British airlines within the international air transport system.[17]

The United States remained unmoved and proceeded to try to outmanœuvre the British. In early January President Ford rejected the CAB recommendation that Delta and NWA should join America's existing three operators in flying into Britain and suggested that instead the CAB should 'reconsider its policy and . . . look in particular at the possibility of using more European destinations rather than concentrating on services from US cities to British gateways'. Once again the threat of bypassing Britain was used to try to make its recalcitrant leaders accept the American view of things.[18]

This hard line was ominous for Britain and, as it transpired, things got worse with President Carter and CAB Chairman Kahn. But there were chinks in the American armour. The DOT remained essentially committed to regulation, which caused difficulties with the deregulators at the CAB and in the Carter White House. The new Secretary of Transport, Brock Adams, came to his job with experience of regulating both surface and air transport. An economist and lawyer by profession, he had become a Congressman for Seattle, the home of the Boeing Corporation. In the past he had opposed allowing Concorde into New York and he favoured the development of an American SST, but otherwise his credentials, at face value, looked favourable from the British government's point of view. In fact, notwithstanding friction and division within the US government, Adams proved to be the most aggressive of the negotiators involved in the Bermuda 2 talks and a tough opponent of the British position.[19]

One ray of hope for the fourth round of talks was the favourable view the British had of Special Ambassador Alan Boyd, who led the US negotiators. He was expected to achieve, and

[17] *Flight*, 27 Nov., 4, 18, and 25 Dec. 1976, and 5 Mar. 1977; *The Economist*, 7–13 Aug. 1976, 10–11 and 66; Dell, 'Interdependence'; Dell interview.

[18] *Flight*, 8 Jan. 1977, 52.

[19] Ibid., 25 Dec. 1976; C. Jonsson, *International Aviation and the Politics of Regime Change* (Frances Pinter, London, 1987), 146 ff.; interview with Foreign Office official.

did achieve, a good rapport with his British counterparts, led by Patrick Shovelton, Deputy Secretary of the DOT's Aviation and Shipping Division. Even so, little was achieved in the London session. Boyd summed things up with the quip that all that Shovelton had given away was 'kind words'. But political pressure was mounting and the importance of reaching an accommodation was increasing. Whilst the fourth round was in progress, Callaghan went to Washington for discussions with President Carter, and during these he raised the problems of Concorde and of the Bermuda 2 talks: 'He told the President that the [latter] issue could generate "a great deal of heat and division between us", especially with Concorde in the background.' His fears were soon realized, but both he and Carter, who were generally on good terms, emphasized to their respective negotiators the need to find a solution and avoid a break in aviation services between the United States and Britain.[20]

Talks in Washington that began at the end of March witnessed a further improvement in the atmosphere between the two sides and agreement on non-controversial issues, but it was left to the final round in London, which began on the 16 May, to resolve the main problems.[21] Contrary to some expectations, substantial progress was made. Britain abandoned demands for a fifty-fifty division of Atlantic traffic, and agreement was reached on the makings of what became the final compromise on dual designation. The United States still balked at predetermination of capacity, and difficulties remained regarding fifth-freedom rights and routes in the Pacific. In short, while there was still some way to go, things looked promising. Then, much to the astonishment of British officials, Brock Adams took a most belligerent line speaking in London on 23 May. He said that the Americans might not be willing to continue talks after 2 June, and that the FAA would be unable to decide about Concorde before the 22 June deadline for the end of the Bermuda 2 talks. (When Bermuda 2 was agreed, the Concorde affair was unresolved, but the signs pointed to a satisfactory outcome for the British, and on 22 November Concorde began flights into New York.) Earlier in May a New York district judge had ruled

[20] *Flight*, 5 and 19 March, 1977; Dell, 'Interdependence', 358; Callaghan interview.

[21] *Flight*, 7 May 1977, p. 1236.

against the City Port Authority's objections to Concorde operating into New York, which had raised hopes that British demands for a satisfactory resolution of the Concorde affair before the signing of a new bilateral air-agreement would be met. Now Adams was denying that possibility and bringing great pressure to bear on the British by trying to make it their responsibility to compromise with the United States in order to reach an immediate agreement and avoid a break in air services between Britain and the United States. From this point the negotiations changed from just being difficult to threatening to cause a serious rift between the two countries.[22]

Dell later recalled that one of the things which struck him most about the Bermuda 2 discussions was the ill temper on the American side. Perhaps the Americans had more justification for it than Dell was prepared to allow, given the unfortunate timing and the demands made by the British, but it is difficult not to share his view that the Americans were at times crude in their bargaining and tended to over-react. At one point officials in the State Department threatened to break off all trade links with Britain unless the British government were more accommodating in the aviation field. This was clearly an idle threat, but it is illustrative of the petulance that the British had to suffer with as even a temper as they could muster.

As the situation deteriorated, Callaghan and Carter both became increasingly concerned and on at least two occasions discussed matters over the telephone, presumably in the informal and friendly way Carter had told Callaghan he thought that they ought to whenever anything in Anglo-American or world affairs were troubling them. The result of this in London was that the Prime Minister consulted Dell about how he thought things might develop. 'I told him', recounted Dell, that I didn't expect that civil aviation relations would in fact be broken off. I thought that we'd come to a conclusion. And he [Callaghan] seemed to be satisfied with that.'[23]

In the end, Dell was right, but the situation remained uncertain and critical for longer than he would have liked. On 13 June the United States submitted new proposals to the British which

[22] *Flight*, 21 and 28 May 1977.

[23] Dell interview; Callaghan interview.

constituted a retreat from their previous, more acceptable, position, and so the British rejected them out of hand and the talks went into recess. Three days later in Washington, Adams said: 'We'll call a halt [to air services between the United States and Britain]. We have reached the bottom line; the President has reached the bottom line. . . . Sure this is a tough time between our countries.'[24]

Strangely, after criticizing the British for denouncing Bermuda 1 and thus imposing a one-year limit on the talks, in the end it was the Americans who insisted on keeping absolutely rigidly to that timetable. The British were prepared to 'stop the clock' on the 22 June and keep to Bermuda 1 until negotiations were complete, but the Americans were not. It was all part of the pressure that they wanted to put on the British government in order to get it to move closer to the US position. However, whether or not this was a bluff, it had to be made credible, which involved arranging alternatives to direct flights into London. The Americans approached the French, asking for permission to increase the frequency of flights for US airlines into Paris, but the French responded with an emphatic 'non'. Dell subsequently commented that 'the annoying thing was the Dutch did agree, when they were approached. Anyhow, we were greatly in love with the French at that moment . . . and we hated the Dutch [said lightheartedly].' Nevertheless, even with permission for more flights into Holland, the Americans were still at a disadvantage compared with the British as far as contingency plans were concerned. Their ability to service the United States from third parties, namely Bermuda and Canada, was much greater than America's to service Britain, especially after France's decision. Realization of this may have played a part in US thinking during the final crisis of the Bermuda 2 talks, edging the Americans towards acceptance of the final compromise.[25]

The Americans did compromise at the last minute and it is not entirely clear why. One factor was perhaps the realization that the British were in a better position to service the United States through third parties than they were to do the same with

[24] *The Times*, 14 and 17 June 1977.
[25] Dell interview.

Britain. Other factors appear to have been the skill and statesmanship of Alan Boyd and the serious and unwelcome consequences that would have flowed from a breakdown in air services between the United States and Britain. If the United States could not reach an agreement with Britain, one of the more liberal aviation-powers, then what hope was there for future liberalization of the international system? And what effect would such a failure have had on negotiations that were pending with the Japanese, the Italians, and others? The Americans had talked themselves into a difficult position. A breakdown in civil-aviation services between Britain and the United States would not have looked good for Dell, but neither would it look good for the United States.[26]

Interestingly, as Dell has pointed out, the Americans may have prejudged the strength of British resolve, without having actually tested it properly. Dell's strategy was to sit tight and see what happened, but his assurance to Callaghan that a solution would eventually be found was the highest level at which matters were considered. The dispute with the Americans never got to the Cabinet, but the United States was not to know that. Dell has speculated that perhaps the Americans got the impression from Callaghan, after Dell had reassured him, that the British government was wholly and fully behind the position adopted by the British negotiators. Dell's point was that this might have been how things would have turned out, but it never actually came to that. The only resolve to be really tested was Dell's, not the collective one of the British government: the matter was never discussed in Cabinet. But the Americans, confronted with the apparent resolve of the British government and the consequences of a breakdown of air services, decided that they had to make concessions. The bottom line remarked on by Adams on Friday 17 June had changed from what it had been on the previous Monday, when the talks went into recess. Over the weekend the talks were resumed on the basis of new instructions from Washington, and they continued into the following week. Progress was made and on 22 June Callaghan stated that it was 'almost unthinkable' that air services should

[26] Dell interview; *Flight*, 2 Apr. 1977; Dell, 'Interdependence', 358; *The Times*, 23 June 1977.

stop. On the following day *The Times* was able to announce 'Victory for All' on its front page: there was agreement on Bermuda 2.[27]

Of the final agreement, Dell later wrote: 'Britain secured more of its objectives than a cool assessment of the relative strength of the two contenders made probable.' One result was that, 'British airlines were able in subsequent years to win more of the market in transatlantic air traffic.' Although both sides had had to make concessions, particularly in the final days of talks, Dell's assessment is fair.[28]

The British gained six new entry-points into the United States, which was important in that it reduced one of the advantages American airlines had, because of their vast domestic geographical area, in attracting transatlantic passengers. Many Americans preferred to travel on US airlines because they could be picked up in their local city and shuttled to their transatlantic point of departure by the same airline that was flying them across the Atlantic. Cabotage prevented British airlines from doing that, but by gaining more entry-points they diminished their disadvantage somewhat.

There was no fifty-fifty split of traffic—the Americans would never accept that—but single designation was agreed, except on two transatlantic routes, with the proviso that if other routes exceeded a traffic level of 600,000 one way over a two-year period (or 450,000 if there was only one airline operating the route), then additional dual designation would be triggered. The American market-share of Bermuda routes was more definitely restricted by the withdrawal of fifth-freedom rights in Hong Kong and in London. Regarding the latter, over a three-year period the United States lost its rights to Austria, Sweden, Norway, Belgium, and Holland; it retained them for Germany and for PAA's round-the-world service. There was also a definite gain by Britain in the vexed area of capacity controls. They only related to the Atlantic, and the British government's original hopes that the airlines might set capacity limits was unacceptable to the United States, because of CAB and White House dislike of direct, rigid controls and also because of the fear of

[27] Ibid.; Dell interview.

[28] Dell, 'Interdependence', 350–9.

antitrust actions in US courts. But the outcome was still satisfactory for Britain. The compromise was embodied in Annex 2 and provided for

> a consultative process to deal with cases of excess provision of capacity, while ensuring that designated airlines retain adequate scope for managerial initiative in establishing schedules and that the overall market share achieved by each designated airline will depend upon passenger choice rather than the operation of any formula or limitation mechanism.[29]

The airlines were to submit their schedules for pre-screening by the US and British governments. If there were disagreement, then the mean of their traffic forecasts was to be taken, plus a right to an increase of at least twenty flights in the summer and fifteen in the winter season.

So, on capacity, and on readjustment through single designation and the withdrawal of fifth-freedom rights, Dell had gone a long way towards realizing his aims of reducing what he saw as American advantages in competing with Britain and of establishing a more equitable distribution of commercial returns between the two countries from the routes reciprocally designated under the Bermuda Agreement. In addition, Britain had gained a number of important new entry-points into the United States.

On the other hand, the Americans had not lost out all down the line by any means. Provisions for fare-setting placed more emphasis on bilateral agreement and on the market and less on IATA, and this was very much the direction in which the United States now wanted to proceed. The United States had also gained freedom to change gauge in London and, more importantly, unrestricted combination rights. The latter meant that US airlines could pick up passengers in London for any destination provided that they had a valid US airline reservation from the United States to their ultimate destination. Some saw this as more than ample compensation for loss of fifth-freedom rights. And finally, at the very end of the negotiations, the Americans had insisted on conditions which undermined the prospects for B.Cal. on its projected route to the south-west of the United

[29] Cmd. 7016, 'Agreement Concerning Air Services' [Bermuda 2], 23 July 1977.

States. Initially, the British hoped that one US airline would operate from Atlanta to London, with an effective monopoly for three years, and that B.Cal. would enjoy the same rights operating into Houston. The Americans decided that this was not acceptable and stipulated that not only would there be a US operator from Atlanta, but also an all-cargo service from Houston to London and a passenger service from Dallas-Fort Worth, which was only 200 miles from Houston. Furthermore, the latter would be able to offer a non-stop flight to London, whereas B.Cal. would have to have a stop-over for the first three years of its operations. According to calculations from B.Cal., which had already had one unhappy experience operating an Atlantic service, Dallas-Fort Worth was likely to drain over 30 per cent of the traffic that would otherwise have had to fly with them from Houston: again their prospects were not good.[30]

The Bermuda 2 Agreement was criticized in Parliament by Conservative spokesmen Norman Tebbit and John Nott, but generally it was well received and considered to be a successful negotiation by all the British, with the possible exception of B.Cal. Judgement as to the merit of these things is always difficult, but perhaps three observations might help establish a clearer perspective. Firstly, BA's share of the Atlantic market increased. Secondly, the Bermuda 2 Agreement was heavily criticized by Kahn and his acolytes, and Congressional dissatisfaction was also vociferous, especially from Massachusetts, as PAA had to withdraw its Boston-to-London service because of the new arrangements. Bermuda 2 was heavily criticized in the United States and the retrospective judgement of the Foreign Office was that it was better than Bermuda 1, both of which facts support the contention that the British did well out of the actions instigated by Dell. Thirdly, there is perhaps continuing disagreement about what Bermuda 2 actually achieved because things were changing so quickly at that time. In the light of America's continuing swing to deregulation, one could say that the Bermuda 2 negotiations in fact came to constitute, whether or not they were initially intended to do so, a pre-emptive strike on the part of Britain. It is doubtful that Britain could have got

[30] Hansard, 23 June 1977, cols. 1754–65; Dell interview; interview with Foreign Office official; Dell, 'Interdependence', 359.

such a satisfactory agreement as Bermuda 2 once the Carter Administration had become properly entrenched and Kahn had achieved the leadership of policy that he later did. If the status quo on civil-aviation policy had been maintained in the United States during 1977, then Bermuda 2 would not have been the success for Britain that it subsequently appeared to be. In short, judgement of the outcome of Bermuda 2 is a particularly relative matter, but whichever way one looks at it, it was a qualified victory for the British.[31]

PROBLEMS, SOLUTIONS, AND PROSPECTS OF THE 1980S

In contrast to what it had done with Bermuda 1, the United States never concluded a Bermuda 2 with anyone else: it was not adopted as a model for the future. As soon as it was signed it was attacked as too restrictive by deregulators led by Alfred Kahn, who had been appointed the new CAB Chairman by Carter in January 1977. This great publicist and advocate of deregulation had already made an impact on world aviation before Bermuda 2 was completed, and although he was unable to get what he wanted from the British in the new bilateral, his influence on international aviation over the next few years was to be very considerable.

Immediately he came to office Kahn began to pronounce critical judgements on US domestic and international controls in civil aviation. He was partly taking the initiative and partly responding to growing unease in Congress and among many sections of the public about too much regulation over the free market, and in particular regarding civil aviation. The reaction abroad to the doctrine of aviation deregulation, however, was overwhelmingly negative. That was very clearly demonstrated in a special ICAO conference—the most important convened since Chicago in 1944—which met in Montreal in the spring of 1977. 'More Control is the Message' was the way one journal summed up its outcome. The United States was virtually isolated, but it remained determined to continue with deregula-

[31] Colvin interview, conducted by the author, 7 Dec. 1989; interview with Foreign Office official.

tion. Liberalization gained momentum in Washington, and in 1978 Congress passed the Airline Deregulation Act, which aimed at minimizing government control over the commercial operations of civil aviation and set a deadline for the demise of the CAB. What regulation remained after that was to pass to the DOT.[32]

The overall effect on Britain of American liberalization was threefold. First of all, the United States brought pressure to bear to get a liberal interpretation of the Bermuda 2 tariff clauses. The immediate cause for raising this was the British contention that the service from Dallas-Fort Worth to London operated by Braniff was competing against B.Cal. unfairly by offering cheap onward flights to destinations in the United States. The British government was sensitive about this because of the criticisms about the poor deal for B.Cal. under Bermuda 2, and so they refused to allow Braniff to continue operations after its inaugural flight. The Americans responded angrily and proceeded to sign liberal bilaterals with Belgium and Holland which, among other things, put pressure on the British Government by holding out the prospect that there countries would drain passengers away from London. In response Britain gave way, and a more liberal interpretation of the tariff clauses was accepted.[33]

Secondly, Kahn demanded that foreign airlines should 'show cause' as to why they should not be liable to US antitrust actions for colluding over fare-setting. The CAB had support for its policy from the Justice Department, the White House, and—with a degree of caution—the State Department, but the DOT continued to be sceptical, as did foreign governments and airlines, including PAA and TWA. Lack of unity in the US government concerning liberalization blunted its thrust a little and international opposition was even more effective in the long term, though not before important changes had been wrought. In particular, IATA was undermined—by the attitude of the US government, by the withdrawal of some American airlines, and by the entry, as a consequency of Bermuda 2, of non-IATA

[32] Ibid.; Sampson, *Empires*, 133–48; *Airline Competition: GOA Report to Congress, May 1986* (GOA, Washington, DC, 1986); *Flight*, 7 May 1977, 1237; Jonsson, *Regime Change*, 124 ff.

[33] Ibid.; Sampson, *Empires*, 145; F. McGowan and C. Trengove, *European Aviation: A Common Market?* (Institute for Fiscal Studies, London, 1986).

airlines like Delta on to the Atlantic route. Laker and its low fares were also destructive of IATA tariff conferences. In 1977 Atlantic fares were in turmoil and IATA was in great difficulty. In the end, Super APEX and standby fares were introduced, in order to enable the scheduled airlines to compete with Laker and charters. Eventually those fares led to the bankruptcy of Laker, in 1982, and resulted in the most celebrated of legal cases concerning civil aviation, when Laker brought antitrust action in the United States against BA, PAA, and others for predatory price-fixing. The case was settled out of court, but it raised the spectre of US antitrust actions against foreign airlines who were involved in IATA fare-setting, and that caused the British government concern when it came to privatize BA in the 1980s.

In 1979 IATA divided its three tariff-conference areas into eleven, and the unanimity rule for setting fare levels was changed to an 80.1 per cent majority. This liberalization, however, was insufficient to mollify the United States, even though the latter retreated from its belligerent position on 'showing cause'. In December 1979 the United States terminated 'show cause' hearings, and the matter was abandoned entirely with the expiry of the CAB on 31 December 1984. However, in 1980 US airlines were forbidden to take part in IATA fare-setting on the Atlantic and this brought conflict with Britain. Once again the United States tried to use Europe as a lever on the British government, this time by offering countries like Germany and Holland more US gateways in return for liberalization and more competitive fares. The United States was determined not to return IATA to the importance it had had in the past. It may have been unsuccessful with its 'show cause' campaign, but its national policy weakened IATA nevertheless. In 1982 the United States discussed Atlantic fares with European countries through the European Civil Aviation Conference (ECAC), which had been set up as a consultative body in 1954, and agreed to take a less hard line towards fare-fixing through IATA, but the role of IATA in fare-fixing had been irredeemably damaged. In 1987 IATA membership was larger than ever, but only 20 per cent of its work-load was to do with tariffs. What the Americans had failed to do through the 'show cause' tactic they had largely achieved through a more piecemeal approach. In the course of that, they had created many worries for the British, but as the

1980s progressed, ideas in the two countries about international civil aviation began to converge again, as the liberalizers in the Thatcher Government built up a head of steam and decided that they would respond positively to the more competitive system the United States had promoted with its attacks upon IATA.[34]

Thirdly, the United States entered a new bilateral with Israel which was substantially different from, and more liberal than, Bermuda 2. The same month that the Israeli bilateral was signed, the US government issued a policy statement which effectively put its contents into a general framework, and this was the model the United States now wanted to follow. It reiterated much of the Nixon policy statement of 1970, but was more liberal. There should be: price competition; liberal charter-agreements; no controls on capacity, routes, or frequencies; elimination of unfair competition; multiple designation; more gateways; and development of cargo services.[35]

The fact that maintaining harmony with British policy was no longer a major priority for the United States, as it had been throughout the post-war period down to the 1970s, was a significant development in the aviation relationship between the two countries. It was also a sign of Britain's relative decline, but the United States was still eager to garner support for liberalization, and although the example set by Britain in the international sphere might have diminished in importance, its potential for influencing the EC had grown, and that soon became a significant matter in both British and American thinking. The EC was committed to the Single European Market due to begin in 1992, and as that date got nearer, the implications for civil aviation were considered more. EC members, apart from Britain and Holland, were notoriously protectionist, but if Britain, the leading European civil-aviation power with the most important route-network, became more liberal, this would have a beneficial impact upon the way the EC's civil-aviation relationship developed with the United States. In fact, after Margaret Thatcher's general election victory in 1979, Britain moved towards greater liberalization, but British and American ideas

[34] Ibid., 144–5; Pryke, *Competition*, 8; *Flight*, 27 Aug., 17 Sept., and 8 Oct. 1977, 577, 813, and 991 respectively, 14 Nov. 1987, 8; Jonsson, *Regime Change*, 124–46.

[35] Ibid., 123; Gidwitz, *Politics*, 76, quoting *Aviation Daily*, 237 : 19, 25 May 1978, 147–50.

about liberalization were not always the same. Like any other assertion of an abstract doctrine, it was put into practice in such a way as to promote national interest as well as altruism, and where liberalization conflicted with national interest it was not promoted. Consequently, there continued to be heated differences over specific issues. This was the case even after Reagan came to power in the United States in 1981, an event which inaugurated a similar conservative dispensation to Thatcher's and also renewed the Special Relationship, largely because of a strong friendship between the two leaders.[36]

The Conservative government in Britain inaugurated the most radical changes in policy since the Attlee Administration. The emphasis on market forces, individual responsibility, and competitiveness was politically ubiquitous. The effect this had on civil aviation was soon clear to see. In 1979 John Nott, the Minister for Trade, introduced what became the 1980 Aviation Act, the main points of which were the encouragement of a more competitive and commercial aviation-system and the eventual privatization of BA. The provision of the 1971 Act for the Minister to give guidance to the CAA was abolished and the CAA took more direct responsibility for licensing policy, though the airlines could appeal decisions to the Minister. In November 1979 the CAA issued its own policy statement, which was in line with the government's desire to cultivate a more liberal system; but, as things turned out, Nott played a more prominent role in the development of policy than some had originally expected.

Decisions which he took in 1980 by virtue of his appeal authority lifted the general tone of the new licensing policy to a more highly competitive one. In the view of Michael Colvin, Chairman of the Conservative Aviation Committee, 'probably the first step towards a sort of deregulated international civil aviation regime was John Nott's decision on Hong Kong in 1980'. The CAA had allowed B. Cal. to compete with BA on the London-to-Hong Kong route but had disallowed applications from Cathay Pacific and Laker. Nott amended the decision on appeal and said that he wanted the market to decide things: if Laker and Cathay Pacific wanted to compete as well, they were to be allowed to do so. The Conservatives had not just

[36] McGowan, *Common Market*, generally.

readopted dual designation, but were promoting multiple designation on routes where they thought it viable. The ethos of competition was embraced by them more wholeheartedly than by any British government since before the war.[37]

In Anglo-American relations, despite a convergence of general policies on aviation, disagreements still persisted. Controversy over fares in 1980 has already been referred to, but in addition there was the lingering distaste in the United States for the capacity controls in Annex 2 of Bermuda 2. The British government was now also unhappy with them, and the Transport Secretary, Nicholas Ridley, who was an ardent advocate of a freer market, took the opportunity of the Annex's imminent expiry to seek a renegotiation of its provisions. On the whole, the British wanted more liberal controls, but they were constrained by the need to safeguard the position of B. Cal. On the American side, by the end of 1985, the drive for international deregulation was losing steam, particularly after a Congressional Report in August 1983 had demonstrated that some foreign airlines had gained more than their US counterparts from deregulation and that American airlines still had to contend with the problem of operators which were government-owned and often highly subsidized. Under these circumstances liberalization was only exposing the United States to more unfair foreign competition, and the Reagan Administration thus began to pull back from deregulation in the international sphere. So, it was not only Britain that had moved towards deregulation; the United States had also pulled back from its more extreme position.[38]

The British negotiators for the Annex 2 talks were led by Handley Stevens, Under-Secretary at the DOT, and he was advised by a Foreign Office team led by R. C. Beetham, Head of the Maritime, Aviation and Environment Department. The political atmosphere between the two sides was better than it had been during the Bermuda 2 talks. Ronald Reagan and Margaret Thatcher had renewed the Special Relationship, and both administrations shared more of a common political disposition than their predecessors had done.

[37] Colvin interview; Baldwin, *Regulating*, 237–47.

[38] Interview with Foreign Office official; Sampson, *Empires*, 146; N. K. Taneja, *US International Aviation Policy* (Heath, Lexington, Ky., 1980).

Initially, the British tried to engage their counterparts from the American DOT and the State Department in broader talks, which would have included the sensitive matter of liability for British airlines under American antitrust laws. This had come to prominence because of Laker and was now a matter of concern, as it could have an adverse effect on the privatization of BA by depressing the market for its shares through fear of expensive antitrust actions. Britain's attempt failed and the matter has still not been satisfactorily resolved so far as it is concerned (though that did not prevent the British government from going ahead with privatization). With Annex 2, the British achieved a more satisfactory outcome.[39]

The talks were by no means easy and the American DOT in particular was difficult, suspicious of British policy, and unenthusiastic about deregulation. There were also prickly personalities on the British side. In March 1986 in a speech before representatives of the American Chamber of Commerce, Aviation Minister Michael Spicer berated the United States for maintaining its cabotage and criticized other aspects of the US aviation system which, in his view, discriminated unfairly against foreign operators. Nevertheless, progress was made, partly because of the good relations which existed between Foreign Office and State Department officials—in particular between their leader Jeffrey Shane, Deputy Assistant Secretary for Transport Affairs, and Beetham. In September 1986 a new Annex 2 agreement was announced and it has proved successful.

Summing up some three years later, a senior Foreign Office official said; 'we both felt we'd got a satisfactory deal and indeed it has worked very well, no problems with it on either side [the Americans] certainly talked about our aviation relationship following that in a much happier way than previously'. The British had to make some concessions, but they achieved their main goal, namely liberalization with a safety net. All scheduled

[39] Interview with Foreign Office official. One of the secondary aims of the talks was to try to clear the decks for BA's privatization, especially concerning the danger of antitrust actions against BA in US courts. Despite a report in *Flight*, 22 March 1986, 4–5, suggesting the contrary, this was only of fairly minor significance in the minds of government officials. M. Ashworth and P. Forsyth, *Civil Aviation and the Privatisation of British Airways* (Institute for Fiscal Studies, London, 1985).

airlines were granted a daily frequency as of right, thereafter capacity was controlled in a proportional way between British and US airlines. On the same route one airline could not exceed by more than 150 per cent the other's subsonic service capacity. If there were disagreement about that rule, then an airline could increase its capacity unilaterally by thirty and twenty flights respectively in its summer and winter schedules. This safety net was provided specifically with B. Cal. and its weak position on the route to the US south-west in mind, but in fact it became redundant when BA bought B. Cal. in 1988. But that does not detract from the success of the Annex 2 talks: there have been no capacity problems under its provisions.[40]

In fact, in terms of high policy, the 1980s saw little else to disturb the relationship between the two countries, with the exception of the problem that began to loom with regard to the EC and the development of a European civil-aviation policy, but that did not really come to the fore until 1989. Before then, there were two difficulties, largely of a commercial nature, which were resolved in the end outside the political arena, but which for a time played a part in it.

The first problem arose out of the privatization of the British Airports Authority and its user charges. Because of the way flights from the United States to Britain are scheduled, most flights arrive in London in the early hours of the morning and the Americans allege that BAA's charges discriminate against carriers landing at such times. BA and other British carriers have to pay the same charges, but nevertheless the United States made a big issue out of this. Attempts failed to settle the dispute before privatization, and after a number of 'hairy' situations the matter was referred to arbitration (where it still lay at the time of writing).

The other commercial matter was Computer Reservation Systems (CRSs) and their potential for discriminatory use, which for a time became of political significance. CRSs were very much a consequence of deregulation, rather like the hub-and-spoke configuration of routes domestically within the United States. By the early 1980s concerns were being expressed about their

[40] Interview with Foreign Office official; *Flight*, 29 Mar. 1986, 2, and 20 Sept. 1986.

unfair use. For example, American Airlines' Sabre, the largest CRS (by 1990 it carried over 10 million individual airfares), might give preference to American flights on its display screen, to the disadvantage of other airlines. In 1984 the American DOT responded to the situation by imposing rules of conduct for CRS users. However, problems persisted, as a report from the US General Accounting Office showed in 1986. The report was drawn up in response to requests from Nancy Kassebaum and Norman Mineta from the Senate and House respectively: they both had official interest in civil aviation. The report recommended further studies by the DOT and action 'to enforce compliance with or to strengthen the CRS rules'. However, by this time CRSs were causing problems in the international sphere, and in particular between BA and American Airlines.

BA and members of the British government felt that Sabre was being used in a way that discriminated against BA. Towards the end of 1987 the Americans claimed that DOT regulations had rendered Sabre and other American CRS systems neutral, but the British remained unconvinced and BA retaliated against what it saw as discriminatory American use of CRSs by developing Travicom-BABS. Travicom was a means by which British travel agents could be patched into CRS systems, including BABS, which BA developed as a temporary stop-gap before the more advanced Galileo System came on line. However, BA refused to allow BA tickets to be issued by any other system in Britain, which encouraged British travel agents to use BABS at the expense of both American CRS systems and US airlines.

By 1988 there had arisen from this a serious dispute between BA and American which was beginning to draw in their respective governments. American, the largest free-world airline, under the aggressive leadership of Robert Crandall, brought legal action against BA under the fair-trading clause of Bermuda 2, and also asked the American DOT to retaliate against BA for its discriminatory use of Travicom-BABS. The situation began to look ugly. As a Foreign Office spokesman put it, 'I think the problem [was] one of our feeling that the way the American system operated favoured American airlines in the USA over ours and it got exacerbated because British Airways retaliated.'

The matter had already been taken up in Parliament by the Transport Committee well before things came to a head. And just as measures had been taken in the United States to regulate the use of CRSs, so in Britain things progressed along a similar path, though largely through the good offices of ECAC, which agreed upon a code of conduct for the use of CRSs in 1988. Before the Transport Committee's report was published on 28 July 1988, BA and American agreed to an out-of-court settlement of their differences largely based on a compromise made possible through ECAC rules. The Committee explained the agreement as follows:

> BA has allowed Sabre to issue its tickets although, outside the UK, this agreement will be subject to either a period of notice or to a moratorium and notice depending upon the region involved. The agreement opens up the UK market to Sabre and is in line with the ECAC code . . . , American Airlines has agreed to abide by the ECAC code for screen displays, despite the USA not being a signatory to ECAC. Sabre has also agreed to improve the display of direct flights and inter-line connecting flights in the USA and the rest of the world. This will be of benefit to BA. . . . The issue of access to information is also resolved. Within Europe Sabre will be subject to any future European Commission (Transport) regulations.[41]

The government still believed that the system was unfair, but for the time being they withdrew from the matter, being unwilling to 'second guess' BA. The problem that remained in 1989 was exacerbated by the hub-and-spoke system, which, in combination with the effectiveness of US systems like Sabre, resulted in customers being attracted to US rather than to other airlines, because they could be picked up from their local airports and taken to their point of departure for London and other destinations by the same airline and vice versa on incoming flights. The excellent service American airlines offer to the hubs, and the advantage this gives them, is difficult for foreign airlines to offset. The British are presently seeking to cope with this problem by breaking into the US interior—either by getting

[41] Short articles about both BAA and the CRS problem appeared from time to time in *Flight*, e.g. 10 Oct. 1987 and 23 Jan. 1988; Interview with Foreign Office official; Colvin interview; GOA Competition Report; House of Commons Transport Committee, *Airline Competition: Computer Reservation Systems*, 3rd report, 28 July 1988 (2 vols.; HMSO, London, 1988); BBC 2 documentary 'Airline', 25 Mar. 1990.

more gateways, or by gaining rights to run feeder operations to the gateways, or by arrangements such as the one between BA and United Airlines made in December 1987, which dovetails the former's transatlantic schedule with the latter's US domestic network. This last tactic has been successful, but the other two are still under consideration and of growing importance as the impact which the Single European Market might have on civil-aviation relations between the United States and Britain attracts more and more attention.[42]

Since 1946 Britain has done well in her aviation relations with the United States, given their respective sizes. Bermuda 2, for some people, seemed to represent an equality of treatment between the two countries when it was patently obvious that they were not equal. Judgements about that vary, but one thing that is not in dispute is that the vast US domestic cabotage represents an advantage over which the British have never been able to counter fully. The result of different geographical positions and sizes has meant that British airlines fly into the United States but then have few destinations to fly on to. If they go to the west coast, they are confronted by the vast reaches of the Pacific, if they go south they are on commercially unviable routes. US airlines, on the other hand fly into London and find themselves on the doorstep of the large European market. A further problem for British airlines is that they have to compete against American airlines which have domestic US networks that feed into their foreign operations by shuttling passengers to and from the gateway airports. However, with the development of the EC and the deadline for the Single European Market in 1992, Britain, along with the rest of Europe, will soon be in a position where it will have similar advantages to those enjoyed by the United States, namely the possibility of a European cabotage of comparable significance, if not actual size, to that of the United States.

The impact of the creation of the Single European Market in 1992 and pressure from Britain and Holland for deregulation within the EC has caused considerable reflection on both sides of the Atlantic during 1988 and 1989. And these matters have

[42] Interview with Foreign Office official; *Sunday Times*, 10 Sept. 1989, 'BA tries to stall United's rivalry'.

been given some focus in Anglo-American negotiations about access to more airports.

From the mid-1980s British pressure for a measure of deregulation has mounted. In 1984 the government published a White Paper on airline competition, and at the Fountainbleau Summit Margaret Thatcher called for European deregulation and there were moves by Britain and Holland to introduce lower fares. Since then the EC has moved gradually and with much protest towards a more liberal system. In July 1989 Sir Leon Brittan, the Community Commissioner for Competition, put forward plans that would 'dismantle the maze of restrictions currently preventing competition in the air'. At the time, the likelihood of such proposals succeeding was widely regarded with scepticism, but developments in late November and early December showed that the transport ministers of the Community could and did agree that liberalization had to get underway in order to meet the 1992 deadline. John Moorhouse, a British Euro-MP and someone much committed to liberalization, issued a circular on 8 December which stated:

> The breakthrough last week in Brussels was fantastic for us. Britain has been leading the fight for cheaper air fares against strong opposition from the French and Germans for many years. In Parliament we won the debate, and now we have won it in Council. It is British ideas of a competitive market which have made all this possible.[43]

While Britain was notching up some hard-earned success in the EC, the British government was also continuing to develop its competition policy at home, although the take-over of B.Cal. by BA was something of an embarrassment—but really not surprising if one had paid heed to the consequences of deregulation in the United States. Civil aviation there is vastly larger, but following airline deregulation in 1978 new airlines entered the market and mergers and bankruptcies followed, and indeed that process continues though at a slower pace. The system that emerged was characterized by a hub-and-spoke configuration of routes, the dominance of over 80 per cent of the domestic

[43] Cmd. 9366, 1984, 'Airline Competition Policy'; *The Independent*, 31 July 1989, 'Sharing the pie in the sky', David Black; Circular, James Moorhouse MEP, 8 Dec. 1989. 'Cheaper Air Fares thanks to British Initiative'; Interview with Foreign Office official; Colvin interview.

market by six mega-carriers, and a greater number of American airlines entering the foreign market. The British situation is very different, but some of the effects of deregulation have been, and may continue to be, similar to those experienced in the United States. The market for British airlines is essentially an overseas carrier market, and it may not be possible to sustain more than one operator there—though EC liberalization may provide a larger domestic base than Britain alone provides, which could allow more operators to establish themselves in a substantial way. After taking over B.Cal., BA had something like 90 per cent of Britain's overseas routes. The only other British airline licensed as a scheduled carrier on the Atlantic was Richard Branson's Virgin Airlines, which only has five Boeing 747s, and although it has been highly successful, its owner has committed it to the idea of 'small is beautiful, successful, and manageable'. Other, more serious, contenders for second-force status are British Midland and Air Europe. Despite this lack of large-scale competitors, the CAA in 1988 published a major review, authored largely by its Economic Policy Chief, Ray Colegate, which reasserted the importance of cultivating competition and made it plain that preferential treatment might be accorded to small independent airlines over BA in order to do that. It was also CAA policy, the review stated, to control fares where necessary to protect consumer interests.[44]

By 1989, in some ways Britain was taking the initiative on liberalization in talks with the United States. In early 1988 the Americans sought greater access to Manchester airport in order to provide more routes for the greater number of their airlines that could ply the Atlantic under the Bermuda 2 bilateral. However, much to the annoyance of the Manchester Airport Authority, which wanted to develop its transatlantic operations (it eventually took the government to court over the matter), the DOT and the Foreign Office were unwilling to allow more American airlines into British airports until they received what they considered to be an adequate quid pro quo. In the House of Commons on 16 March Transport Secretary Peter Bottomley said:

[44] *Flight*, 6 Feb. 1988; BBC 2 'Airline'.

In negotiating wider access for United States carriers to Manchester international airport, the Government are committed, by the 1985 airports policy White Paper, to securing benefits of equivalent value for United Kingdom carriers in return.[45]

So far as the British government was concerned, that was not possible at that time, and Bottomley told the House later in the month that talks with the Americans on 17–18 March had failed to achieve agreement.

The problem of Manchester rumbled on and was taken up again in talks held from 29 November to 1 December 1989. By then, matters had developed and broadened out. The British, knowing of American concerns that a 'fortress Europe' might emerge in 1992 involving economic protectionism in a whole range of things—including civil aviation—wanted to use that concern to try to strike a wide-ranging agreement with them on civil aviation. Put simply, the British wanted to offer themselves as a European hub for US airlines and provide them with liberal operating rights and access to the EC after 1992: American airlines would be allowed to operate short-haul flights into the rest of the EC from Britain and more regional British airports would be opened up to them. Possibly the main political priority for British civil aviation for the near future is to ensure that the London airports constitute one of the hubs, if not the main hub, of the EC's civil-aviation system. Two of the most important necessary conditions for that are that Britain continues to be the main transatlantic gateway, and that the British Airports Authority invest sufficiently to provide an adequate and efficient ground-support-service—and that is by no means definitely going to be the case on the evidence of present practice.

In return for British concessions, the Americans were asked to take two steps to reduce the competitive advantage of US airlines in having a large domestic cabotage. Firstly, the United States was to open more American airports to British operators such as Midland and Air Europe, as well as BA; secondly, BA should be allowed to extend its marketing agreement with UA to allow further co-ordination of their schedules 'and also to sell through-flights to many American cities from London as if they

[45] Hansard, 16 Mar. 1988, vol. 129, Written Answers, cols. 619–20, and 23 Mar. 1983, vol. 130, Written Answers, col. 131.

were BA's own, despite a change of aircraft [i.e. from BA's to United's at the US gateway airport]'. In the longer term the British also wanted 'transatlantic flights to be conducted in the same way as those to many parts of Europe and the Far East, with airlines free to decide on airports and, within limits, fares'.

The Americans would not accept this. They were fearful that they might expose American airlines to too much competition while the EC remained too regulated for them to gain comparable advantages there. That is where things rest in Anglo-American civil-aviation relations at the moment, though the Foreign Office is still optimistic of drawing the United States into an agreement along the above lines before 1992. The British government believes that there is something on offer for both sides and that the Americans will much prefer to get their foot in the EC door through negotiations with Britain rather than wait and have to deal with the European Commission. In fact, the United States may find that it has to deal with the EC earlier than might be expected.[46]

One of the interesting aspects of the November–December 1989 Anglo-American talks was the clear implication that Britain preferred to talk about civil aviation with the United States bilaterally rather than as part of the EC. In civil aviation Britain is the strongest of the member states, but instead of using its negotiating-power on behalf of the Community in dealing with the Americans, the British government broke ranks, in an attempt to further British national civil-aviation interests at the expense of interests formulated by the cautious and protectionist dispensation reigning in Brussels. It was probably no coincidence that the EC Transport Commissioner, Karel Van Miert, proposed in January 1990 that the Commission should take responsibility for all member states in negotiating air-traffic rights with non-members. In particular, he had the matter of bargaining with the United States in mind. Of course, the net result of that might be to push the United States into the arms of the British, as it seeks to strike the best deal it can before things

[46] Interview with Foreign Office official; see also *The Times*, 28 Nov. 1989, 'Deal to liberalise air routes to US may be achieved', H. Elliott. A copy of this was handed to the author by a Foreign Office official with the comment: 'That is what we might have liked to achieve'.

are taken over by the Commission, where the liberalizers will be outnumbered.[47]

SOME CONCLUDING REMARKS

In the seventy years since the Great War, international civil aviation has come of age and flourished. But it has done so in a way different from most commercial enterprises. At every turn it has had to come to terms with political matters of one kind or another. The attempts, such as they were, to depoliticize international civil aviation failed. The last concerted attempt was in 1947, when Britain and the United States tried to get the ICAO to agree on a multilateral agreement that would have embodied the principles of Bermuda 1. Even if that had been agreed, there would still have been great scope for the play of politics in world aviation. In the event, it failed, and politics and the national interests of states continued to vie with each other for advantage. Internationalism has singularly failed to provide a framework for commercial regulation and control, though, as we have seen, some of its principles have had an impact in a more piecemeal way. In the period from 1945 to the late 1970s internationalism had more success in the technical sphere and in fare-setting, but now IATA has lost much of its influence there, though it still has much to its credit. As one author has pointed out, the wonder of the IATA ticket needs to be recognized, for it is too often taken for granted. ICAO also now suffers from lack of support from the main civil-aviation power—the United States—both in political and financial terms. And even the Warsaw Convention, the main function of which is to regulate insurance for accidents, has never been wholeheartedly embraced by the United States, which has consistently called for higher compensation-rates than those espoused by the Convention.

In the late 1970s depoliticization was tried in a new form, namely deregulation to remove government controls and create a commercial, as opposed to a politico-commercial, industry out

[47] *Independent*, 25 Jan. 1990, 'EC Seeks Control of Air Rights'; Colvin interview.

of the airlines. It too had impact upon civil aviation, but also failed to remove politics.

Over the years, some of the political aspects of civil aviation have diminished in importance. In particular, missile technology and spy satellites have reduced the military and intelligence significance of civil aviation. Nevertheless, the civil-aviation industry is still of military value to a country in a broad sense. It is also important for commercial and status reasons, and while countries continue to maintain airlines through subsidies for a range of political reasons, it will be impossible, as the United States found in the early 1980s, to make civil aviation a purely commercial affair. In the absence of strong international controls, one has no option but to fight fire with fire.

Both the role and the status of Britain and the United States, and their mutual relationship within the international civil-aviation system, have also changed between 1919 and 1990. Both of them have played major parts in determining the character of world civil aviation, though Britain's has steadily diminished in importance over the years and it is likely that that of the United States will never be as dominant as it was in the post-war period up until the 1970s. Nevertheless, no matter how impenetrable the future may be, it is safe to say that the potential still remains for both countries to have a moulding influence on the character of civil aviation, and, given the contemporary importance of the industry, that in itself will demand great attention.

Tourism is now the world's largest single industry; a fact which assures civil aviation's future. But it is a future that is less likely to be dominated by the United States and one in which, if Britain plays a leading role it will be mainly by virtue of its position in the EC rather than because of its own intrinsic importance or because of an exclusive bilateral relationship with the United States. The winds of change that have buffeted civil aviation through deregulation continue, though they sometimes blow from different sources.

In the immediate future the greatest potential for change appears to lie in three factors: firstly, Far Eastern airlines such as Japan Airlines (JAL), Cathay Pacific, and Singapore, which continue to grow rapidly through their highly competitive operations; secondly, the potential for route developments in a more liberal Eastern Europe and Soviet Union; and thirdly, the relationship which develops between the EC and the United States after 1992. Whatever character the latter acquires will have an important general impact on whether or not international civil aviation follows a liberal or protectionist pattern.

If the British Foreign Office were to get its way and craft a liberal arrangement with the United States which formed the basis of the latter's relationship with the EC as a whole, then once again Britain and the United States could help to determine the character of international civil aviation in a manner reminiscent of the heyday of their influence, in 1947, when they presented the Bermuda 1 Agreement to the world as a model to follow. But to make such a comment is to enter the realms of speculation and that is not the historian's job. For the time being at least, international civil aviation and the relationship in that field between Britain and the United States must be left to develop as they will. I hope that this account will be valued for what it has had to say about the past, but perhaps it may also help the reader to reach a better understanding of whatever takes place in the future.

Bibliography

PRIMARY SOURCES

British

Archival

House of Lords Record Office: Beaverbrook Papers.
Public Record Office: CAB 22, 23, 24, 27, 65, 66, 87, 128; FO 371/ relevant files for 1940s and 1950s.

Interviews

Rt. Hon. James (now Lord) Callaghan MP (26 Feb. 1987).
Michael Colvin MP (7 Dec. 1989).
Rt. Hon. Edmund Dell (8 Dec. 1989).
Senior Official of the Foreign Office (8 Dec. 1989).

Published Material

BOAC Annual Report and Accounts (HMSO, London, 1949, 1953, 1963).
Sir Alec Cairncross (ed.), *Sir Richard Clarke: Anglo-American Collaboration in Peace and War 1942–49* (Clarendon, Oxford, 1982).
Command Papers:
9218, 1918, 'Civil Aerial Transport Committee Report'.
266, 1919, 'Convention Relating to International Air Transport'.
449, 1919, 'Imperial Air Routes'.
467, 1919, 'Note by the Secretary of State for Air on a Scheme for the Permanent Organisation of the Royal Air Force'.
554, 1920, 'Education and Research in Aeronautics'.
770, 1920, 'Government Assistance for the Development of Civil Aviation'.
1170, 1921, 'Air Estimates: Explanatory Memorandum'.
1739, 1922, 'First Report on the Imperial Airmail Service'.
1811, 1923, 'Government Financial Assistance to Civil Air Transport Companies'.
5351, 1937, 'Report of the Committee on the Development of Civil Aviation in the United Kingdom' [Maybury Report].
5685, 1938, 'Report of the Committee of Inquiry into Civil Aviation' [Cadman Report].

6038, 1939, 'Production of Civil Aeroplanes'.
6321, 1941, 'Joint Declaration'.
6391, 1942, 'Principles Applying to Mutual Aid'.
6561, 1944, 'International Air Transport'.
6605, 1945, 'British Air Transport'.
6712, 1946, 'British Air Services'.
6747, 1946, 'US, UK, Civil Air Services Agreement Bermuda'.
7209, 1947, 'Exchange of Notes Amending Bermuda'.
7307, 1948, 'Report on Tudor Aircraft'.
7478, 1948, 'Report on Tudor Aircraft'.
7389, 1948, 'Agreement on Military Bases'.
5, 1963, 'The Financial Problems of BOAC'.
2853, 1964, 'Report of the Committee of Inquiry into the Aircraft Industry' [Plowden Report].
3015, 1966, 'Exchange of Notes Amending Bermuda'.
4018, 1969, 'Report of the Committee of Inquiry into Civil Air Transport' [Edwards Report].
4899, 1972, 'Civil Aviation Policy Guidance'.
6400, 1976, 'Future Civil Aviation Policy'.
7016, 1977, 'Agreement Concerning Air Services'.
9366, 1984, 'Airline Competition Policy'.

P. and G. Ford, *A Breviate of Parliamentary Papers 1917–19* (Basil Blackwell, Oxford, 1951).

Hansard.

House of Commons Transport Committee, *Airline Competition: Computer Reservation Systems*, 3rd report, 28 July 1988 (2 vols., HMSO, London, 1988).

H. G. Nicholas (ed.), *Washington Dispatches 1941–45* (Weidenfeld & Nicolson, London, 1981).

Parliamentary Sessional Papers 1921–39, Air Estimates.

E. L. Woodward and R. Butler (eds.), *Documents on British Foreign Policy*, 2nd ser., vols. 3 and 4 (HMSO, London, 1948, 1950).

Periodicals, Newspapers, and Ephemera

BBC2 documentary 'Airline', 25 Mar. 1990.

Circular, James Moorhouse MEP, 8 Dec. 1989.

Correspondence with Rt. Hon. Edmund Dell, 26 Apr. 1990.

The Daily Telegraph

The Economist

The Independent

Flight International

The Sunday Times

The Times

American

Archival

Library of Congress: 'US Maritime Commission: Aircraft and the Merchant Marine', 1937—the Grover Loening Report; papers of W. D. Leahy, J. L. Landis.

National Archives: State Department Decimal Files 841.796/, 811.796040/, 811.79640/, 800.796/, 711.4127/, 841.79653/, 811.79641D/, 811.79641/, 841.79600/, 841.79603/, 399.72ICAO/, 911.5200/; RG 40, Secretary's Office Commerce Department.

Presidential Libraries:

D. D. Eisenhower: Presidential Central Files, Confidential File (CF, CF) and Ann Whitman File (AWF); H. R. McPhee Papers.

L. B. Johnson: Presidential Central File, Confidential File (CF, CF), National Security File (NSF) Country File, and General Correspondence (GEN CO); Harry McPherson Office Files.

J. F. Kennedy: Office (OF) and Central (CF) and National Security Files (NSF).

F. D. Roosevelt: Presidential Map Room (MR), Official File (OF), and President's Secretary's File (PSF); A. A. Berle Papers; H. Hopkins Papers.

H. S. Truman: President's Secretary's File (PSF) and Official File (OF); President's Air Policy Commission; R. B. Adams Papers; W. L. Clayton Papers; G. P. Baker oral history interview.

The Smithsonian National Aeronautical and Space Museum Archives: Papers of Juan Trippe.

Published Material

B. B. Berle and T. B. Jacobs (eds.), *Navigating the Rapids 1918–71: From the Papers of A. A. Berle* (Harcourt Brace Jovanovich, New York, 1973).

Public Papers of Herbert Hoover 1929 (US Government Printing Office, Washington, DC, 1974).

W. F. Kimball (ed.), *Churchill and Roosevelt: The Complete Correspondence* (3 vols., Princeton University Press, New Jersey, 1984).

W. Millis (ed.), *The Forrestal Diaries* (Viking, New York, 1951).

Report of the President's Aircraft Board, 30 November 1925 (US Government Printing Office, Washington, DC, 1925).

US General Accounting Office, *Airline Competition: GOA Report to Congress, May 1986* (GOA, Washington, DC, 1986).

Newspapers

The New York Times

SECONDARY SOURCES

Books

ASHWORTH, M., and FORSYTH, P., *Civil Aviation and the Privatisation of British Airways* (Institute for Fiscal Studies, London 1985).

BALDWIN, R., *Regulating the Airlines: Administrative Justice and Agency Discretion* (Clarendon, Oxford, 1985).

BENDINER, E., *A Time for Angels: The Tragicomic History of the League of Nations* (Alfred Knopf, New York, 1975).

BROAD, L., *Eden: The Chronicles of a Career* (Hutchinson, London, 1953).

BULLOCK, A., *Ernest Bevin: Foreign Secretary* (OUP, Oxford, 1985).

CALLAGHAN, J., *Time and Chance* (Collins, London, 1987).

CAMPBELL, J. C., *et al., Council on Foreign Relations: The United States in World Affairs 1947–48* (Harper, New York, 1948).

CARR, E. H., *International Relations Since the Peace Treaties* (Macmillan, London, 1937).

CHUANG, R. Y., *The International Air Transport Association* (A. W. Sijthoff, Leiden, 1972).

CORBETT, D., *Politics and the Airlines* (George Allen & Unwin, London, 1965).

CROSS, J. A., *Sir Samuel Hoare: A Political Biography* (Jonathan Cape, London, 1977).

—— *Lord Swinton* (OUP, Oxford, 1982).

DALEY, R., *An American Saga: Juan Trippe and His Pan American Empire* (Random House, New York, 1980).

DALTON, H., *High Tide and After: Memoirs 1945–60* (Frederick Muller, London, 1962).

DAVIES, R. E. G., *Airlines of the United States Since 1914* (Putnam, London, 1982).

DEMPSEY, P. S., *Law and Foreign Policy in International Aviation* (Transnational Publishers, New York, 1987).

DIMBLEBY, D., and REYNOLDS, D., *An Ocean Apart* (Hodder & Stoughton, London, 1988).

DOBSON, A. P., *US Wartime Aid to Britain 1940–46* (Croom Helm, London, 1986).

—— *The Politics of the Anglo-American Economic Special Relationship* (Wheatsheaf, Brighton and St. Martins, New York, 1988).

DUNNE, M., *The United States and the World Court 1920–1935* (Pinter, London, 1988).

EDEN, A., *Memoirs: Facing the Dictators* (Cassell, London, 1962).

ELLISON, A. P., and STAFFORD, E. M., *The Dynamics of the Civil Aviation Industry* (Saxon House, Farnborough, 1974).

FARLEY, J. A., *Jim Farley's Story* (McGraw Hill, New York, 1948).

FORSYTH, P., *Civil Aviation and the Privatisation of British Airways* (Institute for Fiscal Studies, London, 1985).

FRATER, A., *Beyond the Blue Horizon* (Penguin, Harmondsworth, 1987).

GABRIEL, J. M., *The American Conception of Neutrality After 1941* (Macmillan, London, 1988).

GARDNER, L. C., *Economic Aspects of New Deal Diplomacy* (Beacon Press, Boston, 1964).

GIDWITZ, B., *The Politics of International Air Transport* (Heath, Boston, 1980).

GILBERT, M., *Winston S. Churchill*, iv and vii, *Companion* (Heinemann, London, 1977).

GORE-BOOTH, P., *With Great Truth and Respect* (Constable, London, 1974).

HARLE, V., and SIVONEN, P., (eds.), *Europe in Transition* (Frances Pinter, London, 1989).

HATHAWAY, R. M., *Ambiguous Partnership: Britain and America 1944–47* (Columbia University Press, New York, 1981).

HAYWARD, K., *Government and British Civil Aerospace* (Manchester University Press, Manchester, 1983).

HIGHAM, R., *Britain's Imperial Air Routes 1918–39* (Shoe String, Hamden, Conn., 1961).

HOARE, Sir S., *Empire of the Air: The Advent of the Air Age 1922–29* (Collins, London, 1957).

HURST, R., (ed.), *Pilot Error: A Professional Study of Contributing Factors* (Granada, London, 1978).

HYDE, H. MONTGOMERY, *Baldwin: The Unexpected Prime Minister* (Hart-Davis McGibbon, London, 1973).

JOSEPHSON, M., *Empire of the Air: Juan Trippe and the Struggle for World Airways* (Arno Press, New York, 1972).

JONSSON, C., *International Aviation and the Politics of Regime Change* (Frances Pinter, London, 1987).

KENT, R. J., *Safe, Separated and Soaring: A History of Civil Aviation 1961–72* (US Department of Transport, Federal Aviation Authority, Washington DC, 1980).

LEAHY, W. D., *I Was There* (Victor Gollancz, London, 1950).

LEE, R. A., *Dwight D. Eisenhower: Soldier and Statesman* (Nelson Hall, Chicago, 1981).

LONGMATE, N., *GIs: The Americans in Britain 1942–45* (Scribners, New York, 1975).

MCGOWAN F., and TRENGOVE, C., *European Aviation: A Common Market?* (Institute for Fiscal Studies, London, 1986).

MIDDLEMAS, K., and BARNES, J., *Baldwin: A Biography* (Weidenfeld & Nicolson, London, 1969).

MILLER, J. A., 'Air Diplomacy: The Chicago Civil Aviation Conference of 1944 in Anglo-American Wartime Relations and Postwar Planning', (Ph. D. thesis, Yale University, 1971, Univ. Microfilms International, NBA71–22342).

MILLER, R., and SAWERS, D., *The Technical Development of Modern Aviation* (Routledge & Kegan Paul, London, 1968).

MURRAY, R. K., *The Harding Era: Warren G. Harding and His Administration* (University of Minnesota Press, Minneapolis, 1969).

MYERS, W. S., and NEWTON, W. H., *The Hoover Administration: A Documentary Narrative* (Scribner's, New York, 1936).

NEWHOUSE, J., *The Sporty Game* (Alfred Knopf, New York, 1983).

OFFNER, A. A., *The Origins of the Second World War: American Foreign Policy and World Politics 1917–41* (Praeger, New York, 1976).

PELLING, H., *Winston Churchill* (Macmillan, London, 1974).

PRESTON, E., *Troubled Passage: The Federal Aviation Administration During the Nixon-Ford Term* 1973–77 (US Department of Transport, Washington DC, 1987).

PRYKE, R., *Competition Among International Airlines* (Gower, Aldershot, 1987).

READER, W. J., *Architect of Air Power: The Life of the First Viscount Weir of Eastwood 1877–1959* (Collins, London, 1968).

RICHARDSON, R., *The Evolution of British Disarmament Policy in the 1920s* (Frances Pinter, London, 1989).

RICHMOND, S. B., *Regulation and Competition in Air Transportation* (Columbia University Press, New York, 1961).

ROCHESTER, S. I., *Take-off at Mid-century: Federal Aviation Policy in the Eisenhower Years 1953–61* (US Department of Transport, Federal Aviation Authority, Washington DC, 1976).

SAMPSON, A., *Empires of the Sky: The Politics, Contests and Cartels of World Airlines* (Hodder & Stoughton, London, 1984).

SIMON, Viscount, *Retrospect: Memoirs of the Right Honourable Viscount Simon* (Hutchinson, London, 1952).

SIMPSON, M., *Franklin D. Roosevelt*, (Basil Blackwell, Oxford, 1989).

SOLBERG, C., *Conquest of the Skies: A History of Commercial Aviation* (Little, Brown, and Co., Boston, 1979).

STEBBINS, R. P., *et al. Council on Foreign Relations: The United States in World Affairs 1963* (Harper, New York, 1964).

SWINTON, Viscount, *I Remember* (Hutchinson, London, 1946).

TANEJA, N. K., *US International Aviation Policy* (Heath, Lexington, Ky., 1980).

TAYLOR, A. J. P., *Beaverbrook* (Hamish Hamilton, London, 1972).

—— (ed.), *Off the Record: Political Interviews 1933–43*, (interviewer W. P. Crozier) (Hutchinson, London, 1973).

THORNE, C., *The Limits of Foreign Policy: The West, the League and the Far Eastern Crisis 1931–33* (Macmillan, London, 1973).

WARFORD, J. J., *Public Policy Toward General Aviation* (Brookings Institute, Washington DC, 1971).

WASSENBERGH, H. A., *Aspects of Air Law and Civil Air Policy in the Seventies* (Martinus Nijhoff, The Hague, 1970).

WHEATCROFT, S., *Air Transport Policy* (Michael Joseph, London, 1964).

WHEELER-BENNETT, J. W., *The Disarmament Deadlock* (Routledge & Kegan Paul, London, 1934).

WILBUR, R. L., and HYDE, A. M., *The Hoover Policies* (Scribner's, New York, 1937).

Articles

ALLEN, R. G. D., 'Mutual Aid Between the United States and the British Empire 1941–45', *Journal of the Royal Statistical Society*, 109 (1946), 243–7.

BREWIN, C., 'British Plans for International Operating Agencies for Civil Aviation, 1941–45', *International History Review*, 4 (1982), 91–110.

CARLTON, D., 'The Problem of Civil Aviation in British Air Disarmament Policy 1919–34', *Royal United Services Institute Journal*, 664 (1966), 307–16.

Contemporary Record, 3 (1989), 39–45, '1976 IMF Crisis Symposium'.

COOPER, J. C., 'Some Historic Phases of British International Civil Aviation Policy', *International Affairs*, 23 (1947), 189–202.

DAY, DAVID A., 'P. G. Taylor and the Alternative Pacific Air Route, 1939–45', *Australian Journal of Politics and History*, 32 (1986), 6–19.

DELL, E., 'Interdependence and the Judges: Civil Aviation and Antitrust', *International Affairs*, 61 (1985), 355–73.

DOBSON, A. P., 'A Mess of Pottage for Your Economic Birthright: The 1941–42 Wheat Negotiations and Anglo-American Economic Diplomacy', *Historical Journal*, 28 (1985), 739–50.

—— 'The Export White Paper, 10 September 1941', *Economic History Review*, 39 (1986), 59–76.

FEARON, P., 'The Growth of Aviation in Britain', *Journal of Contemporary History*, 20 (1985), 21–41.

GROVES, P. R. C., 'The Influence of Aviation on International Affairs', *International Affairs*, 8 (1929), 289–318.

LOWENFELD, A. F., 'A New Take-off For International Air Transport', *Foreign Affairs*, 54 (1975), 36–50.

MACKENZIE, D., 'Canada and the Civil Aviation Discussions During the 1937 Imperial Conference', *British Journal of Canadian Studies*, 1 (1987), 97–109.

MCCORMACK, R. L., 'War and Change: Air Transport in British Africa 1939–45', *Canadian Journal of History*, 24 (1989), 341–59.

—— 'Missed Opportunities: Winston Churchill, the Air Ministry and Africa 1919–1921', *International History Review*, 11 (1989), 205–28.

MEGAW, M. R., 'The Scramble for the Pacific: Anglo-US Rivalry in the 1930s', *Historical Studies*, 17 (1977), 458–73.

MROZEK, D. J., 'The Truman Administration and the Enlistment of the Aviation Industry in Postwar Defence', *Business History Review*, 48 (1974), 73–94.

PUGH, M. C., 'Lord Davies and the British International Relations Debate in the 1930s', *International Relations*, 9 (1988), 335–51.

Round Table, 138 (1945), 130–6, 'After Chicago: Imperial Interests in Civil Aviation'.

SMITH, M., 'Planning and Building the British Bomber Force 1934–9', *Business History Review*, 54 (1980), 35–62.

STANNARD, H., 'Civil Aviation: A Historical Survey', *International Affairs*, 21 (1945), 497–511.

THORPE, A., 'Arthur Henderson and the British Political Crisis of 1931', *Historical Journal*, 31 (1988), 117–39.

Index